Teaching Exceptional Adolescents

Ervin

James E. Smith, Jr.
Virginia State University

James S. Payne
University of Virginia

Charles E. Merrill Publishing Company
A Bell & Howell Company
Columbus   Toronto   London   Sydney

Published by Charles E. Merrill Publishing Co.
A Bell & Howell Co.
Columbus, Ohio 43216

This book was set in Avant Garde Medium and Helvetica
Cover Design Coordination: Will Chenoweth
Production Coordination: Sandy Rawson Smith

Library of Congress Catalog Card Number: 79-93164
International Standard Book Number: 0-675-08128-9
Printed in the United States of America

1 2 3 4 5 6 7 8 9 10—85 84 83 82 81 80

Preface

More and more exceptional pupils are remaining in school through the secondary level. Since this is the case, teachers and others must be concerned with educating these pupils to refine the social and academic skills acquired at the elementary school level. Thus, one goal of this book is to expose the teacher to methods and materials that are especially useful with special students at the secondary school level.

In order for teachers to work effectively with exceptional adolescents, these teachers and other school personnel must understand how the secondary school developed and what its general goals and objectives are. Thus, in the first section of the book we describe the development of the secondary school in America, and programs that were specifically developed for exceptional adolescents. The next two sections focus on various teaching and career provisions aimed at enabling the exceptional adolescent to become an independent contributing member of society. Specifically, the second section of the book addresses various concerns related to teaching exceptional youth. The third section takes a look at many factors concerning career preparation.

It is our belief that unless a pupil receives as good an education at the secondary level as at the elementary level, then these prior efforts are in vain. Thus, the exceptional students entering secondary school are like all other students—they must be exposed to a systematic and structured program if learning is to continue to develop and be refined. The authors of this book have gathered together proven educational strategies and techniques to help provide this system and structure.

Acknowledgments

For their comments, ideas, and time given generously at various stages of this book, we would like to thank our colleagues Laurence Coleman, Charles Hargis, and William Coffield. We would especially like to thank James R. Patton for his help with chapters 4–6.

For their love and encouragement, we are grateful to our wives Mary and Ruth Ann.

We also want to thank our editor at Charles Merrill, Marianne Taflinger, for her wisdom, constant support, and patience during the completion of this project.

To
Milton W. Hinton
and
William R. Carriker,
Educators of the First Order

Contents

Prologue

In an anecdote entitled "Miracle at Herbert Hoover High," William W. Purkey (1973) tells the story of a youth named Max Coleman who is in many ways similar to the adolescents who concern us in this book.[1] Max is failing in school. He is perceived as disruptive and a major discipline problem. Thus, he is often sent to the principal's office for disciplinary action. As the story begins, our attention is directed to a discussion in the teacher's lounge where Max is depicted as a mean, rotten troublemaker who has continually caused a number of teachers to develop all sorts of problems. All of this supposed factual information has been related to Miss Wren, a first-year teacher, who is to begin working with Max as soon as school commences for the new year.

A very brief span of time passes before school opens. As the story continues, Max, who wants to "clean up his act," enters Miss Wren's class. Subsequently, Miss Wren overreacts to Max's nonchalant attitude during their initial conversation. As a result, Max ends up in the principal's office once again, still the loser of Herbert Hoover High.

[1] W. W. Purkey, "Miracle at Herbert Hoover High," Alpha Delta Kappan, 1973, 3(2), 9–12. Dr. Purkey indicated that the idea for this article was formulated from an address by Dr. H.F. Lowry, entitled "The Mouse and Henry Carson." Retold by permission of Alpha Delta Kappan.

Now, based on the title of this story, one would expect some type of unusual event to take place. Further, one would probably expect this unusual event or "miracle" to be something good that happens to Max because at this point in the story he has only experienced trouble and misery. In the next part of the story, these expectations are fulfilled when Max attains perfect scores on all factors of an achievement test. Only the readers know that the "miracle" occurred because of a computer malfunction. The result of this miracle is that the entire school, others in the community, and Max's family begin to act in a more positive manner toward him. Due to these more positive actions and reactions of others, Max begins to feel better about himself. He begins to seek knowledge. Max begins to achieve!

Even though this story has an ending that most of us would like to see take place for all troubled youth, most teachers who work closely with adolescents with learning and behavior problems will state that, in a very large number of cases, a miracle does not occur at their high school or for their students. In fact, the point of retelling this story is to state emphatically that good teaching, a structured environment, and an understanding and cooperative administration are three of the many factors that must be brought together to insure that learning takes place for adolescents with learning and behavior problems. This book demonstrates how personnel can provide their own miracles for the Maxes at their school.

part one

Introduction

The first three chapters of this book introduce the reader to various aspects of the total secondary school. Chapter 1 describes the evolution of the American secondary school and its present-day organization. Several trends and issues that are presently of concern to the area of secondary education are also discussed in this chapter. Chapter 2 focuses upon a number of characteristics that show the similarities and differences of exceptional youth and other adolescents. Additionally, a definition of what constitutes a mildly handicapped adolescent is delineated in this chapter. Chapter 3 takes a close look at past and present program options that have been used to deliver services to exceptional adolescents.

1

Secondary Education

In 1976, the National Center for Educational Statistics of the Department of Health, Education and Welfare reported that the 1973 total enrollment in grades 9 through 12 for all schools, public and private, was about 15.5 million students.[1] This group also reported that 10.7% of the total school population were exceptional children (Grant & Lind, National Center for Educational Statistics, 1974).[2] Combining these two figures, one can approximate the number of exceptional pupils at the secondary level, at about 1.7 million students.[3] Because this population is so large, a determination is in order regarding endeavors to educate exceptional youth at the secondary level.

It is clear at the present time that many special educators at the secondary level are hampered by a number of factors in their attempts to ameliorate the problems of exceptional adolescents. Primarily, there is a general lack of understanding of the overall function, purpose,

[1]The actual figure is 15,426,526 pupils. This figure does not include students in grades seven and eight. These grades are viewed as part of the total secondary program.
[2]All categories of exceptionality were included in this figure.
[3]This is a very conservative approximation since it does not include pupils from grades seven and eight.

and organization of the secondary school. Thus, one major purpose of this chapter is to provide present and future special educators, and other interested persons, with a realistic view of the inner workings of secondary education programs.

OVERVIEW OF SECONDARY EDUCATION

Depending on one's geographical location, secondary education programs are organized in a number of different ways. One grouping indicates that children attend an elementary school for the first eight grades and attend a high school for their last four years. However, in other areas, 4–4–4, 6–3–3, 6–2–4, or 7–5 groupings are used. The term *secondary education,* as used in this book, refers to grades 7 through 12. This view is taken because it is at the age of about 12 to 13 that children begin to assume many of the characteristics associated with secondary level students. This is not to say that the 12- or 13-year-old boy or girl who is observed in the seventh grade is the same person when he or she is observed in the 9th grade or even 12th grade, but the observed 7th-grade youngster is on the way to becoming that 9th- or 12th-grade person.

Traditionally, secondary students earn a specified number of units, points, or credits in order to fulfill requirements for graduation. While there are several different types of curriculum organization used to aid students in acquiring graduation credits and organizing a plan of study, much of the curriculum content in the high school is subject-matter oriented. Additionally, pupils in high school are usually age-grade grouped for instruction (Rollins & Unruh, 1964). The secondary school day is usually organized around a fixed schedule of five to seven periods, during which pupils take required and elective subjects. More specific details of the organization of the secondary school are discussed in following sections. Initially, however, a brief historical review of secondary education will reveal antecedents of today's secondary educational programs.

A BRIEF HISTORY OF SECONDARY EDUCATION

In tracing the development of education at the secondary level, Reinhardt (1966) stated that "in the United States, the history of secondary education centers around three institutions: the Latin grammar school, academy, and the high school" (p. 11). Two other prominent educational historians have arrived at much the same conclusion (Brown, 1909; Douglass, 1964). Further, all of these authors agreed that the following were characteristics of Latin grammar schools: (1) they were transplanted from Europe; (2) they were college preparatory schools for men; (3) the curriculum was restricted to classic Latin and

Greek; and (4) these schools were attended mainly by members of prosperous and aristocratic families.

However, due largely to the rise of the middle class and to discontent with the great emphasis placed on the classics to the exclusion of practical matters, the academy gradually took the place of the Latin grammar school. Capitalizing on the popular opinions of the day, Benjamin Franklin published his *Proposals Relating to the Education of Youth in Pennsylvania* in 1749. This paper clearly delineated reasons for establishing a new type of secondary school. Two years later, Franklin chartered the first academy at Philadelphia in 1751. Characteristics of academies included: (1) they were usually under private, denominational control; (2) these schools began to admit women; (3) the curriculum in this type of school was expanded to include practical and vocational subjects; and (4) they continued the teachings of the elementary school, as opposed to operating in a parallel manner, which was the case with the Latin grammar school.

The academy, like its predecessor the Latin grammar school, was replaced by a new institution more in line with the wishes of the rising middle class; this particular group sought to make education more available to the general public in order to elevate the position of their sons and daughters in society. The new institution was called the high school and was mainly tax supported. The first high school, established in Boston in 1821, was named English Classical School (Cubberley, 1920). This name was changed to English High School three years later (Reinhardt, 1966). In 1827, the legislature of Massachusetts enacted a law that provided for the establishment of high schools in towns with 500 or more families. In 1835, this law was amended to permit smaller towns to form high schools (Cubberley, 1920). Most of the high schools developed during this and later periods were modeled after the ones initiated in Massachusetts (see Table 1.1).

Although high schools began to grow rapidly after the passage of the Massachusetts legislation, these schools were not tax supported or under public control in all states. Shortly after the end of the Civil War, a controversy ensued as to whether public, tax-supported high schools were legal entities. Finally, in 1872, a case that began in Kalamazoo, Michigan, that sought to address this question reached the Supreme Court. The court ruled that indeed the concept of a public, tax-supported high school was legal. This decision signaled the beginning of a more rapid rise of high schools throughout the entire United States.

Conant (1966) has indicated that by the 20th century the idea of the American high school was fully perfected. In commenting on the period of secondary education from about 1905 to 1930, Conant stated that in 1905, 9% of an age group graduated from high school. In 1905, the curriculum was mainly academic in orientation; whereas by 1930 the emphasis had changed to developing marketable skills.

Table 1.1
Characteristics of the Latin Grammar School, the Academy, and the High School

Latin Grammar School	Academy	High School
College preparatory school for men	College preparatory for men and women	College and/or life preparation for all
Curriculum restricted to classic Latin and Greek	Curriculum expanded to include some practical and vocational subjects	Broad curriculum
Curriculum parallel to elementary school	Curriculum built on that of elementary school	Curriculum built on that of elementary school
Attended mainly by upper class	Attended mainly by individuals from upper classes and those with superior intellect	Attended by all
Under public control	Under private denominational control	Under public control—tax supported

During the first and second quarters of the 20th century, a number of profound events began to shape the future of secondary education. Among these events were the passage of numerous child labor laws, the great depression of the 1920s and 1930s, and the participation of the United States in two world wars. Enactment of child labor laws created a situation in which adolescents could not enter the work force until their late teens. Coupled with the child labor laws were compulsory school attendance laws requiring children to attend school for a specified number of days as well as a certain number of years. The net result was that there were more pupils in the schools and these students stayed in school for longer periods. Consequently, there was a general shift away from college preparation as the central aim of secondary education to a goal of general preparation for all. This general preparation allowed individual students to decide whether their preparation in the secondary schools would be used as an access to a college or university, or for development of work skills to be used immediately after graduation. The Great Depression furthered the trend of keeping youngsters in school since there were not enough jobs even for the adult population. The two world wars that preceded (World War I) and followed (World War II) the Great Depression took large numbers of persons out of the labor pool. When hostilities ceased, industry was unable to assimilate all the returning veterans. In many cases, government funding provided the impetus and means for many of the veterans to finish their education, at least through the secondary level. By the third quarter of this century, the secondary school had evolved to its present-day position as a comprehensive high school (see Table 1.2).

PURPOSES AND OBJECTIVES

In order to understand secondary education fully, one must at some point ascertain its purposes and objectives. Rollins and Unruh (1964) have indicated that a general aim of secondary education is to aid students in their efforts to continue to learn. These two writers also indicated that in a specific sense the American secondary school should:

1. provide opportunities for all boys and girls to receive at least a twelfth-grade education.
2. attempt to help boys and girls to develop powers of independent, critical thinking.
3. present boys and girls with opportunities to learn the traditions, the ideas, and the processes of American democracy.
4. help boys and girls to understand and appreciate American and world society, their art, their literature, their history, their science, their customs, and their people.
5. help boys and girls prepare for the roles they will assume after they leave it. (pp. 20–24)

Dumas and Beckner (1968) reported that in 1938 the National Education Association listed four main objectives of education. These objectives centered around "development of the learner"; "home, family and community life"; "economic demands"; and "civil and social duties" (pp. 157–158). Dumas and Beckner also stated that in 1961 these four objectives were reduced to one broad objective for secondary education. This broad objective attempted to develop to the maximum an individual's ability to think or use his or her rational powers. Conant (1959, 1967) has suggested that

Table 1.2
Some Important Events in the Development of the Modern High School

Latin Grammar School	Academy	High School
1635—Founding of first Latin Grammar School (Boston), forerunner of modern high school 1635 until Revolutionary War—Period of greatest influence (Douglass, 1952)	1749—Benjamin Franklin published *Proposals Relating to the Education of Youth in Pennsylvania*—a document advocating the establishment of the academy as an alternate means for educating students at the secondary level 1751—First academy established at Philadelphia by Franklin 1751 until about 1875—Period of greatest influence (Douglass, 1952)	1821—First high school established at Boston 1826—First high school for girls established at Boston 1827—Massachusetts legislature enacts law providing for common secondary schools in towns of 500 or more families 1835—Massachusetts law amended to provide for secondary schools in towns of less than 500 families 1872—Tax-supported, public secondary education supported by court in Kalamazoo case 1910—First junior high schools started in Ohio and California 1959—J.B. Conant published *The American High School Today*

the three main objectives of a comprehensive high school are: *first,* to provide a general education for all the future citizens; *second,* to provide good elective programs for those who wish to use their acquired skills immediately on graduation; *third,* to provide satisfactory programs for those whose vocations will depend on their subsequent education in a college or university. (p. 17, 1959)

From these examples of how authorities in the field view the purposes and objectives of secondary education, one can readily determine that there is no one set of purposes and objectives in this area on which everyone agrees. Yet, there are some common threads interwoven into many of the predominant views of the purposes and objectives of secondary education.

One of the common viewpoints held by many knowledgeable persons is that the secondary school is meant to serve the individual *and* the society at large. This means that in a number of instances, the individual pupil is trained to assume a job immediately after graduation from high school. In the effort to prepare a certain student for the above role, teachers, counselors, the student, and other interested persons first evaluate the abilities, interests, and skills of the entering secondary school student to determine the program that will be *best for this particular student.* Likewise, school personnel attempt to design and implement a specific program of study and training for the student who will engage in some type of post-secondary education, such as, a vocational-technical school, college, or university. In these two instances, the secondary school has engaged in efforts to serve the individual.

As the school devises individual programs to meet the needs of students, society is taken into consideration; individuals are taught skills that will enable them to become productive, contributing members of society. At the same time that students actively participate in the educational process, they learn many of the social and civic skills that they will use later in their adult lives. Thus, another purpose of the secondary school is to develop certain social and civic skills in the individual that will ultimately serve the needs of society.

The preceding paragraphs also describe another common element listed within the stated purposes and objectives of secondary education, that is, the preparation of adolescents for future roles in the society. Skills and abilities are not developed and refined in the high school just for the sake of the exercise, but are fostered in preparation for something. In general, this preparation focuses on developing an active, knowledgeable citizenry. Specifically, this same preparation focuses on developing skills that will serve the individual as a custodian, dietician, or airplane pilot.

Throughout the stated purposes and objectives of secondary education, many writers stress the goal of educating all adolescents until at least the 12th grade. While this objective may seem to be universally accepted, this has not always been the case, even in the United States, and is not a recognized goal in a number of countries today.

The preceding paragraphs provide guidelines to the general and/or specific purposes and objectives of secondary education. Yet it is suggested that local groups of concerned teachers, administrators, parents, and students develop their own set of purposes and objectives for the local secondary school. These groups should tailor goals to meet the needs of their particular school district, or community, as well as the needs of the adolescents concerned.

CURRICULUM

Stiles, McCleary, and Turnbaugh (1962) have stated that there are several different views of what the curriculum of the secondary school should be; many different and conflicting opinions exist as to what should be taught in the secondary school. These authors further stated that "in order to attain some consistency, as well as to include the many new phases of the educational program, schools began to define the curriculum as every activity planned and provided by the school" (p. 201). However, this definition seems to be somewhat broad. Stiles et al. further defined the curriculum "as what society requires to be taught, including intellectual skills, knowledges, attitudes and values" (p. 203).

Rollins and Unruh (1964) operationally defined curriculum "as that part of the school program specifically designed to provide planned learning experiences for the children in the school" (p. 29). Using a broader definition than those proposed by Stiles et al. or Rollins and Unruh, Dumas and Beckner (1968) claimed that their definition was "one that allows for specific planning on the part of school personnel" (p. 170). In defining this concept, Dumas and Beckner stated that "the secondary school curriculum includes all those activities and experiences of pupils which occur under the guidance and direction of the school as a result of the planned school program" (p. 170).

MacDonald (1969) attempted to eliminate some of the confusion in this area by distinguishing between the concepts of curriculum and instruction. He stated that

> the curriculum is both a plan and a set of constructed conditions within which instruction takes place. It is prior to instruction but is both more and less than instruction. It is more than instruction in the sense that instruction takes place within certain curriculum conditions; but it is less than instruction in that it cannot include the quality of personality and interpersonal relations unique to individuals and groups that so obviously affect the learning that takes place in schools. The curriculum is thus a directive and a setting, but only a part of the instructional context. (pp. 37–38)

Though particular definitions of curriculum may differ on a number of points, there are still some common elements. The secondary school curriculum is composed of: (1) a formal plan, (2) directed activities and experiences, and (3) a specific setting (the school and its environs). The plan provides the framework under which school personnel work; the directed activities and experiences provide the means for implementing the plan; and the school in most cases is the place where these events take place.

Curriculum Organization

Rollins and Unruh (1964) have indicated that although there are a number of different patterns of curriculum organization, these patterns can be grouped under the following four categories: (1) subject-centered, (2) broad-fields, (3) core, and (4) experience curriculums.

Subject-centered curriculum.

As its name implies, the subject-centered curriculum is organized around the traditional subjects taught in the secondary school, for ex-

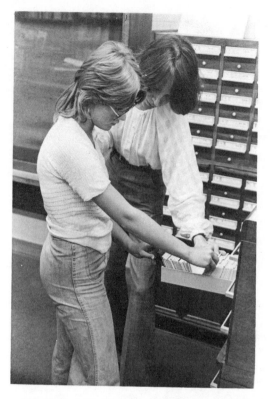

ample, algebra, science, and history. This type of curriculum organization aims at helping the pupil to acquire specific knowledge and skills. An aid to this acquisition of knowledge and skills is the sequential ordering of courses. For example, in the area of science a typical subject-centered curriculum would probably start with general science in the 9th grade, biology in the 10th grade, and so on. Regardless of the subject concerned, one subject is taught at a time during the five to seven periods of the academic day. This organization is somewhat rigid since the teacher is usually concerned with developing skills in only one content area. Thus, students instructed within such a framework often do not see the relationships between subjects. Despite this major disadvantage, the subject-centered curriculum is the one most widely used in American schools.

Broad-fields curriculum.

The broad-fields curriculum attempts to eliminate some of the nonintegration of a subject-centered curriculum by correlating subjects. For example, language arts activities and fine arts activities might be taught together. This approach enables students studying English literature of the period from 1800 to 1850 to also engage in creative activities associated with that period in their fine arts classes. In other words, the broad-fields curriculum cuts across strict subject matter boundaries and allows students to discover the relationship(s) of different facets of the educational program. Since teaching is not as textbook oriented with this type of organization, the teacher has more flexibility in planning experiences for pupils.

Core curriculum.

Douglass (1964) has stated that a core program "involves organizing two or more subjects around problems" (p. 25). Another characteristic of the core curriculum is that it attempts to provide a set of learning experiences that are necessary for all pupils. Core programs also provide the learner with a large variety of learning experiences. These learning experiences are designed to facilitate the problem-solving abilities of the individuals enrolled in this program.

In many respects the broad-field's and core curriculums are similar. However, Rollins and Unruh (1964) have postulated that the core curriculum has a number of distinguishing characteristics:

1. It involves knowledges and skills needed by all pupils.
2. It is scheduled for two or more consecutive periods.
3. The learning experiences are based on broad units of work, usually organized around a common problem.
4. A greater variety of learning experiences are used.
5. Instructional methods are more flexible.
6. Subject matter divisions are eliminated.
7. Teaching and guidance are coordinated, rather than considered separate functions.
8. It involves problem-solving techniques.
9. It considers the study of values as important as the study of content. (p. 47)

Experience curriculum.

"The experience curriculum assumes that the skills and attitudes that are valuable to a pupil in solving a problem or satisfying a need are those that are learned best and most effectively by the pupil" (Rollins & Unruh, 1964, p. 52). This points out that an experience curriculum is much more student centered than the three types previously mentioned. Another attribute of an experience curriculum is its tremendous dependence on teacher perceptions and effectiveness. This particular curriculum assumes that a teacher is perceptive enough to recognize the heretofore unknown skills and attitudes of the pupil. After this, the teacher must also be able to devise and implement strategies to develop these skills and attitudes. Since an experience curriculum demands so much of the teacher's time and energy, not many teachers or school systems elect this particular curriculum option.

EDUCATIONAL ACTIVITIES IN THE SECONDARY SCHOOL

While the curriculum provides the framework for numerous school activities, these activities exist in many forms and even taken alone constitute an important part of the total program. The authors' view is that there are essentially two types of curriculum activities that take place within the school—inclass and extraclass activities.

Inclass Activities

Inclass activities are those planned activities that are more directly associated with the formal portions of the curriculum plan. Therefore, many people have a good conception of what these activities entail. Inclass activities are usually associated with the subject or group of subjects presently being taught to a set of students. For example, students in a math class would be engaged in math-related activities; students in a science laboratory would be involved with science activities.

Regardless of the curriculum organization (subject-centered, broad-fields, core, or experience), all students are expected to complete a number of required courses during their secondary schooling. Required courses and their concomitant activities are usually taken from the following subject areas: English and language, mathematics, science, health and physical education, and social studies. A typical individual four-year program might include the following:

9th Grade
English I
General Science
General Math
Civics
Health

11th Grade
Literature
Physics
Geometry
American History
Physical Education II

10th Grade
English II
Biology
Algebra
World History
Physical Education I

12th Grade
Public Speaking (Elective)
Chemistry
Trigonometry
Economics

The above schedule of courses presupposes that an individual following this program, or any other one for that matter, has acquired at least the minimum skills for entry into such a study program. Depending on whether an individual planned to terminate his or her formal education after graduation or planned to pursue a higher education, the sample schedule of courses could be modified.

Extraclass Activities

Again referring to the sample schedule of courses listed above, one can readily determine that if a student takes one course per period and there are six or seven periods in the school day, then the student has room in the schedule for one or two more courses or activities. In this instance, the student can choose to fill the schedule with another strictly academic or inclass activity or with some type of extraclass activity.

While the concept of inclass activities is clear to most people, extraclass activities have been called a number of different things, such as, "extracurricular" activities (activities occurring outside the curriculum) or "cocurricular" activities (activities that have equal status with curriculum activities). According to Dumas and Beckner (1968), some of the most important characteristics of extraclass activities are: these activities are usually done on a voluntary basis; credit is usually not given for such activities; scheduling for these activities is less formal than for inclass activities; and all schools include these activities in the planned school program.

Examples of extraclass activities that a student might choose are:

1. Student Government Association/Student Council
2. Academic Clubs
   - Foreign Language
   - Mathematics
   - Science
3. Nonacademic Clubs
   - Library
   - Athletics
   - Band Booster
   - Student Publications

It should be stressed at this point that while participation in the above activities is usually voluntary, provisions are made in the school schedule so that all students may, in fact, choose one or several of these activities. For this reason, such activities are considered a part of the curriculum even though they often do not take place in a formal classroom setting.

A Typical Daily Schedule of Activities

Payne, Polloway, Smith, and Payne (1977) have indicated that a typical secondary class schedule includes such activities as: a homeroom period where administrative matters and other concerns are taken care of; several brief periods of time for class changes; instructional periods; and time for extraclass activities. The following is an example of a typical class schedule.

8:15—8:30	Homeroom _____ *	12:15—1:05	Health/Physical Education _____
8:35—9:25	English _____	1:10—2:00	Social Studies _____
9:30—10:20	Mathematics _____	2:05—2:55	Elective/Activity Period _____
10:25—11:15	Science _____	3:00—3:10	Homeroom _____
11:20—12:10	Lunch _____		

* Class change

While this class schedule would probably be used by upper-level secondary students (grades 9–12), students in the seventh and eighth grades would also follow a similar schedule. Usually these students would not have the choice of elective subjects. However, they might have an "activity" period fixed in their schedule that would allow for certain extraclass activities, such as, band / choir, working on a school newspaper, or similar activities. As the students proceed through the secondary school, their schedules become less fixed, that is, graduation requirements are fulfilled giving the individual student more opportunity to participate in elective portions of the educational program.

LEADERSHIP IN THE SECONDARY SCHOOL

The board of education through its appointed or elected administrative agent, the superintendent of schools, is responsible for the total operation of the school system. In much the same way that the board of directors of a large corporation delegates some of its authority to the president of the corporation, a board of education delegates some of its authority to the division superintendent. The superintendent, in turn, delegates a large amount of this same authority to principals and supervisors (as well as to the immediate assistants to the superintendent). Thus, the principal of today's secondary school is no longer just a glorified clerk or disciplinarian. Rathe, he or she is responsible for the entire operation of the school. Duties of the principal include: developing a sound budget, selecting an adequate staff, evaluating the total school program including teachers, providing for discipline, and informing the public about programs and policies of the school.

    According to Dumas and Beckner (1968), seven of the most important tasks of a principal, listed in their probable order of importance, are:

1. Leadership in the professional improvement of the staff.
2. Improving classroom instruction.
3. Building and improving the curriculum.
4. Pupil supervision and administration.
5. Public relations.
6. Plant administration.
7. Business management and office routine. (p. 329)

Although the employment of faculty and staff is ultimately vested in the local board of education, a building principal must have some direct input as to who will work at the school. This gives the principal a chance to select compatible persons. At the same time, the principal acts as a "quality control expert" by selecting professional staff who will work diligently to foster the aims of the curriculum the school has developed. By selecting certain persons for the professional staff, the building principal strives to insure that good classroom instruction will be maintained, at the very least, and improved in many cases.

The task of improving classroom instruction also depends on "building and improving the curriculum." If the curriculum has been developed along the lines advanced earlier in this chapter, that is, developed with input from students, teachers, administrators, and interested citizens, and developed with concern for the local community as well as society, then the task of curriculum building and improvement is that much easier.

In the effort to provide administrative and supervisory support in the pupils' activities area, the principal is responsible for developing student schedules for inclass and extraclass activities as well as insuring a balance between the two. Often, many of these responsibilities are delegated to subordinates, such as, guidance personnel, athletic directors, and others who actually structure or schedule activities. Discharging this task also requires that the principal be ultimately responsible for student discipline and conduct.

Through public relations endeavors, the principal informs the community of policies and practices of the school, as well as important events directly and indirectly connected with the school calendar. This task is accomplished by a number of means, such as, written communications, speeches to interested community groups, and face-to-face meetings. Effective public relations present a school-related perception of certain events, but do not entail distortion of facts. Viewed in this way, good public relations attempt to improve communications between all persons concerned with the well-being of the school.

Perhaps the two tasks of the principal that take the greatest amount of time are plant administration and business management and office routine. This is unfortunate, but in these times of unstable school finances, it is readily apparent why such a situation exists. As school systems begin to develop plans for more cost efficient use of school plants, instead of continuing the mad rush to build new structures, this unfortunate situation may be corrected.

The Department Head

The department head or chairperson usually coordinates the activities of a number of teachers in a given subject area, for example, English or mathematics. Aside from the immediate assistants to the principal, the department head is usually the next link below the principal in the administrative organization (see Figure 1.1). Primary duties of the department head include: assisting the school principal with administrative details, such as, distributing and interpreting memorandums, coordinating textbook distributions, or planning overall schedules for the department; advising the principal, for instance, conveying the wishes of department members concerning new material adoption or curriculum revisions; and coordinating activities within the department, such as, insuring that all teachers have the necessary equipment and materials, and maintaining communication with each teacher in the department so that students are exposed to a comprehensive program, not one that is piecemeal.

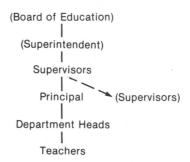

Figure 1.1
A typical secondary school administrative
arrangement.

In smaller school systems, and sometimes in larger ones, the role of department head is not well defined nor a part of the formal administrative structure. For these reasons, the department head, in many instances, has a title and is expected to perform certain duties, but receives no compensation or release time to perform these duties. This results in a situation that is unsatisfactory, and in which the department head is little more than an administrative conduit for the principal. This role makes the department head an administrative buffer rather than a facilitator. A number of steps can be taken to alleviate this problem, including: formalization of the position so that all persons concerned have a more definite idea of what the position entails and what can reasonably be expected of a person in such a position; provision of compensation—if the position is needed and taken seriously, a salary is in order; and provision of release time to allow the designated person sufficient time to accomplish the job. In a number of instances, the position of department head could be a part-time position, with some release time from regular teaching responsibilities and a salary above that of a regular teacher.

The Supervisor

To a large extent, the role of the supervisor is determined by the local school division. For this reason, the supervisor's position in the typical administrative arrangement is also determined by that same division (see Figure 1.1).

However, some generalizations concerning the role of the supervisor can be made. One of the main jobs of the supervisor is to provide consultative services to schools and teachers within the district. Sometimes these consultative services are provided to the building principal and the administrative staff; more often these services are provided directly to the classroom teacher. In providing consultative services, the supervisor makes an effort to coordinate learning activities in the school division. For example, the secondary supervisor endeavors to make the different units of the secondary school work together harmoniously throughout the entire division. On the other hand, a reading supervisor would strive to coordinate reading activities in the division. No matter what the specific duties of a supervisor are, one main task is to develop resources in a specified area. These resources may consist of outside personnel conducting inservice programs, the development of new subject matter materials, or helping a teaching committee decide on the appropriate textbook for local students.

The Teacher

In military parlance, the teacher is the "on-line commander" or the last officer (of the school) in the formal chain of command who is responsible for insuring that adequate learning occurs for each student. Thus, the primary goal of the teacher is to provide appropriate instruction to pupils in the school. The importance of this goal cannot be overemphasized. Unless the student is actually provided with an appropriate educational experience, the role of the teacher, and all subsequent persons in leadership positions in the school, is in question. From the student's perspective, the teacher is the first person encountered in most school situations. Also, the teacher is the school person with whom the student will have the most contact. Therefore, the teacher will, in many instances, provide more than appropriate instruction. The teacher will often be a friend, counselor, and catalyst in the life of the developing adolescent.

TRENDS AND ISSUES IN SECONDARY EDUCATION

There are usually a number of evolving trends and issues in any field being debated by professionals within that particular field. Three trends and issues that presently concern many educators at the secondary level are: (1) the issue of whether today's comprehensive high school is really "comprehensive"; (2) the development of alternative schools; and (3) the rapid rise of the minimum competency testing movement. Each of these topics will be discussed briefly.

During the past few years, an issue that has been hotly debated is whether the comprehensive high school, as delineated by James Bryant Conant (1959; 1967), has really fostered better secondary programming in terms of the educational, social, and financial benefits for today's youth. Passow (1977) has indicated that many educators are concerned about the continued existence of the comprehensive high school because, in many instances, this type of secondary school is too big to meet the needs of a large and often diverse student population. A related criticism is that the programming of the comprehensive high school often fails to meet the needs of many students because it is too general—in other words, no one type of student is gaining an appropriate or sufficient education. Even though some educators do not perceive the comprehensive secondary school as being really comprehensive, others claim that in many cases this type of school is adequately comprehensive in the area of college preparatory programming (Passow, 1977).

However, these same educators feel that the needs of students not in the college preparatory segment of the program are not being fully met. Regardless of the position one takes regarding the effectiveness of comprehensive secondary schools, one point seems nondebatable—a large number of students are not being served adequately by these schools. We draw this conclusion from the fact that the National Commission on the Reform of Secondary Education (1973) reported that at least one million youth drop out of school each year. While a vast number of reasons could be cited for this alarming dropout rate, one of the major reasons has to be the fact that secondary schools, as they presently exist, are not meeting the needs of many of today's youth.

Because present-day secondary schools have failed to reach a large segment of the adolescent population, other types of secondary schools have been created. While these schools have been referred to as "free schools" or "storefront schools," the name applied most often is "alternative schools." The one overriding characteristic of these schools is the uniqueness of each of the schools that make up the group we call alternative schools. These alternative schools often: provide programming options beyond those of the standard secondary school; focus more closely on individual needs, skills, and talents; exist in various forms, such as, open schools, schools without walls, or learning centers; and often exist outside the public school system (V. Smith, 1973). Alternative schools should not be confused with such parallel secondary schools as parochial schools or private schools. For all practical purposes, these parallel schools cannot be distinguished from public secondary schools.

In concluding these initial comments on alternative schools, it can be said that these schools are primarily committed to meeting the needs of some locally specified population; students usually voluntarily enter these schools; and any evaluation of each school is predicated on how effectively it meets the needs of its students (Smith & Cox, 1976).

It should be noted that alternative schools have come into existence with much criticism. Mortimer Smith, a leading critic of the alternative school movement, feels that it moves too far away from the concept of basic education, that is, instruction primarily focused on the development of numeration, language, and thinking skills (M. Smith, 1973).

In discussing the topic of minimum competency testing, Mary Berry (1979) has noted many lay persons as well as educators are currently concerned that overall student achievement appears to be declining. She further stated that by early 1979 at least 35 states had passed laws that required school districts to administer competency examinations to determine the level of achievement of pupils in certain academic areas. According to Pipho (1978), one goal of minimum competency testing is to improve student achievement and/or instruction. However, to this date, no one has shown how student testing at any level will lead directly to higher achievement or better instruction.

While minimum competency testing laws differ from state to state, there are a number of common elements. For example, in most states several (at least two different sets) examinations are to be administered periodically throughout the academic career of the student. For those students who do not score at a suitable level, remediation is to be provided. In many cases, the timetable for provision of remediation is extremely fuzzy; it is unclear how remediation will be provided and when it will take place. Many states have tied the minimum competency examinations to high school graduation requirements—all students who graduate from high school must pass these tests at a certain predetermined level, for example, the eighth-grade achievement level. Additionally, the tests that make up the competency examinations tend to center on math and reading skills. Lastly, most if not all of the examinations will become compulsory in the early 1980s (Pipho, 1978).

In addition to these problems associated with minimum competency testing, Brickell (1978) and Wise (1978) have noted a number of factors that must be addressed if any positive benefits are to be gained from this movement. Two of the questions that Brickell has raised have to do with which competencies will be measured and how these selected competencies will be measured. Although many states have mandated that testing be done in such areas as math and reading skills, few states have clearly delineated the competencies that are to be assessed or how they will insure that these competencies have been adequately assessed. Wise has claimed that this movement is already doomed to failure because of our ignorance about teaching and learning; that is, it does not always follow that when the teacher teaches, the student learns. Obviously, we have not covered all the intricacies or ramifications of the trends and issues discussed. Nor have we explored all of the many trends and issues currently being debated in the field of secondary education. However, we have attempted to set the stage for later discussion of these and other topics as they relate to exceptional adolescents.

SUMMARY

Secondary education in the United States evolved from the traditional Latin grammar school, which was upper-class in orientation, to the academy, which was more middle-class in outlook, and finally to the high school of today, which is geared to providing college or life preparation for all students. While there are a number of different stated purposes and objectives of secondary education, one of the major goals of professionals in this area is to prepare adolescents for future roles in this society. In line with this stated goal is the belief of many educators that the secondary school should strive to meet the needs of the individual student *and* society.

The curriculum of the secondary school usually includes a formal plan of directed activities and experiences that occur in or near the school environment. The most widely used types of curriculum organizations are the subject-centered, broad-fields, core, and experience curricula. The subject-centered curriculum is the option in use in most schools. A major criticism of this curriculum is that it does not promote generalizations from one subject to another.

All of the curricula mentioned are implemented through formal planned activities, which are usually referred to as inclass activities, or through extraclass activities, which are less closely associated with the formal curriculum. Even though extraclass activities often do not occur in a formal classroom setting, these activities are considered part of the curriculum.

Three trends and issues that were discussed in this area were the "comprehensiveness" of the comprehensive high school, alternative schools, and the minimum competency testing movement. Of these trends and issues, minimum competency testing was least clearly defined in terms of what it is, what it specifically attempts to accomplish, or how it can be accomplished.

REFERENCES

Berry, M.F. Student competency testing. *The High School Journal,* 1979, *62,* 166–172.

Brickell, H.M. Seven key notes on minimum competency testing. *Phi Delta Kappan,* 1978, *59,* 589–592.

Brown, J.F. *The American high school.* New York: MacMillan Co., 1909.

Conant, J.B. *The American high school today: A first report to interested citizens.* New York: McGraw-Hill, 1959.

Conant, J.B. *The comprehensive high school: A second report to interested citizens.* New York: McGraw-Hill, 1967.

Conant, J.B. *The revolutionary transformation of the American high school.* In L.E. Metcalf, J.J. Deboer, & W.V. Kaufers (Eds), *Secondary education: A textbook of readings.* Boston: Allyn & Bacon, 1966.

Coombs, J.R. Can minimum competency testing be justified? *The High School Journal,* 1979, *62,* 175–180.

Cubberley, E.P. *The history of education.* Boston: Houghton Mifflin, 1920.

Douglass, H.R. *Secondary education in the United States* (2nd ed.). New York: The Ronald Press, 1964.

Dumas, W., & Beckner, W. *Introduction to secondary education: A foundations approach.* Scranton, Pennsylvania: International Textbook Co., 1968.

Grant, W.V., & Lind, C.G. *Digest of educational statistics.* Washington, D.C.: HEW (OE), 1974.

Macdonald, J.B. The high school in human terms: Curriculum design. in N.K. Hamilton & J.G. Saylor (Eds.), *Humanizing the secondary school.* Washington, D.C.: Association for Supervision and Curriculum Development, NEA, 1969.

The National Commission on the Reform of Secondary Education. *The reform of secondary education: A report to the profession.* New York: McGraw-Hill, 1973.

Passow, A.H. *American secondary education: Conant influence.* Reston, Virginia: National Association of Secondary School Principals, 1977.

Payne, J.S., Polloway, E.A., Smith, J.E., & Payne, R.A. *Strategies for teaching the mentally retarded.* Columbus, Ohio: Charles E. Merrill Publishing Co., 1977.

Pipho, C. Minimum competency testing in 1978: A look at state standards. *Phi Delta Kappan,* 1978, *59,* 585–588.

Reinhardt, E. Development of secondary education. In L.E. Metcalf, J.J. Deboer, & W.V. Kaulfers (Eds.), *Secondary education: A textbook of readings.* Boston: Allyn & Bacon, 1966.

Rollins, S.P., & Unruh, A. *Introduction to secondary education.* Chicago: Rand McNally, 1964.

Smith, F.R., & Cox, C.B. *Secondary schools in a changing society.* New York: Holt, Rinehart & Winston, 1976.

Smith, M. CBE views the alternatives. *Phi Delta Kappan,* 1973, 54, 441–443.

Smith, V.H. Options in public education: The quiet revolution. *Phi Delta Kappan,* 1973, *54,* 434–437.

Stiles, L.J., McCleary, L.E., & Turnbaugh, R.C. *Secondary education in the United States.* New York: Harcourt, Brace & World, 1962.

Wise, A.E. Minimum competency testing: Another case of hyperrationalization. *Phi Delta Kappan.* 1978, *59,* 596–598.

2

Characteristics of Exceptional Youth

Traditionally in the past, exceptional adolescents have been divided into categorical groups in a manner similar to the division of elementary age exceptional children. These divisions often reinforced our conceptions of what exceptional adolescents should be like because many of our ideas about these youth were based on knowledge directly associated with younger children. However, as one attempts to deal with these youth, it becomes readily apparent that even though a categorical label such as "learning disabled" can be applied to young children as well as to adolescents, the two groups may not learn or behave in a like manner. This dilemma leads us to the main purpose of this chapter—to discuss the characteristics of secondary special students that distinguish them from other students.

The first section of this chapter examines several categorical definitions of exceptionality to set the stage for the material that follows. The second section discusses arguments and counterarguments for combining several groups (which we refer to as the "mildly handicapped"), for example, the mildly mentally retarded (EMR), the learning disabled (LD), and the mildly behavior disordered (BD). At the end of this section we offer our opinion on this matter and our proposed definition of what constitutes a mildly handicapped learner. Following this discussion, a brief examination is made of different theories that seek to explain adolescence and some of the behaviors of adolescents. Next, a list of developmental tasks associated with adolescence is described in an attempt to take a more specific and detailed look at one of the theories of adolescent development. Since adolescents, like all other humans, have a number of basic needs that they try to fulfill, these basic needs will be closely scrutinized in the section following the examination of developmental tasks. The material on basic needs is followed by a discussion of general characteristics of exceptional youth, as well as a review of selected studies concerning the various groups that make up the larger group we call the mildly handicapped. The chapter closes with a number of implications about interactions of exceptionality, adolescence, and school and societal demands. Throughout this chapter, anecdotes concerning exceptional youth present "real life" examples of the points under discussion.

CATEGORICAL DEFINITIONS OF EXCEPTIONALITY

For our purposes, the following definitions of behavioral disabilities, learning disabilities, and mental retardation provide the overall framework that will be used later in reporting studies that have sought to identify characteristics of persons in these groups.

Behavioral disabilities, as defined by Graubard (1973), refer to

> a variety of excessive, chronic, deviant behaviors ranging from impulsive and aggressive to depressive and withdrawn acts (1) which violate the perceiver's expectations of appropriateness, and (2) which the perceiver wishes to see stopped. (p. 246)

While there are a number of definitions of *learning disabilities,* the definition proposed at the DCLD Board of Trustees meeting in April of 1977 seems the most appropriate in terms of actually defining the population under discussion; it also seems the least discriminatory toward children and youth who may have additional handicaps. This definition states:

> Specific learning disabilities are serious impediments that are intrinsic to the individual. These conditions are manifested in wide discrepancies among developmental and/or academic skill areas. Such

disorders may exist independently of or in addition to other handicapping conditions or lack of opportunity to learn. Specific learning disabilities are of such severity that special remedial or compensatory
education programming is required. The problems are demonstrated
by markedly depressed performance in such developmental areas as
perceptual-motor ability or language acquisition and in those
academic skill areas related to reading, spelling, written expression,
and arithmetic. Specific learning disabilities may be found in children and youth who are mentally retarded, emotionally disturbed,
sensorially impaired, or otherwise handicapped. (p. 3)

Mental retardation as defined by the American Association on
Mental Deficiency (Grossman, 1973, 1977) refers to "significantly sub-
average general intellectual functioning existing concurrently with
deficits in adaptive behavior, and manifested during the developmental period" (p. 5). Since we are concerned mainly with the mildly
retarded whom Zigler (1967) has hypothesized as being essentially
normal in most respects, that is, no specific pathological agents or
genetic mechanisms can be shown to cause this type of retardation,
the above definition is further restricted to include only those persons
who have measured IQs in the range of about 60 to 70 IQ points and
who have only slight deficits in adaptive behavior.

At this time it seems wise to include a definition of juvenile delinquency, since many of the youth that we are concerned with will come
into conflict with our legal system at one time or another. According
to Briggs and Wirt (1965) a delinquent is

a person whose misbehavior is a relatively serious legal offense,
which is inappropriate to his level of development and is alien to the
culture in which he has been reared. Whether or not the individual is
apprehended or legally adjudicated is not crucial. (p. 23)

THE MILDLY HANDICAPPED LEARNER

A number of educators have extensively examined the question of
whether it would be more advantageous to combine the many categorical groups of exceptional children and youth with mild learning problems into one group called the mildly handicapped, or some other
generic name (cf. Epstein & Cullinan, 1979; Hallahan & Kaufman,
1976, 1977, 1978; Lilly, 1977, 1979; MacMillan, 1973; Smith, Polloway, & Smith, 1978). The arguments of these writers for development
of a generic category are: techniques for teaching the several groups
are similar; regardless of any attached label, many of the persons who
would be included in a mild generic category display behavioral prob-

lems that are associated with their learning problems; and a continued emphasis on specifically defining categorical groups will always exclude some undefined group of learners with mild learning problems from educational services that they may need (MacMillan, 1973; Smith et al., 1978).

On the other hand, a number of educators have argued that specific categories such as LD, BD, and EMR are worthwhile and necessary for the best education of these exceptional individuals. The arguments of this group revolve around the following points: specific categories are needed for research purposes to insure the highest amount of reliability and generalizability of results; combining the several groups would promote heterogeneity rather than homogeneity (homogeneity is needed if similar teaching methods are to work with these children and youth); and generic groupings would call for matching learners in development and learning. According to Becker (1978), if the last point were followed to its logical conclusion, then a large difference would often exist in the chronological ages of the students who would be matched on mental age. For example, if two students with mental ages of 12 and IQs of 100 and 70 respectively were placed in the same classroom, then we would assume a similarity in stage and style of learning because these students were matched on mental age. Yet, just as Becker has indicated, our example would result in a chronological age (CA) of 12 for the youngster with the IQ of 100 and a CA of approximately 17 for the youngster with the IQ of 70. Since we know that there is a difference in social behaviors and expectations of 12 year olds and 17 year olds, it is quite natural to expect differences in learning styles of these two youth. Thus, it would seem that the two students in our example are matched on one important variable (MA), but not on another (CA), which may be equally important.   •

In the above arguments for and against generic groups of youngsters with mild learning problems, one point that has not been sufficiently dealt with by either of the two major sides is the relationship of and grouping on common characteristics. Both sides in this continuing debate have implied that these two factors must always be linked; that is, if you group certain learners according to some predetermined characteristics, then these same learners will be taught in the same environment or they will always be placed together. This simply is not the case. Proponents of generic groupings would agree that once a set of common characteristics is determined, for example, responsiveness to similar teaching strategies and materials, mild learning and behavior problems, and approximately equal mental ages, then the next obstacle to be faced is to insure that divergent characteristics do not interfere with learning. At least two strategies come to mind relative to eliminating this obstacle. The first strategy involves teaching students in extremely small groups (two to four pupils). This strategy would allow the teacher to begin grouping on the predetermined characteristics, and then to minimize other divergencies by limiting the number of members in an instructional group. This strategy is frequently employed in the noncategorical, resource room approach used for teaching exceptional children and youth. A second strategy is to begin grouping students on common characteristics, and then continue to group these pupils according to other significant criteria. For example, we might start with a very large group of mildly handicapped learners; then, in this case, restrict our class placement or teaching to adolescents who have approximately the same mental and chronological ages, and who are interested in vocational programs for repairing automobile engines. This second strategy has been used in the past to educate categorical and noncategorical groups at the secondary level. By using one or both of the above strategies, general characteristics as well as specific individual characteristics can be accounted for and dealt with effectively. We do not believe that this is the case with the numerous categorical definitions and placements that presently exist. These definitions and subsequent placements frequently have failed to move beyond a set of obvious and general characteristics to deal with the large amount of heterogeneity that is also found in categorical groupings.

A Proposed Definition

It should be poignantly clear from this discussion that the issue of creating a generic grouping for children and youth with mild learning problems has not been resolved, nor is it closed. In fact, Hallahan and Kauffman (1978) have noted that the field of special education is at an impasse on this issue. Our position is that since a large amount of heterogeneity continues to exist, even within specifically defined categorical groups, it is more logical to use a generic category to meet the needs of the many unserved and underserved children and youth in our schools. In line with this opinion, the following definition is proposed. *Mildly handicapped learners are those learners who display slight but persistent learning problems, which may be of a specific or general nature and which are associated with negative behavioral manifestations, or maladaptive behaviors, and failure in school. Additionally, the specific cause of the learning problem is unknown in the vast majority of cases.*

Admittedly, this definition is a compromise solution to many of the definitional problems that presently exist. However, it is our belief that this definition has at least three positive features. First, it allows us to provide services for those youngsters who presently fall between the cracks of traditional categorical definitions, for example, those youngsters who are too smart to be labelled mentally retarded, yet not smart enough to be labelled learning disabled, and who do not act weird enough to be labelled behavior disordered. Second, this proposed definition would not exclude youngsters with other handicapping conditions from this generic grouping. In this instance, a student previously labelled mentally retarded or behavior disordered can still have a specific learning problem and be eligible to be served under this generic label. Third, since our proposed definition is not as restrictive as preceding ones, it will permit the use of more fluid placement options. This fluidity will allow all youngsters with mild learning problems to be served in the least restrictive environment, as mandated by PL 94–142 (Ballard & Zettel, 1977). Additionally, since many of the categorical definitions previously referred to will continue to exist, researchers have the option of using the specific populations derived from these definitions for study. This action would be similar to the situation in which mentally retarded individuals are divided into several groups (mildly, moderately, and severely retarded) for study.

ADOLESCENT DEVELOPMENT

Since the pupil who concerns us is an adolescent or is nearing the adolescent stage of development, it appears that before a general or specific determination is made of the potential problems of the exceptional youth, the larger dimensions of adolescence must be examined. The period of adolescence is generally conceived of as extending from puberty (about 12) to approximately the 18th to 20th year of life. Pollard and Geoghehan (1969) have suggested that persons at this stage of development make a gradual shift of social orientation away from the family to the peer group. Youngsters in this group begin to seek in earnest to develop an identity of their own (Erikson, 1963); they begin to quest for adulthood. In this quest the adolescent begins to attain physical and social maturity and moves from a conforming person to a more self-governing individual. It is at this stage that age-mates and models assume a position of great importance. This is easily seen in the attempts of many adolescents to dress and talk like their peers; no one at this stage in our society seems to want to be too different from "the crowd."

While it is generally accepted today that the passage through the period of adolescence varies in different cultures, the earlier writings

of persons such as Granville Stanley Hall (1904) indicated that this was a time of "Sturm und Drang," or storm and stress, and that this was probably true for all cultures. However, Garrison (1965) has firmly stated that this viewpoint is no longer held in high esteem. According to Erikson, as quoted by Evans, adolescence is the period in life when the youth seeks to reconcile two conflicting identities, to fashion a realistic whole out of the positive and negative sides of his or her personality (Evans, 1967). Havighurst (1972) has theorized that the primary lessons of youth during this period are social and emotional, rather than intellectual. Regardless of the views that one may hold regarding this period, it seems clear that the persons we are discussing are no longer children; yet, they have not attained full adult status; and these youth must fit themselves into the existing culture as well as fit the culture to themselves.

Developmental Tasks

In line with the more general task of adolescence just mentioned, Havighurst (1972) has reported that there are a number of specific tasks associated with adolescent development. These tasks are:

1. achieving new and more mature relations with age-mates of both sexes
2. achieving a masculine or feminine social role
3. accepting one's physique and using the body effectively

4. achieving emotional independence of parents and other adults
5. preparing for marriage and family life
6. preparing for an economic career
7. acquiring a set of values and an ethical system as a guide to behavior—developing an ideology
8. desiring and achieving socially responsible behavior. (pp. 45–75)

*Achieving new and more mature relations with
age-mates of both sexes.*

This task suggests that the individual, whether male or female, will begin to look on age-mates as persons to work with in accomplishing common goals. In these pursuits, the adolescent discovers that at times he or she is expected to lead or provide some direction to the group. Yet, at other times, this same leadership may not be necessary. Thus, the adolescent must develop a knowledge of certain group dynamics to know what specific role must be assumed in a particular group. At the same time, many adolescents are moving toward the goal of identifying males and/or females as individuals and not just as members of their sexual group or the "other" sexual group.

Achieving a masculine or feminine social role.

During the period of adolescence, boys and girls begin to change into physically mature males or females. There is a clear biological basis for this change, or more precisely these changes, since several physical as well as mental alterations take place within the adolescent at this time. For example, the maturing male begins to develop body hair on the upper torso as his sexual organs develop, and the maturing female begins to develop enlarged breasts and experiences her first menstrual cycle as her sexual organs develop.

As the adolescent matures physically, psycho-social development also takes place. This psycho-social development leads the perceptive youth to discover how adult males and females act differently from each other. Through these perceptions, the young man or woman is enabled to define gradually an appropriate social role.

*Accepting one's physique and using the body
effectively.*

The goal in this instance according to Havighurst (1972) "is to become proud, or at least tolerant, of one's body; to use and protect one's body effectively and with personal satisfaction" (p. 51). This means that at this juncture in time, and in the future, the individual must be aware that, barring an unfortunate incident, this is the body that one will have for a lifetime and that it must be taken care of and protected. Thus, health and safety lessons that occur in or out of school become very important at this time. Matters of how to use the body in work and play also assume much importance.

Achieving emotional independence of parents and other adults.

This task causes a certain amount of friction in the family as well as in situations where other adults may assume the role of the parent. Often this friction is caused by the ambivalence of both the adult figures and the adolescent; for example, both the parents and adolescent may have many emotion-laden ideas about the relative amounts of freedom and protection needed by the youth involved. However, the goal of the adolescent at this time is to achieve an emotional state of being in which he or she can rationally decide when help is or is not needed. A complementary task of parents, educators, and others is to help the maturing individual reach this goal by providing opportunities for positive growth. If adults as representatives of the culture really want the youth to "grow up," then the youth must be provided with adult-like tasks in order to accomplish this goal. In much the same way that a neonate is gradually moved away from total reliance on a liquid diet to one that includes solids, the adolescent must be helped to move away from the total emotional and physical dependence of childhood to the independence of adulthood. Since the adolescent is, in many cases, capable of performing this task, provisions must be made to insure that it in fact takes place. Examples of activities that would help the adolescent to accomplish the task include: (1) requiring the youngster to assume more responsibility in caring for the home or members of the family, such as, younger brothers and sisters—at the same time, this individual should be given more freedom in deciding how to handle such matters as dating and curfews; and (2) providing opportunities in the school for the student to make decisions about school-related matters, such as, membership on athletic teams or curriculum revisions.

Preparing for marriage and family life.

In general, this task requires that the evolving adult begin to develop relationships with the opposite sex that will ultimately result in marriage. Going through the courtship ritual, learning to understand and tolerate the actions of others, and gradually acquiring the ability to love and share this love with another individual are all positive steps that may lead to marriage.

While the institution of marriage is still held in high esteem by most members of our society, the ultimate results of the marriage partnership are not as fixed as in the past. A marriage of today will not necessarily result in the partners having children. In quite a few instances, today's marriages result in a family composed of the marriage partners only. This indicates that the family is not as stable a concept as in the past. Thus, an added component to the task of preparing for family life is that of deciding what the family life of a specific marriage will be composed of, or how this particular family will be like or different from other families. The changing concept of the family is due in part to the availability of contraceptive devices, as well as the changing roles of males and females in our society.

Preparing for an economic career.

Achievement of this task centers around attempts of an individual, and other supportive persons, to organize one's work potential and obtain a job. There are many possible avenues for achieving this task, and one subgoal is to eliminate gradually unwanted choices as one moves nearer to finding the right job.

Havighurst (1972) has also indicated that a primary goal associated with this task is for the adolescent to feel able to work. It is not enough to possess work-related skills; one must feel that these skills are useful and that one can use them.

Acquiring a set of values and an ethical system
as a guide to behavior—developing an ideology.

In line with several of the other adolescent developmental tasks, this task compels the individual to formulate an ideological system for guiding behavior. That is, since this person is striving to achieve an identity separate from parents and other adults, is attempting to develop positive relationships with peers and others, and is moving toward an economic career, then the youth must have some systematic way of dealing with self-behavior as well as the behavior of others. Unless the adolescent develops a set of ethical values, he or she will act in an erratic and often confusing manner in social exchanges. In other words, the adolescent must develop a kind of personal, ethical, and moral "road map" as a guide to behavior; this personal map is contrasted with the one previously imposed by parents and other authority figures.

Desiring and achieving socially responsible
behavior.

This task requires the person to want to interact socially in the community and to achieve this interaction through some responsible behavior. Ways of accomplishing this task include: working as a member of a local political party; being active in community affairs; or volunteering to work with young children in or out of school.

Even though these developmental tasks, which were described by Havighurst, were formulated through observations of normal or average adolescents, they are just as applicable to the development of mildly handicapped adolescents. Thus, we should expect this specific group of adolescents to work toward achievement of these tasks.

Basic Needs of Adolescents

Along with the developmental task associated with adolescence, there exist a number of physiological and psychological needs that the teenager must also satisfy (Maslow, 1968). Initially the teenager, like all other persons, is concerned with satisfying such physiological needs as those for water, food, and protection from the elements. After these physiological needs are met, Maslow (1968) has postulated that certain psychological needs assume a more dominant role in the life of the individual. The psychological needs that become important are for: (1) safety, (2) belonging and love, (3) esteem, and (4) self-actualization.

Safety needs extend directly from some of the physiological needs; that is, a person not only wants to be protected from the elements, but wants actually to feel safe. For the younger child, safety needs can be met by parents and other authority figures. Yet, these safety needs cannot be met in the same way for the teenager who is trying to be independent. Thus, many youths in this age bracket join cliques, gangs, and other groups to help satisfy some of their safety needs. In this instance, the motto of many teenagers seems to be: "There is safety in numbers." At this time, the adolescent is primarily concerned with being and acting like the peer group instead of trying to define who he or she is.

During the period when safety needs are being reasonably met, belonging and love needs come to the fore in the individual's life. Belonging and love needs cause the person to wish for and seek the affection, love, and trust of others. Satisfying these needs for the developing youth often involves choosing between several sets of people, for example, parents, teachers, siblings, same sex peers, or opposite sex peers. This dilemma occurs because the world of the adolescent is enlarging daily and the goals of these different groups are not always harmonious.

Esteem needs closely follow and are intricately associated with belonging and love needs. The esteem needs are predicated on the individual's evaluation of self, based on personal perceptions of how others feel toward him or her. The individual wants to feel that others value him or her. Feelings of competence, adequacy, and achievement are also associated with a person's esteem needs. Because the maturing youth is in a period of transition, esteem needs are not always met. Consequently, many of the highly competitive behaviors displayed by some adolescents in academic and nonacademic situations are indicative of their attempts to satisfy esteem needs (see Anecdote 2.1).

Maslow (1971) has cautioned that few people ever reach the level of self-actualization; most people are in the process of working toward that goal. This statement makes sense if one realizes that lower needs (lower than self-actualizing needs) are usually met only on a temporary basis. Thus, the teenager who is striving to gratify other needs is also moving in the direction of fulfilling self-actualizing needs. Viewing the transitional period of adolescence in a more precise manner, one can readily conclude that the adolescent is, in most cases, striving to become what he or she is capable of becoming, and this striving usually enables the person to reach for even higher levels of achievement (see Anecdote 2.2).

Anecdote 2.1
Joan

The first thing you would notice about Joan was her sly grin. If you were a male teacher at our school, the grin was a lot easier to notice because she had this disturbing habit of running up to male teachers to say "Hello." Joan seemed to crave attention in and out of the classroom. In the classroom, she delighted in incessant giggling with her favorite girl friend and in defying instructions so that the entire class would have to stop work and pay attention to her. My particular problems with her centered around the fact that she could not wait to get home to call me in the evening. She would call and would want to talk for hours about the most inane matters. I tried every reasonable means to get her to stop calling, but she persisted. Finally I had to call in her guardians with whom she lived. After talking with them for a short time, it was easy to see what a major part of Joan's problem was. Her guardians indicated that Joan's mother had left her with them for several extended periods beginning when Joan was a small child. They expressed the opinion that Joan's mother was a "sinful" woman and that she did not love Joan. From their conversation, it was obvious that while they were providing Joan with a home and care, her guardians did not value her as a person. They seemed to feel that taking care of her was a job that they had to do. Thus, in most instances in the home, Joan was tolerated, but probably not actually loved in the true sense of the word.

THE EXCEPTIONAL ADOLESCENT

The exceptional adolescent lives in the midst of all the developmental tasks and basic needs associated with this period of growth, as well as in the midst of the recurring problems that may be attributed to exceptionality. This places the exceptional youth in a double bind that compounds the intricacies of adolescence and the problems of exceptionality. In other words, it is difficult enough being an adolescent. When the developmental tasks and basic needs of adolescence are combined with some type of learning or behavior problem, such as those of the mildly handicapped youth, then this youth is probably in for academic trouble at the very least (see Anecdote 2.3). Pollard and Geoghegan (1969) have reported that for many children who had gotten by in the primary grades, this period of schooling results in an increased display of learning and behavior problems. While specifically referring to the plight of the learning disabled adolescent, Lerner (1976) made a very cogent comment that could apply to the situation of all adolescent mildly handicapped learners. She pointed out that by

Anecdote 2.2
Rodney

Rodney was a pleasant but extremely shy teenager. To many of his teachers, he seemed to have the ability to perform adequately in the classroom, but for some reason he never quite achieved the level that was expected. After several years of just getting by in school, Rodney was placed in a resource program where he continued to display many of the same below-average behaviors. However, during the months after he had been placed in the resource program, Rodney began to show a number of positive changes in his attitude, appearance, and daily work. Most of his teachers, including the resource teacher, attributed this change in behavior to the fact that Rodney had been placed in a resource program that was meeting his needs. Yet, the resource teacher was still curious about Rodney's change in behavior and subsequently asked him to try and explain it.

Rodney commented that the changes that everyone saw were brought about by the fact that his parents had bought him a "CB" and that he talked on it every chance he could. Rodney further explained that his "handle" or CB name was "Shy Guy," but that since no one actually knew who he was or what he looked like, he no longer felt shy. After he had talked on the "CB" for several weeks, Rodney felt better about himself and his ability to accomplish certain goals, He also explained that, for this reason, he felt he could do better in school. Apparently he was right!

this time in their lives, youngsters who have experienced persistent learning problems frequently have low opinions of themselves, as well as negative attitudes about learning. These same youngsters will also often display concomitant emotional and behavioral problems. Additional comments regarding this situation will follow.

General Characteristics

Epstein and Cullinan (1979) have postulated that mildly handicapped adolescents are generally characterized "by their failure to achieve one or more developmental-educational goals to an acceptable extent within an acceptable period of time" (p. 6). The developmental-educational goals that these authors refer to are *social participation, intellectual competence, community contribution,* and *career preparation.*

Achievement of the first goal, social participation, implies that the maturing adolescent must not only be in school, but must also take an active part in the social milieu of the school. Achievement of

Anecdote 2.3
Lonnie

At the time I first met Lonnie, he was being considered for placement in a high school special education program. The person in charge of the special education program stated that it was more vocationally oriented than the general program of this particular high school. Lonnie was being considered for placement because he had received some very low grades in several subjects during the past year. In fact, his school performance had been marginal for his entire academic career. Yet, despite a number of learning problems, he had never actually failed a grade. He also was a year older than most of the other students in the ninth grade because he had entered the first grade when he was seven. Another factor that made Lonnie's situation unique was that he was steadfast in his belief that he could succeed in the regular high school program.

Lonnie's mother, who was aware of all of the aspects of this matter, had constantly stressed to the school officials involved that she was not worried about "her son going into a special education program," but that she was "more concerned about his total well-being, his academic success or failure, and how he felt about himself." Because of the commitment of Lonnie's mother and the many other factors previously mentioned, the school personnel in this case decided to monitor Lonnie's performance closely in the future and to provide him with remedial help. It was also decided that in the event these actions were not successful, placement in the vocationally oriented program would be tried.

this goal is especially important for the mildly handicapped youth because it allows the youth to work realistically on accomplishing the other three goals. Attainment of the developmental-educational goal, intellectual competence, is the primary reason the student is in school. Obviously, many mildly handicapped adolescents have problems in this area that are serious enough to attract the attention of school personnel. Thus, school personnel and the affected students must require that proper instruction be delivered to these individuals so that the students can develop or strengthen their intellectual powers. Realization of the third goal, community contribution, calls for the adolescent to recognize at least two things. First, most of the adolescent's day is spent in the school, which is a smaller version of the community outside the school. If the youth is to survive in the outside community, then he or she must learn to survive in the school community. This means that social, work, and intellectual skills all have to be used to foster positive relationships with other community members. Second, the adolescent must abstain from negative behaviors and constantly seek to contribute actively in any way to the maintenance of the school society. This can be done through such activities as volunteering to work in the library or another school department, participating in various clubs or on athletic teams, and helping individual teachers or students perform their daily tasks. The fourth goal, career preparation, indicates that the matter of future economic survival should be seriously worked on at this point in the adolescent's life. Therefore, secondary school personnel must help each pupil to determine what the career possibilities are, how to acquire employment skills, and eventually how to acquire the job that the youth is seeking.

As previously mentioned, mildly handicapped adolescents often have great difficulty in achieving developmental-educational goals. For this reason, secondary educators must be especially careful to provide well-planned instruction in social, academic, and vocational areas for these students.

Academic Achievement

At this point, we turn our attention to several areas where some of the specific characteristics of the mildly handicapped can be determined. The two areas that will be closely examined are reading achievement and arithmetic achievement.

Reading.

One area that has been explored quite extensively, relative to exceptional youth, is that of reading. Various reading-related topics and their effect on high incidence secondary youth (Sabatino, Rothman, & Epstein, 1978) have been explored, for example: the relationship of delinquency and reading failure (Hogenson, 1974; Miller & Windhauser, 1971), or the effects of remedial reading instruction (Muehl & Forell, 1973). While these studies are not conclusive in the sense that exact cause and effect relationships were discovered, results of these and similar studies do provide a knowledge base that is increasing and evidence on which tentative conclusions can be drawn.

In an attempt to determine what variables were related to high school reading performance, Muehl and Forell (1973) did a follow-up study of 43 high school students who had been diagnosed originally as disabled readers. These researchers selected three reading tests from the nine parts of the *Iowa Tests of Educational Development,* which are used to evaluate the general educational development of high school students. Muehl and Forell reported that results of their study showed that youngsters who had been diagnosed previously as poor readers continued to be poor readers at the secondary level. These authors further indicated that only 4% of the follow-up group was performing satisfactorily in the area of reading. Results of this study and others by researchers, such as, Balow (1965), and Lovell, Byrne, and Richardson (1963) have consistently indicated that young children labelled as poor readers in their early years continue to read poorly in their later school years. While these studies concerning remedial reading instruction do not offer an overall bright view of the future for children labelled as disabled or poor readers, all of the studies cited above indicate that many of the children labelled as poor readers *did* show some improvement in their reading skills. However, most of the children were still performing below average in reading at the time of the follow-up studies.

Hogenson (1974) and Miller and Windhauser (1971) in a somewhat different vein attempted to show that there is a link between reading failure and juvenile delinquency; juvenile delinquency and reading problems can be shown to exist together in more instances than expected by chance. Indeed, after studying two experimental populations of 48 boys who were randomly selected, Hogenson (1974) compared correlations between reading and manifest aggression. Reading failure was found to correlate positively with aggression in the two groups of boys. That is, the more reading failure a boy manifested, the more likely he would also manifest aggression. Miller and Windhauser (1971) examined personality characteristics of disabled readers and delinquent youth. They concluded that these "two types of students possess many similar personality characteristics such as emotional maladjustment, hostility, and suspicion. Also, both groups of youth usually have a negative self-concept and low tolerance to frustration" (p. 186).

Wiig and Semel (1974) compared 30 learning disabled youth to 30 randomly selected youngsters in grade 6 on their ability to understand or comprehend material that had been read to them. The LD group was composed of 4 females and 26 males who ranged in ages from 12 years 4 months to 16 years 1 month. Grade placements ranged from 6th to 9th grade. After subjects were selected for the study, the authors then read 50 logico-grammatical sentences to each subject. These sentences were divided into 5 groups (10 each) and were concerned with comparative, familial, passive, spatial, and temporal relationships. The analysis of results showed that a significantly larger proportion of LD youth scored below the median than individuals from the comparison group. These results were interpreted to mean that the adolescents with learning disabilities showed deficits in auditory comprehension, logical processing, and semantic coding of these perceptual events.

MacMillan (1977) concluded that for the mildly retarded the following seems to hold true regarding the matter of reading achievement: (1) mildly retarded individuals seem to underachieve in reading in much the same way as normals, that is, the mildly retarded person read below the level of expectancy even when this level of expectancy was based on mental age; (2) the mildly retarded performed best in the area of reading recognition; (3) the poorest performance of the mildly retarded was in the area of reading comprehension; and (4) the same teaching methods used to teach reading to normals were effective in teaching reading to mildly retarded persons. As far as teaching methods were concerned, the crucial factor appeared to be the belief of the teacher that a certain method would be successful. That is, if a teacher was familiar with a certain method for teaching reading and believed that method could be used successfully with a certain student, then the likelihood of success was greatly increased.

In summarizing this brief review of reading achievement among mildly handicapped adolescents, certain conclusions seem inescapable. Poor reading achievement is often associated with negative behaviors such as hostility, suspicion, and aggression. Therefore, it can be concluded that youths who display these behaviors are likely to be poor readers, and poor readers are more likely than not to display negative behaviors. Additionally, the prognosis for the complete eradication of reading problems is not good. If a youngster was labelled a poor reader at an early age, he or she is likely to exhibit poor reading skills in the secondary school.

Arithmetic.

According to Payne, Polloway, Smith, and Payne (1977), researchers are beginning to devote more time and attention to factors that affect achievement in the area of arithmetic or mathematics. At present, however, there is very little firm evidence derived from research in this area to tell us how mildly handicapped pupils learn or fail to learn certain arithmetic concepts. Not only is there a paucity of research in the total area of arithmetic achievement, there is even less research dealing directly with adolescents.

There are a number of reasons for this present situation. First, it is often difficult to separate learning in the areas of language and/or reading from learning in the area of arithmetic. Probably a more correct statement would be that presently arithmetic instruction is closely tied to certain language learnings, and it is also closely tied to one's ability to read or solve word problems. In looking at these relationships, especially between arithmetic and reading, it is clear that when a person experiences reading difficulties, the probability of concomitant problems in arithmetic is very high. Interestingly, the converse is not necessarily true. A person who is experiencing arithmetic difficulties may not have problems in reading. A second problem that has thwarted researchers in this area is how much learning is enough. Ask the following question: After a student has learned the basic computation facts, how much more learning is needed in this area for her or him to survive? For certain individuals, minimal arithmetic skills will be enough if they are going to work in a factory, as a telephone operator, or in a number of similar occupations. However, for those who will become scientists, engineers, or accountants a greater amount of mathematics is required.

Even though there has not been a large amount of research done in this area, Cawley and his colleagues at the University of Connecticut at Storrs have shed some light on this subject (cf. Cawley & Goodman, 1969; Cawley & Pappanikon, 1967; Cawley & Vitello, 1972). In one of their experiments, Cawley and Goodman studied the effects of an 18-week demonstration program on normal and mentally retarded pupils who ranged in age from 127.74 months to 172.52 months. These youngsters were divided into four different groups: Control A—this group included mentally retarded youths who received no special training, nor were their teachers given special training; Control B—this group was composed of normal 4th-grade children; Experimental A—this group was made up of mentally retarded youth who received training from teachers who had been specifically trained to use demonstration materials; and Experimental B—this group included mentally retarded youth who had demonstration materials, but whose teachers had not been specifically trained to use these materials. When pre-post differences for all groups were compared, the Experimental A group showed the greatest gain on a test of verbal problem solving and a test of arithmetic principles and understanding.

Following similar studies with other populations, Cawley and his associates have concluded that: (1) concrete learning is *process* and *product* for many mildly handicapped learners; concrete learning should, however, be part of the process whereby the learner is enabled to generalize to new situations that involve the same type operation or principle (Cawley & Pappanikon, 1967); and (2) teacher education programs must begin to stress development of problem solving skills and understanding, as opposed to a student simply deriving a product from his or her arithmetic work. From their work in this area, these researchers have also developed a model for arithmetic learning that emphasizes process activities rather than product-related activities, and that can be used with many mildly handicapped pupils (Cawley & Vitello, 1972). The program *Project Math,* which is based on the above mentioned model, is described in detail elsewhere (Cawley, 1977). In general, the materials and procedures that have been developed for use in the *Project Math* series are meant for all mildly handicapped learners.

In summarizing the preceding discussion, one can conclude that more research is presently being conducted in the area of arithmetic achievement, especially by Cawley and his associates, and that this research will provide us with new information on how to help mildly handicapped adolescents learn arithmetic concepts.

Behavioral and Personality Characteristics

Unlike the previous area of academic achievement, quite a few researchers have studied the behavioral and personality characteristics of mildly handicapped youth. In many cases, these particular characteristics have been looked at as they relate to other variables, such as, academic achievement and juvenile delinquency.

Based on the previous factor analytic work of Quay and his colleagues (Quay, 1964; Quay, Morse, & Cutler, 1966; Quay & Quay, 1965) concerning personality patterns of different groups of youth, McCarthy and Paraskevopoulas (1969) studied the behaviors of three groups of learning disabled, emotionally disturbed, and average youngsters. The youngsters ranged in age from 6 years 2 months to 13 years, and ranged in IQ from 68 to 132 points. After comparing the three groups on the *Behavior Problems Checklist* developed by Quay and Peterson (1967), it was determined that all groups were rated as being significantly different on the factors of: (1) unsocialized aggression, (2) immaturity-inadequacy, and (3) personality problems. Results also showed that both groups of handicapped youngsters had conduct-related behavior (acting out, aggressiveness, and hostility). Both groups also showed a relatively high level of immaturity. An important point based on results of this study is that the negative behaviors of the mildly handicapped groups continued into adolescence.

In a somewhat different vein, a number of investigations have sought to determine the relationship of behavior in the classroom to general academic success. Noteworthy among these efforts have been a series of studies by Swift and Spivack (1969a, 1969b, 1973). In these studies, Swift and Spivack attempted to show that behaviors that are related to academic success are the same for all youth, regardless of the educational setting. However, as will be indicated shortly, mildly handicapped youth tend to display many behaviors that do not enhance their possible academic achievement.

In one study, Swift and Spivack (1969a) compared the behavior patterns of underachieving and achieving youngsters based on the dual criteria of (1) teacher assigned grades and (2) achievement test scores taken from the *Iowa Test of Basic Skills.* Using the above criteria, as well as comparing all subjects on the *Devereux Elementary Behavior Rating Scale,* the following results were obtained: (1) achievers displayed less behavior problems than any other group, (2) persons with A and B grades displayed less problem behaviors than others, and (3) persons with D and F grades displayed more behavior problems than any other comparison group.

In a related study, Swift and Spivack (1969b) held weekly discussions with teachers of 1,554 youth who were between the ages of 12 and 19 and who were either in regular public school classes (N = 882) or in special classes for the emotionally disturbed (N = 672). From these ratings, a behavior rating scale consisting of 45 items grouped into 13 factors was developed. Twelve factors were common to both settings; one factor, verbal negativism, was found only in the special class setting. The authors drew the following conclusions from the study: behaviors related to academic success were the same for youth in regular and special classes at the secondary level; boys exhibited more disturbance/restlessness behavior and had poorer work habits, whereas girls tended to exhibit more quiet, withdrawn, and anxiety producing behaviors; and originality diminised significantly as students progressed from 7th to 12th grade.

In a later report, Swift and Spivack (1973) analyzed two different comparisons of urban and suburban high school students on the *Hahnemann High School Behavior Rating Scale* (HHSB). After comparing the two groups in the first study, Swift and Spivack indicated that, in a practical sense, there were no differences in behavior between the two groups. It was hypothesized in the second study that underachieving and achieving urban students would display significantly different behavior patterns as measured by HHSB scores. Results from this study were similar to ones obtained in suburban schools; that is, achievers displayed fewer problem/disturbing behaviors than did underachievers. Other results of the second analysis revealed that high teacher grades were associated with mid to high group test scores (69 of 86 cases), low teacher grades were associated with low group test scores (25 of 38 cases), and urban students were more active, verbally negative, and restless than suburban students. However, urban students were less likely to display anxiety in school.

While most writers have resisted the urge to equate mildly handicapped youth with juvenile delinquency, several have indicated that there is considerable overlap in the behavior and personality characteristics of these groups (Berman & Siegal, 1976; Mauser, 1974). For example, Berman and Siegal compared the performance of 45 adjudicated juveniles and a matched control group on the *WAIS* and *Reitan Neuropsychological Battery* for adults. With the exception of one subtest of the Reitan battery, the juvenile delinquents' performance was inferior to the control group's Berman and Siegal summarized the results of this study by concluding that "it appears that the delinquents as a group showed deficits with respect to controls in their ability to comprehend, manipulate and utilize conceptual material which is of a verbal nature" (p. 587). Other conclusions drawn from this study included the fact that the juvenile delinquents studied did not seem to use good judgment, nor did they seem to profit from experience, and lack of skills seemed to be associated with the backgrounds of most of these youths. Apparently, many of the mildly handicapped youth that concern us will manifest problems similar to those mentioned in the above study.

In an attempt to show the similarities between groups of youth classified as delinquent or learning disabled, Mauser (1974) reviewed an extensive amount of literature concerning these two groups. From this review he concluded that: (1) both groups were mainly composed of males; (2) both sets of youth showed a low tolerance for frustration and tended to have negative or low self-concepts; (3) each group was low in measured academic skills; (4) low achievement had existed for both these groups since shortly after they had started school; and (5) there did not appear to be a single cause or cure associated with either juvenile delinquency or with learning disabilities.

Implications

In reviewing the material cited in the two previous sections, relating to academic achievement and behavioral and personality characteristics of exceptional youth, one can readily deduce that as a group the mildly handicapped tend to perform poorly in academics when compared to their peers. They also tend to display inappropriate classroom behaviors that seem to have a negative correlation with academic success (acting out, aggressiveness, making negative remarks toward others) and there is a striking similarity between the behaviors displayed by mildly handicapped youth and juvenile delinquents.

Several implications seem inescapable. First, since many exceptional youths are likely to be underachievers and to display behavior problems, systematic and long-term measures must be taken to eradicate these problems. Second, since many of these youths will have had these problems for quite some time, the individual and the problem will probably resist change. Third, because this population is so heterogeneous, we must be prepared, as Mauser (1974) stated, to institute a large number of different treatment strategies with these youths. A number of these treatment strategies will be discussed in chapter 3.

Additionally, these conclusions indicate that teachers who work with exceptional adolescents must resist the temptation to look for or expect immediate solutions to their problems. Teacher trainers in this area will also have to make a number of adjustments in the training of special and general education teachers if the present situation is to be changed. General educators at the secondary level will have to be less subject oriented in their teaching procedures and perceptions of adolescent learners. Special educators at this level need to become more familiar with the inner workings of the secondary school and to work actively to define their place in the instructional environment.

SUMMARY

In this chapter, the exceptional adolescent has been looked at vis-à-vis his or her status as an adolescent and as a person who is mildly handicapped. Initially in this regard, three categorical definitions of learning disabilities, behavioral disabilities, and mental retardation were cited to provide a framework for later discussions in the chapter. A definition of what constitutes a mildly handicapped learner stated that such a learner displays slight, but persistent learning problems, which may be of a specific or general nature and which are associated with negative behavioral manifestations, or maladaptive behaviors, and failure in school. Following this discussion, an overall look was taken at a number of general and specific tasks of adolescence. Fitting oneself into the culture and fitting the culture to oneself was seen as one general task to be accomplished. Some specific developmental tasks that all adolescents strive to accomplish are: achieving emotional independence from adult figures, achieving an appropriate social role (masculine or feminine), and preparing for an economic career.

The last sections of the chapter focused on a number of general and specific characteristics of exceptional youth. Generally, mildly handicapped youth were characterized as having failed to achieve the developmental-educational goals of social participation, intellectual competence, community contribution, and career preparation within a reasonable amount of time. Lastly, it was shown that in a large number of instances mildly handicapped youth displayed chronic problems in the area of achievement. Many of these youth also displayed behaviors that were very similar to those of juvenile delinquents. However, no specific relationship was shown to exist between juvenile delinquency and mildly handicapping conditions.

REFERENCES

Ballard, J., & Zettel, J. Public Law 94–142 and Section 504: What they say about rights and protections. *Exceptional Children,* 1977, *44,* 177–184.

Balow, B. The long term effect of remedial reading instruction. *The Reading Teacher,* 1965, *18,* 581–586.

Becker, L.D. Learning characteristics of educationally handicapped and retarded children. *Exceptional Children,* 1978, *44,* 502–511.

Berman, A., & Siegal, A.W. Adaptive and learning skills in juvenile delinquents: A neuropsychological analysis. *Journal of Learning Disabilities,* 1976, *9,* 583–590.

Briggs, P.F., & Wirt, R.D. The meaning of delinquency. In H.C. Quay (Ed.), *Juvenile delinquency: Research and theory.* Princeton, New Jersey: Van Nostrand, 1965.

Cawley, J.F. Curriculum: One perspective for special education. In R.D. Kneedler & S.G. Tarver (Eds.), *Changing perspectives in special education.* Columbus, Ohio: Charles E. Merrill Publishing Co., 1977.

Cawley, J.F., & Goodman, J.D. Arithmetical problem solving: A demonstration with the mentally handicapped. *Exceptional Children,* 1969, *36,* 83–88.

Cawley, J.R., & Pappanikon, A.J. The educable mentally retarded. In N.G. Haring and R.L. Schiefelbusch (Eds.), *Methods in special education.* New York: McGraw-Hill, 1967.

Cawley, J.F., & Vitello, S.J. Model for arithmetical programming for handicapped children. *Exceptional Children,* 1972, *39,* 101–110.

Division for Children with Learning Disabilities Newsletter, 1978, *3* (3), 3.

Epstein, M.H., & Cullinan, D. Education of handicapped adolescents: An overview. In D. Cullinan & M.H. Epstein (Eds.), *Special education for adolescents: Issues and perspectives.* Columbus, Ohio: Charles E. Merrill Publishing Co., 1979.

Erikson, E. *Childhood and society* (2nd ed.). New York: Norton, 1963.

Evans, R.I. *Dialogue with Erik Erikson.* New York: Harper & Row, 1967.

Garrison, K.C. *Psychology of adolescence.* New York: Prentice-Hall, 1965.

Grubard, P.S. Children with behavioral disabilities. In L.M. Dunn, *Exceptional children in the schools: Special education in transition* (2nd ed.). New York: Holt, Rinehart & Winston, 1973.

Grossman, H. (Ed.). *Manual on terminology and classification in mental retardation.* American Association on Mental Deficiency Special Publication Series No. 2, 1973, 1977.

Hall, G.S. *Adolescence: Its psychology and relations to physiology, anthropology, sociology, sex, crime, religion, and education.* New York: Appleton, 1904.

Hallahan, D.P., & Kauffman, J.M. *Exceptional children: Introduction to special education.* Englewood Cliffs, New Jersey: Prentice-Hall, 1978.

Hallahan, D.P., & Kauffman, J.M. Labels, categories, behaviors: ED, LD, and EMR reconsidered. *The Journal of Special Education,* 1977, *11,* 139–149.

Hallahan, D.P., & Kauffman, J.M. *Introduction to learning disabilities: A psycho-behavioral approach.* Englewood Cliffs, New Jersey: Prentice-Hall, 1976.

Havighurst, R.J. *Developmental tasks and education* (3rd ed.). New York: David McKay Co., 1972.

Hogenson, D.L. Reading failure and juvenile delinquency. *Bulletin of the Orton Society,* 1974, *24,* 164–169.

Lerner, J.W. *Theories, diagnosis, teaching strategies: Children with learning disabilities.* Boston: Houghton Mifflin, 1976.

Lilly, M.S. Learning and behavior problems: Current trends. In S.M. Lilly (Ed.), *Children with exceptional needs: A survey of special education.* New York: Holt, Rinehart & Winston, 1979.

Lilly, M.S. A merger of categories: Are we finally ready? *Journal of Learning Disabilities,* 1977, *10,* 115–121.

Lovell, K., Byrne, C., & Richardson, B. A further study of educational progress of children who had received remedial education. *The British Journal of Educational Psychology,* 1963, *33,* 3–9.

MacMillan, D.L. Issues and trends in special education. *Mental Retardation,* 1973, *11*(2), 3–8.

MacMillan, D.L. *Mental Retardation in school and society.* Boston: Little, Brown and Company, 1977.

Maslow, A.H. *The farther reaches of human nature.* New York: Viking Press, 1971.

Maslow, A.H. *Toward a psychology of being* (Rev. ed.). Princeton, New Jersey: Van Nostrand, 1968.

Mauser, A.J. Learning disabilities and delinquent youth. *Academic Therapy,* 1974, *9,* 389–402.

McCarthy, J., & Paraskevopoulas, J. Behavior patterns of learning disabled, emotionally disturbed, and average children. *Exceptional Children,* 1969, *36,* 69–74.

Miller, W.H., & Windhauser, E. Reading disability: Tendency toward delinquency? *Clearinghouse,* 1971, *46,* 183–186.

Muehl, S., & Forell, E.R. A follow-up study of disabled readers: Variables related to high school reading performance. *Reading Research Quarterly,* 1973, *19,* 110–123.

Payne, J.S., Polloway, E.A., Smith, J.E., & Payne, R.A. *Strategies for teaching the mentally retarded.* Columbus, Ohio: Charles E. Merrill Publishing Co., 1977.

Pollard, M.B., & Geoghegan, B. *The growing child in contemporary society.* Milwaukee: Bruce Publishing Co., 1969.

Quay, H.C. Dimensions of personality in delinquent boys as inferred from the factor analysis of case history data. *Child Development,* 1964, *35,* 479–484.

Quay, H.C., Morse, W.C., & Cutler, R.L. Personality patterns of pupils in special classes for the emotionally disturbed. *Exceptional Children,* 1966, *32,* 297–301.

Quay, H.C., & Quay, L.C. Behavior problems in early adolescence. *Child Development,* 1965, *36,* 215–220.

Sabatino, D.A., Rothman, S.G., & Epstein, M.H. Youth in trouble. In D.A. Sabatino & A.J. Mauser (Eds.), *Specialized education in today's secondary schools.* Boston: Allyn & Bacon, 1978.

Smith, J.E., Polloway, E.A., & Smith, J.D. The continuing dilemma of educating children with mild learning problems. *Special Children,* 1978, *4*(2), 52–60, 63.

Swift, M.S., & Spivack, G. Achievement related classroom behavior of secondary school normal and disturbed students. *Exceptional Children,* 1969, *35,* 677–684. (a)

Swift, M.S., & Spivack, G. Clarifying the relationship between academic success and overt classroom behavior. *Exceptional Children,* 1969, *36,* 99–104. (b)

Swift, M.S., & Spivack, G. Academic success and classroom behavior in secondary schools. *Exceptional Children,* 1973, *39,* 392–399.

Wiig, E.H., & Semel, E.M. Logico-grammatical sentence comprehension by adolescents with learning disabilities. *Perceptual Motor Skills,* 1974, *38,* 1331–1334.

Zigler, E. Familial mental retardation: A continuing dilemma. *Science,* 1967, *155,* 292–298.

3

Secondary Programming for Exceptional Youth

During the last few years, there has been a tremendous increase in the amount of concern expressed about programming for exceptional adolescents. Unfortunately, this expressed concern has had little effect on the actual development of new secondary programs. At this point, one might question how this present situation came about and speculate on the future direction of secondary special education.

Prior to the present burgeoning concern about secondary programs for exceptional adolescents, the entire field of education literally "looked the other way." For example, the first author is reminded of his initial two years of teaching in the public school of a small town. During this time, I worked with the "intermediate" educable mentally retarded (EMR) class at one of the local elementary schools. Although this class was housed in an elementary school, most of the pupils that I worked with were between 12 and 16 years of age. Not only were these students older than the typical elementary pupil, but the two different classes were composed almost entirely of males (there was one female in the class during the second year). The first-year class of 15 pupils included: a behavior disordered boy whose father physically beat him on numerous occasions; a 13-year-old boy who could do arithmetic problems with the greatest of ease but who could not read on a third-grade level; an aspiring basketball player who did want to do anything except play basketball; and at least one boy who was below average in all areas. The second-year class included: one male who was in our class solely because he was a behavior problem and no regular classroom teacher would work with him; one female who never spoke above a whisper and who was waiting to leave school when she turned 16; and several adolescents who were taller, bigger, and stronger than I was. After being in my class for one or two years, these various individuals were then "promoted" to the local high school. Some of them stayed at the high school for a few weeks, others stayed for a semester, while a few held on for the entire year. The problems that all of these young people encountered centered around the fact that there was no specific program at this particular high school to meet the needs of these special students. Indeed, this was not and probably still is not an atypical situation or way of handling exceptional adolescents.

Even in geographical areas that have been able to have specific programs aimed at meeting the needs of mildly handicapped adolescents, the programs that were developed were often haphazardly conceived. A clear set of program objectives, program direction, and program evaluation were often lacking. Also, training programs to prepare teachers to work in this area and to build on the established secondary level programs have been virtually nonexistent. Thus, many of the secondary school programs that sought to serve the needs of the mildly handicapped were ill-conceived and probably staffed by persons untrained to work in such programs.

Another problem that has caused much consternation is that of deciding what teaching methods and materials to use in programs serving these youth. Compounding this problem has been the concern of how to determine systematically the adequacy of the methods and materials being used in many of these programs. In other words, although educators in this area needed a data base to make program decisions, results from such a data base were not forthcoming. A respectable amount of research and writing has been done on mildly handicapped children; this is not true for the secondary level exceptional pupil. The paucity of research and writing has created situations in which poorly trained teachers, in often poorly designed programs, use teaching methods and materials that were designed for use either with average secondary pupils or for younger exceptional pupils.

This somewhat bleak picture regarding secondary programming for exceptional adolescents, we believe, accurately reflects present-day realities. However, there are a number of well-established secondary programs and program models for teaching exceptional adolescents. Yet these well-established programs are the exception rather than the rule at the present time. In subsequent portions of this chapter, past as well as emerging program options for working with mildly handicapped youths will be discussed. Following this discussion, there is material reviewing the role of the special educator in the secondary school. Lastly, we will discuss a number of issues and trends of current interest in the field.

TRADITIONAL OPTIONS

As Deno (1970) and Reynolds (1962) have indicated, programs and services for the exceptional student range from those in the regular classroom to those delivered in institutional settings. Traditionally, high school programs for mildly handicapped youth have been handled by use of categorical groupings. For example, in the past, secondary programs for educable mentally retarded, learning disabled, and emotionally disturbed/behaviorally disordered students have often been different in kind and emphasis. Programs for educable mentally retarded adolescents have concentrated on developing work-related skills in academic as well as nonacademic areas. The resource model that teachers of learning disabled children at the elementary level rely on heavily is also used at the secondary level for this group. On the other hand, programs for the emotionally disturbed or behaviorally disordered adolescent have ranged from the resource room approach, to self-contained special classes, to residential schools and other types of institutional settings. Secondary programs relating to these categorical groups will be examined in more detail. Programming for juvenile delinquents will also be described because, as stated in chapter 2, some of the youth that we are discussing have a high probability of becoming delinquents.

High School Programs for EMR Students

The high school work/study program is the educational option that is most often associated with the secondary level mildly retarded pupil (Brolin, 1976; Kolstoe & Frey, 1965). This particular secondary program calls for the student to engage in academic and vocational pursuits aimed at developing entry level job skills for the program trainee. In tracing the history of secondary education for the retarded, Kokaska (1968) has indicated that at least two factors, the Second World War and the federal government, have had a great influence in shaping the present emphasis on early and continuous work experience for this group. Kokaska viewed World War II as having both a propulsive and retardant effect on the development of secondary programs for the retarded; whereas the war created a labor shortage that made it possible for many marginally employable persons to get jobs, it also caused many school age persons to leave the formal school setting in order to take these jobs, preventing some mildly retarded persons from getting these jobs. During the same period, the federal government was instrumental in shaping policy in this area by documenting through publications certain cooperative relationships of state vocational rehabilitation agencies and local school systems. In a number of instances, these cooperative relationships were formed to bridge the gap between the time the vocational rehabilitation program could provide services to the student (about 18 years of age) and the time a student could leave school (usually 16 years of age). Regardless of the particular reasons for the present emphasis on work programs for the EMR youth, professionals in this area seem committed to this option.

The typical work/study program emphasizes developing academic and vocational skills that will either be used directly on the job or as a means for securing future employment (see Table 3.1). Work/study programs usually require the student to spend the first and perhaps second year in the program developing and refining general academic and vocational skills that have some direct relationship to many possible jobs. At the same time, the student is trained to work at different simple jobs in the school setting (helping the janitor, helping in the principal's office, or working in the school cafeteria). Working at these simple jobs provides a means for counselors and the work/study coordinator to assess the job-related capabilities of the student. During this initial phase of the work/study program, the student concentrates on fostering many work-related skills (Smith, 1974). However, the latter phases of the program call for the prospective employee to move out into the community to practice job-related skills in a more realistic and less controlled setting. This on-the-job training may entail working at several different jobs over short time periods, or it may be semi-permanent with the student remaining at the same site for his or her entire training period. Usually, during the latter stages of the program, the worker in training returns to the school for at least one-half of the day. At the end of a three- or four-year program, the successful student graduates and hopefully secures gainful employment (Capobianco & Jacoby, 1966).

For the mildly retarded, the major goal or emphasis at the secondary level has been the development of marketable skills that will enable the individual to obtain a job after graduation. Throughout the high school career of this particular group of adolescents, counselors, teachers, and other professionals strive to help the mildly retarded youth to acquire and demonstrate skills related to preparation for em-

Table 3.1
A Typical Work/Study Program

Grade 10

Academics—Emphasis is on development or remediation of skills in the areas of English, math, or social studies depending on the entry level skills of the student. In most programs, classes or courses associated with these content areas take up about one-half of the school day.

Physical Education/Health—Work/study participants usually take these courses with all other students during one academic period each day.

Preliminary Vocational Training—Specific vocational information concerning the student is gathered at this time (if it has not been secured previously). Basic courses dealing with the fundamentals of work are taken by all students in the program. These basic courses include introductory material relating to the use of hand tools, developing homemaking skills, making simple repairs, as well as other job-related topics. This training encompasses approximately one-fourth to half of the school day.

Grade 11

Academics—Emphasis in this area is shifted to use of basic skills in vocational areas. For example, in the area of English, the student might work on letter-writing skills. In the area of math, the student might work on units concerned with budgeting, buying on credit, or paying taxes. This part of the program continues to require approximately half of the school day.

Physical Education/Health—One period each day.

Vocational Training—Depending on a number of factors, such as, the student's interests and aptitude and the prevailing as well as projected job market, each pupil is offered specific vocational training. This training may be in such areas as the building trades, clerical work, food service, patient care, or materials handling. At this time, students are given the opportunity to display their work skills through inschool job performance. This portion of the work/study program continues to require approximately one-fourth to one-half of the school day.

Grade 12

Academics—Skills directly related to job training continue to be emphasized. These skills include reading newspapers and other written materials to obtain job information, and refining job interview skills through effective use of oral and written communications. This portion of the program begins to require less than half of the school day.

Work Experiences—During this phase of the program, each student participates in a number of specific job experiences in the local community for approximately one-half of the day. Whether at work in the morning or in the afternoon, each student reports to the school every day to participate in academic courses, as well as to receive any necessary counseling.

ployment. In a number of instances, the state vocational rehabilitation agency, as well as other rehabilitation facilities, are instrumental in securing jobs for the EMR student and/or assessing job-related skills (Brolin, 1976).

Secondary Programming for Learning Disabled Students

Scranton and Downs (1975) have noted that program development for LD children and youth has lagged far behind that of other areas of special education. This is especially true for the LD adolescent. This phenomenon may be due, in part, to the recent growth of the field of learning disabilities, or to the fact that our nation's schools have, in many instances, attempted to work with the mildly retarded or juvenile delinquent who displayed more obvious problems. Regardless of the reason, an alarmingly small number of secondary programs are aimed at meeting the needs of this population. Professionals in this area not only face the problem of a general scarcity of programs, but also the fact that many existing secondary programs are in private settings (Marsh, Gearheart, & Gearheart, 1978). In the private setting, the student usually boards at the school, school personnel can work with a pupil for larger amounts of time, and students can also be admitted selectively to the school thereby increasing homogeneity. Thus, in a large number of cases private programs are different from those offered in the public schools. As a result of their individuality, these private secondary programs often cannot be used as program models.

As previously stated, secondary programs for the learning disabled student in the public schools tend to employ the resource model (Goodman & Mann, 1976; Lerner, 1976). The resource model calls for an outside specialist or resource teacher to be directly concerned with and responsible for ameliorating learning problems of this group of students. The resource teacher can assume one of several roles in attempting to eradicate or modify a certain student's learning difficulties. One role is that of direct remediation—the specialist works directly with the pupil on some specific skill or in a specific content area. A second role is that of providing supportive assistance to the regular teacher who, in turn, works with the student. A third role involves acting as a teacher liaison between different specialists and work with a particular pupil, for example, coordinating the activities of a speech clinician, vocational educator, and rehabilitation counselor.

A number of important assumptions underlie the operation of a resource program for learning disabled pupils (and other exceptional students for that matter). These underlying assumptions are: (1) the resource person must have an extensive knowledge of the entire school operation, especially as it relates to teaching of general and specific skills; (2) the resource person must be able to work effectively with others as a number of services are involved in the attempt to solve a particular youth's educational problems; (3) the resource teacher must be technically competent in the areas of assessment and remediation of educational difficulties; and (4) the resource program must be adequately funded. When and if these basic assumptions are violated, the impact of the resource program is drastically reduced (Wiederholt, Hammill, & Brown, 1978).

The major emphasis of most secondary programs for youth who are labelled learning disabled is on normal or near normal achievement (Lerner, 1976). In attempting to achieve this goal, the resource teacher, in conjunction with other school personnel, concentrates on remediating the deficits of the student as well as capitalizing on that person's strengths. However, Goodman and Mann (1976) have convincingly argued that teaching at this level and for this type of student should be mainly compensatory in nature. It was felt that since many of these youth would shortly be terminating their formal schooling, emphasis should be placed on using the academic skills that the students have, rather than remediating weak ones. For more detailed descriptions of secondary programs for learning disabled youth, the reader should consult the following sources: Goodman and Mann (1976), Mann, Goodman, and Wiederholt (1978), Marsh, Gearheart, and Gearheart (1978), Sabatino and Mauser (1978), and Zigmond (1978). In addition, Table 3.2 offers a brief description of one LD program that exemplifies many of the points just discussed.

Programs for Behavior Disordered and Delinquent Youth

Many of the problems mentioned in connection with secondary programs for youth with learning disabilities are also associated with secondary programs for youth with behavior disorders. For example, Nelson and Kauffman (1977) found that there was a scarcity of programs at this level for youth who would fit under the broad category of behavior disordered. They speculated that a number of characteristics of secondary education may contribute to this general scarcity of programs, for example, specialized content teaching, and/or a continued emphasis on academic achievement over other types of learning. Another recurring problem for practitioners in this area—emotional disturbance/behavior disordered—is the inability of this group of professionals to define specifically the population with which they are concerned (Kauffman, 1977). Without a clear definition, there can be no clear pattern for delivery of services to this group of youth. A third

Table 3.2
Example of a Secondary LD Program

Chesterfield County (Virginia) Junior High School
Learning Disabilities Project

In 1972 the Chesterfield County Junior High School Learning Disabilities Project was initiated. The purpose of the project was to assist junior high school learning disabled students in increasing their academic achievement in school. Secondary goals of the project involved improving the self-concept, and reducing the drop-out rate of these students. The project was located in eight junior high schools throughout Chesterfield County. In each of these schools, learning disabled students, students who were viewed as being average or above average in intelligence but who had been experiencing failure in school, were referred to the project staff by their regular classroom teachers. After a referral was made, the pupil was administered a battery of tests to determine his/her present achievement level and areas of need, intellectual functioning, and perceptual-motor performance. When it was determined that a particular youth was in fact learning disabled, then (s)he was assigned to the learning lab located in his/her school. Each student spent at least one period a day in the learning lab where (s)he received individual instruction tailored to meet his/her needs from an LD meet his/her needs. Throughout this process, parents, teachers and administrators were kept abreast of the situation through periodic reports of the project staff. Additionally, teacher orientation sessions were held at the beginning of each year to acquaint regular classroom teachers with the project. The project staff was also available to work with regular class teachers throughout the year, thereby insuring that learning which took place in the learning lab was carried over to the regular class setting.

Results of the project revealed that after two years in the project, students showed general improvement in their grade point average as well as in the academic areas of spelling, paragraph comprehension, work recognition, and arithmetic computation (Goodman & Mann, 1976).

problem that causes additional confusion in this area is the close association between behavioral disabilities and juvenile delinquency. Youth with behavior disorders frequently engage in antisocial and illegal acts that cause some of them to be labelled as juvenile delinquents. On the other hand, many of the behaviors that juvenile delinquents exhibit can be characterized as illegal, aggressive, and potentially harmful to the youth or to someone else. Because of this, these youth would also be perceived as having behavior disorders. Even though there is some similarity in the behaviors of these two adolescent groups, programs for dealing with these behaviors are not always the same, or more precisely these programs do not emanate from the same source. We will return to this point shortly.

Although there is a general scarcity of programs for all maladjusted adolescents, there does seem to be a wide array of programs. Programming for this group includes: (1) the traditional self-contained class where the maladjusted student is educated away from the rest of the school; (2) the day school approach that locates several classes for maladjusted youth in one building; and (3) the residential program that provides around the clock supervision and/or education for this group. Residential programs often exist outside the public school setting and may include programs that are administered in "reform schools," jails, and prisons. Programs for behavior disordered and delinquent youth place a heavy emphasis on eliminating emotional and behavioral excesses as well as eradicating learning problems.

Although, in many respects, programs for juvenile delinquents are similar to those for youth with behavior disorders, one factor usually distinguishes the two. In a large number of cases, programs for juvenile delinquents are handled through the legal system rather than through the educational system. Therefore, we can reasonably infer that most of the youth dealt with by juvenile courts have been charged with the commission of some illegal act. These individuals are often placed in very restrictive settings such as juvenile detention homes. In contrast then, program settings for juvenile delinquents vary from the most restrictive to the least restrictive; programs for youth with behavior disorders tend to move along the continuum from least restrictive to most restrictive. Table 3.3 provides a brief description of three programs for juvenile delinquent and behavior disordered youth.

EMERGING PROGRAM OPTIONS

While traditional secondary programs continue to focus on specific categorical groups, a small number of programs have moved beyond this point in the last few years. Two of these programs are described here to acquaint the reader with the possibilities in this area.

Wood, Meyer, and Grady (1977) described the continuing education program of Broward Community College as it relates to exceptional adults. Students involved in this program attend classes two nights a week during ten-week sessions. The objectives of the program are to increase vocational, recreational, and social adjust-

Table 3.3
Three Programs for Maladjusted Youth

The Woodward Day School

The Woodward Day School was founded in 1970 as a cooperative venture of the Worcester (Massachusetts) public schools, the Worcester Youth Guidance Center, and the Worcester State Hospital. The school was developed as an alternative to institutionalization for behavior disordered adolescents in the age range of 13 to 19. The school has an enrollment of about 30 students and is located on the grounds of Worcester State Hospital.

According to Kennedy, Mitchell, Klerman, and Murray (1976), the school program is composed of three primary components: therapy, education, and vocational training. The therapy component is aimed at reducing undesirable and antisocial behaviors through the use of traditional therapeutic methods. On the other hand, the education component is concerned with aiding all students in the development of "survival skills," whether they will be reintegrated into the public school or will exit from the formal school situation via the Woodward Day School. These survival skills include traditional subjects taught at this level as well as skills associated with "such routine tasks as how to use public transportation, shop economically, read maps, and search for employment" (Kennedy et al., p. 717). Lastly, the vocational training component, which is aimed at older students who will not be reintegrated into community high schools, emphasizes development of vocational skills. The school also provides a means to evaluate its effectiveness by following up clients who are reintegrated into community high schools, or who are placed on jobs in the community. If students experience problems after leaving Woodward, they (and sometimes their parents) are provided with supportive counseling by the staff and others directly and indirectly connected with the Woodward program.

Ashland Senior High Learning Center

The Ashland Senior High Learning Center is a program for youth who might be labelled mildly emotionally disturbed or mentally retarded. This high school program is based in a rural setting in Ashland, Oregon. The total high school services about 725 students. According to Hoover (1978), "the main goal of the learning center is to develop self-sufficient, responsible, independent citizens with healthy self-concepts" (p. 30).

The program is composed of students who are at least 16 years of age and who have shown academic and emotional difficulties in school. All of these students have also failed to function normally in the school's regular or traditional program. Students in the program attend regular classes that meet their needs for academic requirements. These same students attend class sessions in the learning center to work on nonacademic problems. The learning center sessions are guided by a "resource" type teacher who helps the students in their attempts to evaluate and solve their problems. This resource teacher may also bring into the learning center other persons or things that can serve as resources to aid students in solving their problems.

Hoover (1978) also reported that this project has been very successful based on the fact that 30 of the 39 students who were in the program for at least two years graduated from high school. On the other hand, only six students dropped out of school.

Achievement Place

Achievement Place is a group home that was started in the late 1960s by Wolf and his colleagues (Phillips, Fixsen, Phillips, & Wolf, 1979). Clients who are placed in this group home are delinquent and disturbed adolescents who are referred through social service agencies, mental health agencies, and juvenile courts. The house is run by an intensively trained husband and wife team who live at the group home. Major goals of Achievement Place and the many replications of this group home situation are to help all youth placed in the home to develop self-governing skills that will reduce aggressive and/or maladaptive behaviors, while increasing positive self-care and academically oriented behaviors. These goals are fostered through an organizational structure called the "Teaching-Family Model" (Phillips et al., 1979).

ment skills. These objectives are met in courses dealing with vocational adjustment, home management, human growth and development, health education, consumer education, and music appreciation. Courses are also offered for students who want to upgrade their skills in such areas as typing, general office work, and automobile repair. In addition, a sports program that includes swimming, team sports, and other recreational activities is an integral part of the program. Another unique aspect of this program was the development of a summer camp at the college that afforded the participants an opportunity to interact with many of the other students who attended the college. Wood et al. (1977) reported that during this summer program many of the campers began to display extroverted personality traits instead of their former introverted traits.

It is apparent that this program is quite successful. It has grown from the original enrollment of 50 students in 4 courses to 135 students in 17 courses. Students in the program have also stated that they feel good about themselves, that they now have skills in areas where they previously had few, and that this program has made them feel like real people (Wood et al., 1977).

In Lynchburg, Virginia, in a project concerned with junior high school youth, school personnel perceived a need to develop a system-wide program that would meet the needs of youth with learning and behavioral problems. There were at least two unique features of this program: (1) students were not placed in the program based on some categorical label but on the basis of teacher recommendations, past school performance, and low achievement scores derived from a battery of tests; and (2) most students were given academic help in their school by a resource teacher. Students with the most severe problems were also given individual tutoring by master's level interns from one of the local universities. During a portion of the day when these students were not in their regular classes, or in the resource room, they participated in group counseling sessions to help them solve or better understand their behavioral problems. As a result of this project, a number of students who would have terminated their formal schooling at an early age continued on through high school (*Project Genesis*, 1975).

We believe these two examples just described give the reader an idea of what can be done for mildly handicapped young people if we discontinue our heavy reliance on categorical groupings, which do not promote the provision of needed services, and if we also begin to develop secondary educational options, which meet the needs of students, in place of a rigid administrative structure. Obviously, we still have a long way to go.

THE SECONDARY SPECIAL EDUCATOR

In many respects, the special educator at the secondary level performs functions similar to the special educator in an elementary situation. Yet, there are some significant differences between their roles.

Roles of the Secondary Special Educator

The specific roles that the special teacher performs in the secondary school include: (1) direct teaching; (2) operating a resource program; and (3) coordinating different aspects of the secondary program that are meant to eliminate or diminish significantly problems of the mildly handicapped learner.

Direct teaching involves working with the student in a situation where there are few other intervening teaching stimuli. This teaching situation would most likely occur in a self-contained classroom or similar environment, for example, a secondary day or residential school. A direct teaching program can operate parallel to the regular program or supplement it. In the direct teaching environment, the teacher is primarily concerned with assessing, developing, and/or remediating learning skills. The teacher in this position may focus on one skill area, such as, providing instruction in an academic block composed of math, English, and science. Teachers who work primarily in the area of vocational training also fit into this category. For example, business, shop, and home economics teachers would be responsible for teaching certain vocational skills directly to the student.

In order for the teacher who works directly with the special needs student to be effective, a number of variables must be taken into account. First, this type of teaching usually requires a low pupil/teacher ratio to assure that each student receives individual attention and instruction. Secondly, the teacher has to concentrate on the development and/or remediation of specific skills; this implies that each student's skills and abilities will be carefully assessed for program planning and development. Lastly, since this type of teaching arrangement usually takes the student out of the mainstream for a portion, if not all, of the school day, some measures must be taken to insure that the student receives social and academic experiences that will aid his or her adjustment in the mainstream environment. These social and academic experiences might occur in such courses and activities as physical education, health, school dances, or athletic events.

Relative to operating a resource program, Wiederholt, Hammill, and Brown (1978) have indicated that there are "at least five different types of resource programs (that) currently operate in the schools: the

categorical, the cross-categorical, the noncategorical, the specific skill varieties, and the itinerant" (p. 6). The first two types, the categorical and cross-categorical, are meant to serve pupils who have been officially classified as handicapped. In the categorical program, the resource teacher usually serves only one type of handicapped student. On the other hand, two or more types of handicapped groups may be served in a cross-categorical resource program. The noncategorical resource program serves both handicapped and nonhandicapped pupils. Thus students in this type of program might be referred by special or regular class teachers.

According to Wiederholt et al. (1978), the specific skill resource program is "organized around the training of particular skill areas, such as reading, mathematics, or speech. . . . Specific skill resource teachers usually work exclusively with normal students and their teachers; only rarely do they provide services to handicapped children" (p. 9). The overriding characteristic of the itinerant resource program is its mobility, that is, the itinerant teacher usually offers resource services at several different schools. The services delivered by this type of resource teacher may overlap those delivered through any or all of the resource models previously mentioned. In this situation, teachers at the schools visited by the itinerant resource teacher must follow up the actions initiated by the resource person. Since the itinerant teacher must spend a large amount of time travelling and must visit several schools in a limited amount of time, Wallace and Mc-

Loughlin (1975) have suggested that this type of program be used minimally, or only at the beginning stages of program development.

No matter what type of resource program is used in a particular school, the resource person: provides services to mild and moderately handicapped students (and students who in some instances may not be classified as having a handicap); usually works with a small number of pupils for one or more academic periods during the day; and advises regular classroom teachers regarding strategies, methods, and materials that can be used in working with exceptional adolescents.

The role of coordinating secondary programming for exceptional pupils may involve several complementary functions or duties including: (1) developing and maintaining a high school work/study program; (2) providing direct and indirect counseling services to youth enrolled in the program; (3) acting as a liaison between (a) the school program and parents or guardians and (b) community agencies; (4) acting as a student advocate in matters that affect the student and his or her program; and (5) providing follow-up services for program graduates, as well as for persons who have dropped out of the program. In this position, the special educator is responsible for seeing that academic and nonacademic services are provided for and delivered to the exceptional pupil in a relatively smooth and cohesive fashion.

Obviously, the special educator at the secondary level has a number of different roles and the staffing of one position does not preclude the possibility of working in another position. These different roles are not mutually exclusive; they all assume some expertise in the areas of identification, screening, formal and informal assessment, planning individual programs, implementing these programs, and evaluating the results of these programs.

TRENDS AND ISSUES IN SECONDARY SPECIAL EDUCATION

In chapter 1, several trends and issues relating to the entire field of secondary education were briefly discussed. At this point, we will examine a number of these trends and issues to determine how each relates to secondary special education and the special needs adolescent. The discussion is limited to two primary areas that we feel will have a tremendous impact on secondary special education for some time to come. These trends and issues are: (1) minimum competency testing and (2) preparation and certification of secondary special teachers.

The previous discussion on minimum competency testing stated that the requirement that all students attain a predetermined level of competence in certain academic subjects was being tied to graduation requirements in many states. This fact has several implications for the special student at the secondary level. In fact, many educators and parents are concerned that many mildly handicapped students will not be allowed to graduate, since they probably will not be able to meet the minimum competency requirements, or that states and local school systems will begin to issue special diplomas for those students who attend school through a certain number of years (Candor-Chandler, 1978). In other words, some students who have worked up to their highest level will not receive a diploma at all; others will receive diplomas that are different from those received by the majority of students (these special diplomas will probably be couched in terms that indicate the recipient has not achieved at any average level); and some students will only receive a certificate of attendance. In our democratic society this type of situation does not seem fair. Yet, short of abandoning the competency tests altogether, no reasonable solution can be offered at this time. In fact, few special educators have responded to this situation in any comprehensive manner.

Another issue of tremendous importance to the field is the matter of teacher preparation and certification in the area of secondary special education. According to Sabatino (1979), most teacher preparation programs are not training teachers to work with exceptional adolescents. In fact, there are no real models for providing this needed training at this time. Even if there were a large number of training programs, there would still be the problem of teacher certification. One way that we usually differentiate between secondary and elementary level teachers is that of specialization in a content area; secondary teachers usually teach only one subject area, such as history or science, whereas elementary teachers are trained to teach in several subject areas. Should a similar procedure be followed in training and certifying special educators at this level? We think not.

However, there is a need to provide more specific training for the special teacher who will work with mildly handicapped adolescents. For example, the secondary special educator should have a working knowledge of work/study programs, should be aware of procedures that can be used to find jobs in the community, and should be trained to provide counseling services, albeit on a limited basis. Most training programs at this point do not require the development of even these minimal skills, nor do state certification offices list requirements that distinguish between special educators at the secondary level and those in an elementary school. Certainly this situation has to change in the near future if we expect to make real progress in addressing and alleviating the problems of the mildly handicapped adolescent.

SUMMARY

This chapter explored the topic of programming for exceptional adolescents. At the beginning, it was noted that the entire field of education has engaged in avoidance behavior as far as exceptional youth are concerned. Even in those geographical areas where programs did exist, they were often haphazardly developed and many suffered from inadequate evaluation as to the ultimate effect of the program on its participants. Following this discussion, past program options for educating different groups of mildly handicapped youth were discussed. These traditional program options ranged from the work/study program, which is mainly associated with the mildly retarded, to the secondary level resource room, used extensively with learning disabled adolescents, to the vast array of programs associated with behavior disordered and delinquent youth. Programs for the last two groups of youth exist on a continuum from classes in a public school to education in prisons and jails. Next, two secondary programs seen as potential models for the future were described. One of the programs was in a community college setting. This type of program would probably meet many of the needs of pupils requiring a transition program between the high school and a full-time job. The other program was situated in a junior high school setting. Two unique characteristics of these different programs were their noncategorical nature and the fact that both took students from where they were when they entered the program and attempted to meet their needs rather than fit them to the program. The discussion following the program descriptions focused on the many different roles of the secondary special educator. These roles include direct teaching, being a resource person who works with students and/or teachers, and coordinating the many aspects of the secondary program as they relate to the special needs learner. Lastly, two trends and issues considered to have a great potential impact on secondary special education were discussed. These were the minimum competency testing movement and teacher preparation and certification for secondary special educators. It was postulated that, unless these matters are concluded in a positive manner, the education of exceptional adolescents will not progress.

REFERENCES

Brolin, D.E. *Vocational preparation of retarded citizens.* Columbus, Ohio: Charles E. Merrill Publishing Co., 1976.

Candor-Chandler, C. Charleston, West Virginia: Competency requirements for special education students. *Phi Delta Kappan,* 1978, *59,* 611–612.

Capobianco, R.J., & Jacoby, H.B. The fairfax plan: A high school program for mildly retarded youth. *Mental Retardation,* 1966, *4,* 15–20.

Deno, E. Special education as developmental capital. *Exceptional Children,* 1970, *37,* 229–237.

Goodman, L., & Mann, L. *Learning disabilities in the secondary school: Issues and practices.* New York: Grune & Stratton, 1976.

Hoover, J. A rural program for emotionally handicapped students: Democracy in action. *Teaching Exceptional Children,* 1978, *10,* 30–33.

Kauffman, J.M. *Characteristics of children's behavior disorders.* Columbus, Ohio: Charles E. Merrill Publishing Co., 1977.

Kennedy, J., Mitchell, J.B., Klerman, L.V., & Murray, A. A day school approach for aggressive adolescents. *Child Welfare,* 1976, *55,* 712–724.

Kokaska, C.J. Secondary education for the retarded: A brief historical review. *Education and Training of the Mentally Retarded,* 1968, *3,* 17–26.

Kolstoe, O.P., & Frey, R.M. *A high school work/study program for mentally subnormal students.* Carbondale, Illinois: Southern Illinois University Press, 1965.

Lerner, J. *Children with learning disabilities: Theories, diagnosis, and teaching strategies* (2nd ed.). Boston: Houghton Mifflin Company, 1976.

Mann, L., Goodman, L., & Wiederholt, J.L. *Teaching the learning-disabled adolescent.* Boston: Houghton Mifflin Company, 1978.

Marsh, G.E., Gearheart, C.K., & Gearheart, B.R. *The learning disabled adolescent: Program alternatives in the secondary school.* Saint Louis: C.V. Mosby Company, 1978.

Nelson, C.M., & Kauffman, J.M. Educational programming for secondary school age delinquent and maladjusted pupils. *Behavioral Disorders*, 1977, *2*, 102–113.

Phillips, E.L., Fixsen, D.L., Phillips, E.A., & Wolf, M.M. The teaching family model: A comprehensive approach to residential treatment of youth. In D. Cullinan & M.H. Epstein (Eds.), *Special education for adolescents: Issues and perspectives*. Columbus, Ohio: Charles E. Merrill Publishing Co., 1979.

Project Genesis: Program Description. Lynchburg, Virginia: Lynchburg Public Schools, 1975.

Reynolds, M.G. A framework for considering some issues in special education. *Exceptional Children*, 1962, *28*, 367–370.

Sabatino, D.A. Obstacles to educating handicapped adolescents. In D. Cullinan & M.H. Epstein (Eds.), *Special education for adolescents: Issues and perspectives*. Columbus, Ohio: Charles E. Merrill Publishing Co., 1979.

Savatino, D.A., & Mauser, A.J. (Eds.). *Specialized education in today's secondary schools*. Boston: Allyn & Bacon, 1978.

Scranton, T.R., & Downs, M.C. Elementary and secondary learning disabilities programs in the U.S.: A Survey. *Journal of Learning Disabilities*, 1975, *8*, 394–399.

Smith, R.M., *Clinical teaching: Methods of instruction for the retarded* (2nd ed.). New York: McGraw-Hill, 1974.

Wallace, G., & McLoughlin, J.A. *Learning disabilities: Concepts and characteristics*. Columbus, Ohio: Charles E. Merrill Publishing Co., 1975.

Wiederholt, J.L., Hammill, D.D., & Brown, V. *The resource teacher: A guide to effective practices*. Boston: Allyn & Bacon, 1978.

Wood, L.O., Meyer, B.D., & Grady, S.C. Exceptional adults learn in Broward Community College's continuing education program. *Teaching Exceptional Children*, 1977, *10*, 7–9.

Zigmond, N. A prototype of comprehensive services for secondary students with learning disabilities. *Learning Disability Quarterly*, 1978, *1*, 39–49.

part two

Instructional Provisions

This section of the book takes a close look at the different facets of the school and classroom that ultimately cause the student to learn. Chapte 4 examines the processes of assessment and intervention. Such topics as the referral process, gathering assessment data, and procedures for assuring that attempts at assessment and remediation are successful are discussed. Chapter 5 considers various topics relating to structuring academic tasks for learning. This chapter discusses teaching decisions, teaching procedures, and stages of learning, as well as other topics. In chapter 6, numerous aspects of classroom management are discussed, such as, arrangement of the classroom environment and scheduling of nonacademic activities. The basic premise of this chapter is that unless the teacher can successfully bring together or manage the various elements in the classroom, students will not learn.

4

Assessment and Educational Intervention

This chapter examines the dual processes of assessment and remediation of educational difficulties of exceptional adolescents. Although the chapter is divided into two major parts, assessment and intervention, it is crucial to highlight first the major components of the referral process. An arbitrary separation of assessment and intervention has been made, but the authors believe that these two processes are intricately tied to each other. The significance of this idea has been accented by Wallace and Larsen (1978) so that it becomes clear that educational evaluations are made in order to set up appropriate teaching strategies. That is, a teacher assesses the pupil's abilities with a purpose in mind. Usually this purpose is to change teaching strategies so that the learner can learn more easily or more quantitatively, and actually develop skills not formerly acquired or demonstrated.

THE REFERRAL PROCESS

Exceptional adolescents typically do not just appear in our classrooms; usually they are part of a process that has identified them as needing help and referred them to other personnel. This sequence of action initiates the referral process, which can be found in most school settings in the country. This process often provides the link between regular teachers and support personnel by evoking a mechanism to assist a student who is experiencing educational difficulties. However, the referral process is not solely restricted to the use of regular teachers; individuals including parents, special education teachers, assistant principals, and counselors, can refer a student. Just as a variety of people can initiate the referral process, there can be a myriad of reasons for a referral. Acknowledging the many legitimate nonacademic reasons for referring a student, this chapter focuses on the educational reasons.

The Dynamics of the Process

In order to bring structure to a sometimes confusing topic, we refer the reader to Figure 4.1. This figure is a generalized diagram of the important stages intricately incorporated into the referral process. Specificity has been sacrificed since every school system will reflect a vast amount of variation compared to other systems. Hopefully, however, this generalized diagram encompasses the major components of most referral processes.

After a referral is made, regardless of who makes it, someone in the school is responsible for activating the remainder of the process. Ordinarily this is the function of the principal; however, it may be accomplished by another individual. The next stage may involve an in-house staffing that could be described as a regular meeting of specific in-house personnel to review all new referrals or to monitor past referrals. At this point, a preliminary decision is made as to what further action is appropriate. If it is determined that intervention can be accomplished without further information, then this is achieved in an appropriate way (materials or consultation to the original referent). However, if the referral demands further investigation, certain definite procedures are employed. First, the parents of the student must be notified (in their natural language if necessary) that further evaluation is requested. Second, with the parents' permission, the indicated assessment procedures are begun. Very frequently, evaluative information is desired in the following areas: educational, psychological, sociological, and physiological/physical.

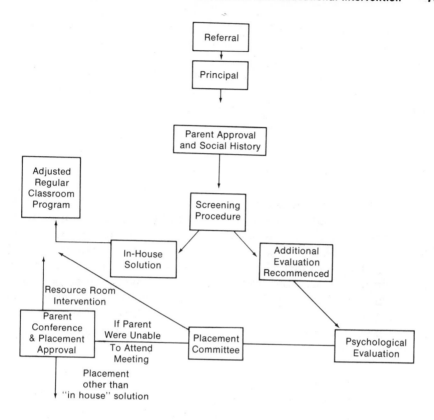

SOURCE: Hawisher, M.F., & Calhoun, M.L. *The resource room: An educational asset for children with special needs.* Columbus: Charles E. Merrill Publishing C., 1978

Figure 4.1
The Generalized Referral Process

Following the accumulation of the various evaluations, a placement committee convenes to provide the referred student with intervention strategies that will guarantee an appropriate education. This committee is responsible for designing an educational program specific to the needs of the referred student. Additionally, this committee must monitor the student's progress and reevaluate the placement at specified times.

This referral process actually includes many aspects of assessment and regulates the implementation of intervention. In keeping with the constitutional mandates of equal protection and due process, the formal application of this referral process becomes imperative.

Now that we understand how some students get to the point where assessment procedures are indicated, it is prudent to mention that quite regularly a teacher may wish to assess a student's performance prior to referring that student for supportive services or alternative placement. Primarily, the teacher may be interested in learning how better to help the student. Therefore, the next section of this chapter explores more closely this assessment process, whether it is accomplished by the teacher or by more specialized personnel.

ASSESSMENT

As just indicated, the primary purpose of educational assessment is to gather data that will help the teacher plan new and more effective teaching strategies. Yet, all types of assessment are not always used for this purpose. For instance, some types of assessment data are used primarily for classification and placement in special programs; for example, IQ tests are freqently used to classify persons as mentally retarded or learning disabled. At this point, we will discuss these different types of assessment, as well as different levels of assessment, assessment in specific content areas, and interpretations of assessment information.

Levels of Assessment

One approach to assessment is to study the different levels of assessment. Usually, assessment procedures are divided into two different levels, a *general level* and a *specific level.* Use of either one or both of these levels of assessment is predicated on the severity of the student's learning problems. General assessment is used to evaluate less severe learning problems; specific assessment is aimed at discovering the vectors impinging on more severe learning problems.

An example of general assessment is the evaluation of a pupil's overall academic achievement by such testing instruments as the *Wide Range Achievement Test* (Jastak & Jastak, 1965) or the *Sanford Achievement Tests* (Madden & Gardner, 1972). In this situation, the teacher is concerned with determining areas in which the student is *and* is not experiencing problems. On the other hand, specific assessment is usually aimed at locating the precise area(s) in which the student is failing to learn. For example, if a general achievement test indicates that a particular pupil is experiencing some difficulty in the area of arithmetic, then the teacher would need to scrutinize closely the different subareas of arithmetic (computation, arithmetic reasoning, or measurement) to determine exactly where the problem is.

At this point, many secondary teachers will be concerned about how to assess the learning of a student in a specific area such as reading, social studies, or history. However, such a specific discussion could encompass an entire book or even several books. This section of the chapter will acquaint the reader with several general guidelines for assessing a student in any area. The individual who is interested in more specific information relative to assessment should consult: *Teaching children with learning and behavior problems* by Hammill and Bartel (1975), *Assessment in special and remedial education* by Salvia and Ysseldyke (1978), and *Educational assessment of learning problems: Testing for teaching* by Wallace and Larsen (1978).

Types of Assessment

Although most of us probably think that assessment implies testing and nothing else, there is indeed more. Clearly, if assessment is inexorably associated with intervention (in an educational realm), then other techniques become diagnostically valuable. Salvia and Ysseldyke (1978) have provided a concise and useful guide, Figure 4.2, for organizing the variety of methods available to those involved with evaluating exceptional adolescents. The two dimensions that distinguish this assessment guide are the type of information desired and the time when the information is gathered. Even though this guide adequately covers many of the methodologies used in assessing an individual, a number of other types of assessment need to be discussed.

TIME AT WHICH INFORMATION IS GATHERED

	Current	Historical
Observations	Frequency counts of occurrence of a particular behavior Antecedents of behavior Critical incidents	Birth weight Anecdotal records Observations by last year's teacher
Tests	Results of an intelligence test administered during the assessment Results of this week's spelling test given by the teacher	Results of a standardized achievement-test battery given at the end of last year
Judgments	Parents' evaluations of how well the child gets along in family, neighborhood, etc. Rating scales completed by teachers, social workers, etc. Teacher's reason for referral	Previous medical, psychological, or educational diagnoses Previous report cards Parents' recall of developmental history, of undiagnosed childhood illnesses, etc.

TYPE OF INFORMATION

SOURCE: From *Assessment in special and remedial education* by John Salvia and James E. Ysseldyke. Copyright © 1978 by Houghton Mifflin Company. Reprinted by permission of the publisher.

Figure 4.2
Sources of Diagnostic Information

Normative-referenced assessment.

Normative or norm-referenced evaluation compares a person's scores to a group norm or set standard. Payne (1975) has stated that norm-referenced tests compare one to a hypothetical average and that this type of test can predict success (or conversely failure) beyond chance. Normative-referenced tests are often used in making classification and placement decisions in the schools. These instruments are standardized, implying that all subjects are taken through the same testing procedure, instructions for the administration of the test are the same, and scoring is done through an objective predetermined system. Norm-referenced instruments are also examples of formal testing de-

---

Table 4.1
Examples of Normative Referenced Tests

Achievement (General)

Peabody Individual Achievement Test (Dunn & Markwardt, 1970)
Wide Range Achievement Test (WRAT) (Jastak, Bijou, & Jastak, 1963)

Arithmetic

Key Math Diagnostic Arithmetic Test (Connolly, Nachtman, & Pritchett, 1971)

Intelligence

Stanford-Binet Intelligence Scale (1974)
Weschler Intelligence Scale for Children—Revised (WISC-R) (1974)

Language

Peabody Picture Vocabulary Test (Dunn, 1959)

Reading

Durrell Analysis of Reading Difficulty (Durrell, 1955)
Gates-McKillop Reading Diagnostic Tests (Gates & McKillop, 1962)

---

vices; that is, they are usually produced by a commercial publisher, and must be administered by persons specifically trained in their use (see Table 4.1). Simply, norm-referenced assessment techniques provide for a distribution of scores that can be used to separate individuals (Salvia & Ysseldyke, 1978).

Although there is no universal format inherent in all normative-referenced devices, this type of instrument usually reports either grade scores, age scores, or both. As a result, an individual can readily be compared to other students relative to the scale chosen or provided.

Interestingly, normative-referenced instruments may yield valuable diagnostic information; however, these tools are not often used for this purpose. Perhaps the two main reasons are that teachers usually have not been trained to elicit this information from this kind of test, and the process of gaining diagnostic information from this type of test is probably more tedious and time-consuming than gathering it from other sources.

Criterion-referenced assessment.

Criterion-referenced testing compares a person's score to a set goal or level. In regard to this topic, Payne (1975) has stated that for this type of testing:

a goal is set and one can determine a child's performance in relation to the goal. Criterion goals are specific and contain the attributes of being observable, quantifiable, and sequential. Since these goals are observable and quantifiable the teacher can determine exactly what is known and what is not known. (p. 7)

A number of authors (Proger & Mann, 1973; Salvia & Ysseldyke, 1978; and Wallace & Larsen, 1978) have cited the ostensible attributes of criterion-referenced assessment. The following is a summary of these points:

1. It affords indices of mastery.
2. Specific behaviors/skills can be evaluated and monitored.
3. There is a close relationship between testing and instruction.
4. The student is considered on an individual basis—relative to himself or herself.
5. Criterion-referenced assessment relates closely with the technique of task analysis (discussed in chapter 5).
6. Efficacious monitoring of the student can be achieved through continual ongoing evaluation.
7. A criterion-oriented instrument can be adapted to a variety of different curricular contexts.

While these attributes of criterion-referenced assessment are attractive, there are some potential drawbacks. Wallace and Larsen (1978) have cautioned that two possible problems concern:

1. Inappropriate criteria.
   a. too difficult—the student grapples with classwork that is too difficult due to unrealistic goals having been set.
   b. too easy—the material presented is well below the instructional level.
2. Problems with analyzing failure to master criteria—a number of factors must be considered (i.e., criteria was [sic] not covered, poor teaching, inappropriate teaching, etc.).

While criterion-referenced tests may be formal or informal, they are usually associated with informal or teacher-produced materials. Whereas norm-referenced instruments are more properly used for screening purposes, criterion instruments are used to gain specific diagnostic information concerning a student's mastery of certain skills in a given area. Table 4.2 lists and describes several criterion-referenced measures.

Table 4.2
Examples of Criterion-Referenced Tests

Arithmetic

Key Math Diagnostic Arithmetic Test (Connolly, Nachtman, & Pritchett, 1973)
Teacher-Made Arithmetic Test
Sample Items:
1. Complete the following: 12 × 6 = _____ 2 × 4 = _____
2. Multiplication is the _____ process of division.
3. Six times four equals what?

Reading

Informal Reading Test
Sample Items:
1. Name the following letters: J b r s a D l m
2. Complete the following sentence: Mary hit the _____. (ball, tall)
3. Read the following sentences and answer the questions below.
   John ran away from home. He was picked up by a policeman. John was glad to be taken back home.
   a. Who ran away? _____
   b. Who stopped John from running away? _____
   c. How did John feel when he was taken home? _____

Spelling

Teacher-Made Spelling Test
Sample Items:
1. Spell the following words: nice twenty return cheerful
2. Complete each sentence below:
   a. Sally is a _____.
   b. We put our money in a _____.

Observational techniques.

Within the last few years, the value of observational methodologies has been recognized and championed. Since observational techniques allow the observer to gain additional information about a student who is experiencing problems, the diagnostic process is even further enhanced. Simply stated, "observations can provide highly accurate, detailed, verifiable information not only about the person being assessed but also about the contexts in which the observations are being made" (Salvia & Ysseldyke, 1978, p. 8).

Observational strategies can be classified on the basis of various systems: Bickman (1976) dichotomizes between "unstructured" (participant observation, specimen records, anecdotes) and "structured" (checklists); Salvia and Ysseldyke (1978) categorize on the basis of "systematic" or "nonsystematic" observation; other authors classify observational strategies as "formal" or "informal." Formal observation may be the type often used where baseline data is being gathered on an individual's typical behaviors in a certain setting, or it may be the type where an individual IQ test is being administered. Informal observation may occur as the teacher casually observes the student's behavior during classroom instruction or in different school-related social situations, such as, the school cafeteria, school dances, and/or school-sponsored athletic events. In any event, the data resulting from observational techniques is only useful when the following factors are acknowledged:

> the value of data obtained . . . depends upon several factors: (1) the accuracy with which observations are made and recorded; (2) the extent to which conditions under which observations occur are noted and considered in interpreting observational data; (3) the degree to which observations focus on important aspects of the child's behavior; and (4) the extent to which the child's behavior is not influenced by the observation procedures. When these conditions are met, the teacher has data which can be useful in assessing the child's general level of effectiveness. (Lister, 1969, p. 184)

Smith and Neisworth (1969) have cautioned that there are a number of potential problems related to behavioral observations. According to these writers, "one major source of inaccuracy is the various biases of the subject and/or experimenter" (p. 23). Another problem in this area is that the observer may not specifically focus on the behavior observed and thus distort the evaluative process; instead of interpreting data based on observed behavior, the observer may resort to overgeneralization, labelling, et cetera.

Bryan and Bryan (1975) and Smith (1969) have pointed out that a number of procedures can be carried out to increase the reliability of observational data. These procedures can be summarized as follows:

1. More than one method should be used for collecting the data.
2. The student should be observed in more than one setting.
3. Observed behaviors should be reassessed frequently.
4. Behavioral data should be collected on a continual basis.

The case study or case history.

This is probably the method least used by educators for gathering information concerning the past and present learning of a student.

Marsh, Gearheart, and Gearheart (1978) have suggested that there are at least three reasons for this situation: (1) teachers usually have not been trained to use this technique; (2) securing needed information via this approach requires a large expenditure of time and energy; and (3) there is a real possibility that certain "sensitive" and confidential information may become available to inappropriate persons. Other concerns associated with this particular technique revolve around the fact that the interviewer soliciting information for the case study must be very adept at using general questions to gain specific information. The interviewer must also be able to communicate effectively with other people through an oral medium. Lastly, since the respondent in many cases must rely on memory for certain details, some of the information gathered through this process must be viewed as speculative.

Regarding the information contained in the case study or case history, Lerner (1976) has indicated that this information is usually grouped into the following categories:

1. Identifying Information
2. Birth History
3. Physical and Developmental Data
4. Social and Personal Factors
5. Educational Factors (p. 78)

Assumptions Inherent in the Assessment Process

Before analyzing the assessment process, a few basic principles must be understood in order to put this topic of assessing the exceptional adolescent into perspective. Smith and Neisworth (1969) refer to five areas worthy of elaboration: examiner knowledge and skill, appropriateness of the assessment technique, errors of measurement, comparable acculturation, and representative samples of behavior. Note that these factors are most closely associated with formal testing techniques.

In order for a given testing session, its results, and interpretations to have any meaningful validity, the above factors must be considered. The examiner, in addition to being familiar with the assessment instrument, must also be aware of the testing "climate" (student's disposition, setting variables that may influence the results, and the examiner-examinee rapport). Implicit in the examiner's familiarity with the instrument is a working knowledge of the test items, the recording/scoring procedure, and the capability of reporting the results meaningfully.

Selection of an appropriate evaluative instrument seems too obvious to even mention. However, there are two cautions worth emphasizing: a given assessment tool must be both age-relevant and content-relevant.

All formal assessments have the problem that error will always be present in any attempt to evaluate an individual. It is thus desirable to use instruments that have been designed to minimize that amount of error.

As far as comparable acculturation is concerned, Smith and Neisworth (1969) state:

> It is assumed that the child being tested has been exposed to essentially the same type of environment as those on whom the test was standardized. . . . The assumption is often difficult to accept, since we all are not reared in the same type of environment. (p. 16)

This point is important when assessing the exceptional adolescent because the instrument used has not always been standardized on populations that included exceptional students.

Any test is merely a sample of behaviors from a large pool of possible behaviors and, consequently, the results cannot imply more than how an individual did at a particular time on a particular compilation of test items. Salvia and Ysseldyke (1978) have aptly captured the essence of what can be inferred from a given testing situation:

> When we give a test, we observe only the test taker's performance on one sampling of behavior, at a particular time, under particular testing conditions, and in a particular situation. We observe what a person *does*; we may or may not observe what that person is capable of do-

ing. We sample a limited number of behaviors and generalize the individual's performance to other, similar behaviors. (p. 20)

The Assessment Process

The preceding sections of this chapter examined the diverse components of assessment (types and levels of assessment) as well as a number of assessment techniques. However, we contend that unless these components are successfully combined, the ultimate goal of assessment will not be realized; that is, the teacher will fail to develop educational strategies aimed at helping the student to learn. Figure 4.3 outlines the overall process of assessment and its major components. Through this process, the student's abilities are carefully observed and plans for developing or remediating skills are formulated. In the following examination of the various components of the assessment process, our purpose is to determine how these components can be successfully combined by the classroom teacher.

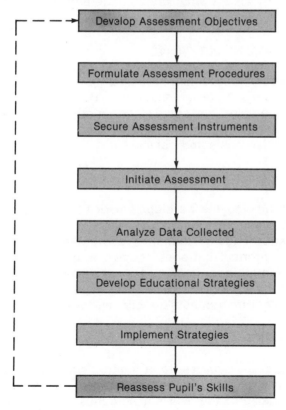

Figure 4.3
The Assessment Process

Develop assessment objectives.

Educational assessment does not, or should not, take place simply because someone arbitrarily decides that it should. In general, someone (usually the teacher) expresses a belief that the student is failing to learn. This apparent failure does not necessarily indicate or even imply that there is something wrong with the student. In fact, the student may be the victim of poor teaching, may be placed in an inappropriate learning environment, or may not be learning for any number of reasons. The overriding point is that no one really knows what the potential problem (or solution) is. Therefore, one of the first concerns is to develop a plan to determine what factor(s) are causing the student's failure to learn.

In securing assessment data regarding a certain student, one need not go through all the same stages that would be required for working with every student. Thus, a primary goal in developing the plan mentioned above would be to develop assessment objectives, that is, to specify clearly what the ultimate aims of this assessment are.

Formulate assessment procedures.

After objectives for assessment have been specified, the next step in the process requires the development of some systematic procedures to insure that the objectives are reached. In other words, once a decision is made about what to do, the next step involves deciding how best to accomplish goals and objectives.

Secure assessment instruments.

Immediately following the development of assessment procedures, pertinent assessment instruments must be secured. In this instance, the teacher's knowledge of normative- and criterion-referenced tests, or formal and informal batteries, comes into play. Depending on whether the ultimate goal is to classify the student or to determine what subskills the student may or may not have in a certain area, particular assessment instruments are chosen for a given student.

Initiate assessment.

After objectives, procedures, and instruments are selected, the teacher actually has to perform the assessment. In the initial assessment, the teacher probably will not be concerned with testing each and every hypothesis about what is causing the student to display learning problems. A primary goal of assessment at this point is to gather enough information so that reasonable and realistic decisions can be made about the student's perceived problems.

Analyze data collected.

Sometimes what a person believes to be true is in fact not true. But because the person has no way of checking that belief, truth is not found. The teacher is in somewhat of an analogous situation before a student is assessed: beliefs are held about the pupil, but these beliefs cannot be proven false nor substantiated. However, after the abilities of a person have been analyzed, then the teacher has some data on which to base at least tentative conclusions. The teacher sorts through the information in order to determine pupil strengths and weaknesses.

Develop educational strategies.

From the assessment data and its analysis, teaching strategies should be developed. Since more precise information is now available concerning the student's abilities, these teaching strategies should closely match the needs of the student. This point of matching teaching strategies and methods to the student's abilities is a very important one. If teachers randomly assign the student to any teaching method within a particular content area, or if the student is placed in a program simply because it exists and not because it meets his or her needs, then both student and teacher have gone through the assessment process for nothing. Thus, the *student and the teaching strategies* that have been developed *must be matched*.

Implement teaching strategies.

After completing the previous phase, the teacher is ready to put into effect the teaching strategies that were devised. As implementation occurs, it is important that other variables that do not directly concern the new or different technique(s) are controlled. By doing this, one can be certain that any change that takes place was brought about by the introduction of the new teaching strategy rather than some other variable.

Reassess the student's skills.

Perhaps the most critical step in this whole process is the last step. As seen in Figure 4.3, once the steps from stating specific assess-

ment objectives to implementing teaching strategies have been accomplished, we are pretty much back where we started. Interestingly enough, however, this is probably where we want to be because, at this very point, a determination can be made as to whether the original objectives have been met. Even if the first objectives have been met, there will be other possible problems to correct—students usually do not have one problem that exists in isolation.

The School Psychologist

In the recent past, the school psychologist did not participate directly in evaluations aimed at developing an educational program for a student. This professional most often administered normative reference instruments (Payne, 1975) aimed at classifying a student as having some type of handicapping condition, for example, mental retardation, a behavior disorder, or a learning disorder. However, the role of the school psychologist is rapidly changing. Presently, this professional: (1) helps the classroom teacher to determine a pupil's strengths and weaknesses in certain academic areas by administering appropriate assessment devices; (2) provides the teacher and other concerned school personnel with information that will assist in planning and developing a pupil's individualized education program (IEP); and (3) serves as a consulting member of the IEP team.

A Special Issue in Assessment/Evaluation of the Exceptional Adolescent: Competency Testing

With the present movement toward making graduation (and promotion for that matter) contingent on the demonstration of certain competencies, the question must be asked, What competency criteria should be required of the exceptional adolescent? In Virginia, many opponents to the competency issue have charged that these tests are racially/culturally biased. Thus, the battle can be waged on many fronts.

As far as the mildly handicapped adolescent is concerned, perhaps Goodman's (1979) ideas are worth contemplating when we try to deal with setting competency requirements:

> As regards curriculum, the CBE [Competency Based Education] movement's emphasis on mastery of basic skills is certainly compatible with priorities in special education, which have long included mastery of basic skills. I suggest that regular education's minimal competencies may well become special education's terminal competencies for mildly handicapped pupils. (p. 117)

The era of competency and accountability (to the public who supports education and to the students, parents, and families whom we serve) is most certainly here. What must be done is to advertise the goals that we are trying to assist our students in achieving and to nurture a positive, reciprocal, active relationship between regular and special education.

EDUCATIONAL INTERVENTION

Discussion of the matter of educational interventions for exceptional youth with other educators often reveals a very puzzling situation. Much the same situation exists for educators who work primarily with mildly mentally retarded students of any age. Some of these educators argue that teaching methods used with this group are different from those used with other pupils, others argue that the basic teaching is the same. Our position is that teaching methods are the same for exceptional children and youth, and for that matter, most average pupils. Yet, the strategies for teaching exceptional adolescents differ because, as a group, these youth share a number of characteristics that distinguish them from other learners; for example, reward systems differ for this group, and exceptional adolescents display a number of chronic learning problems. Thus, in order to teach certain math skills to a youth who has displayed learning problems in this area, a teacher has to recognize that instruction may need to be: (1) broken down into smaller units; (2) paired closely with a rich or nearly continuous reinforcement schedule; and/or (3) tied to current interests of this particular student. In this particular case, the actual methods for teaching math to the student would not change even

though the teacher strategies are aimed at achieving a strong interface between the student's characteristics and instruction.

A second dilemma that comes to mind is related to the question teachers often ask following assessment procedures, What should be done after the assessment process is completed? While the answer may seem blatantly obvious, that is, correct whatever problems need to be corrected, some teachers have a tendency to quit after John's or Susan's educational problems have been closely analyzed and possible causes have been found. Other teachers may respond hesitantly to this question because they are not sure whether an attempt should be made to remediate certain skills or whether new skills should be developed. Other teachers may not feel qualified to engage in remedial endeavors, or may feel that remediation is the responsibility of specialists, such as, remedial reading teachers or speech therapists. While these concerns are legitimate in many cases, we feel that teachers should do more than just assess a student's skills. Teachers should attempt to correct deficiencies that might prevent the student from learning other material or from acquiring other skills; they should engage in intervention, some more than others, and should not regard intervention as the sole province of specialists. These and other matters relating to educational intervention are more closely scrutinized in the following discussion.

Delivery of Services

To a great extent, the most efficient type of intervention program that seeks to assist the adolescent with learning problems will be predicated on the setting in which the student exists or is placed. On the secondary level, there has been and continues to be a paucity of programs for the exceptional adolescent. Historically, the mildly retarded adolescent has been provided more services than the behaviorally handicapped or learning disabled student. A study that surveyed secondary learning disabilities programs in the United States during the school year of 1973–74 reported that of the 37 state departments of education that responded, only 9% of the total number of school districts had established secondary level programs (Scranton & Downs, 1975). These same authors suggest a number of factors that relate to this lack of services; however, these factors do not justify the situation. Since this study, much has happened—most notably PL 94–142, which mandates appropriate education for secondary students (by 1978 up to age 18, and by 1980 up to age 21).

For mildly handicapped adolescents, the alternatives of service delivery that are available include special class placement, resource room support (categorical or noncategorical), or regular classroom placement. Of course, variations of these three principal systems and other possibilities exist; however, for the sake of clarity these other alternatives will not be covered at this point.

While certainly more restrictive on a physical setting dimension, the special class should offer a curriculum characterized by "(1) specially trained teachers; (2) special materials; (3) methods emphasizing individualized instruction with a workable teacher-pupil ratio" (Mauser, 1978, pp. 204–205). Although this service delivery model has been criticized in recent years, it can be used effectively when an appropriate amount of regular class integration is also present.

The resource model on the secondary level has attracted a number of advocates recently. Even though differing somewhat from the model used on the elementary level, there are some substantive similarities. The salient characteristics of regular short-term intervention on an individual basis or in a small group setting, with a specific individualized program in operation, are similar regardless of the level of schooling. Important differences are also recognizable, including a different school organization, different needs of students (Hawisher & Calhoun, 1978), and different demands put on the resource teacher.

Some mildly handicapped adolescents can function with little difficulty in regular classes for the entire day. Other exceptional students can operate well in the regular setting with minimal support from support systems. Whether a student can compete successfully or, more importantly, progress on an individual basis in regular classes will principally depend on the nature and severity of the problem(s) that this student experiences.

Teaching Orientations

Just as the type of service model determines to a great extent how intervention occurs, the teaching orientation or intervention ideology also influences the specific components of any secondary level program involving exceptional students. How then do we best intervene with these youths? Goodman (1979) approaches this issue with the goal of functional literacy as a paramount feature of secondary programs.

> Secondary remedial programs cannot undertake the tasks of both regular and special education and do them well. The scope of a special academic program intended for secondary pupils with minimal cognitive impairments should be restricted to instruction in basic skills at lower grade levels one through six. Students who function beyond the sixth grade level, even if their academic achievement is still below grade, age, or I.Q. expectancies held for them, should be considered candidates for other types of educational intervention, such as tutorial help. Special education academic instruction is thus restricted to students with severe academic deficiencies who are functioning below the seventh grade level. (p. 110)

Another system for analyzing the thrust of services centers on how the educational problems of the student should be addressed. There seem to be three major orientations that exist in various programs: remedial, developmental, or compensatory. At one time or another, all teachers are concerned as to whether they should remediate skills in a certain area, whether they should continue to develop new skills in some other area in which the student may be progressing satisfactorily, or whether they should address the problematic area indirectly by bypassing it in terms of remediation and substituting compensatory strategies. This predicament of remedial, developmental, or compensatory teaching is not easy to resolve. Up to this point, research has not provided a clearly documented, rational choice. Since this is the case, all of these strategies are described in more detail.

Remedial strategies.

Basically, the function of remedial teaching is to strengthen directly the skill areas in which the exceptional adolescent is having problems. For example, if a student is having difficulty copying material from the blackboard, then intervention techniques would attempt to help this student copy more masterfully. Without a doubt, change is desired within the student, demonstrated extrinsically by performance measures. Weiderholt and McNutt (1979) list three strengths and three weaknesses of this remedial approach:

Strengths:
1. It pinpoints the skills that students lack or have not mastered.
2. It attempts to ameliorate weaknesses rather than dismissing or avoiding them.
3. It offers an option to those students who are not able to cope with the regular classroom program.

Weaknesses:
1. It may tend to disregard or fail to acknowledge confounding variables that may be responsible for the problem.
2. It may concentrate on skills that have little or no applicability to other aspects of the student's schooling or needs.
3. It frequently uses materials, tests, and methodologies that have not been conclusively validated by research.

Developmental strategies.

Techniques that reflect this orientation presuppose a very low level of achievement, whereby the intervention program incorporates a more extensive, structured, and sequential presentation of skills to be mastered. This type of intervention would most likely be reserved for those adolescents whose educational problems were of such severity that a comprehensive program was indicated. Thus, this situation suggests that a student in need of a developmental program (as presented in this context) probably still needs to acquire very basic skills. We would like to think that there are only a few secondary level students lacking many of the very basic skills usually mastered on the elementary level, but unfortunately there is a significant number of adolescents who possess such characteristics. Table 4.3 graphically illustrates the instructional differences between developmental and remedial strategies. Three factors are inherent in the instructional preference depicted in Table 4.3: age, preparation, and previous learning history.

It is evident that in dealing with younger children, remedial and developmental teaching are not that far apart; for example, a third grader who is reading on a first-grade level is actually only two years behind in reading. On the other hand, the closeness of remedial and developmental teaching does not usually exist at the secondary level—a ninth grader who is reading on a third-grade level is in the same relative position as the youngster who was previously mentioned (both are reading at a level that is one-third of what is expected). However, in real terms, the older student is farther behind.

Table 4.3
Comparison of Developmental and Remedial Strategies

Classifying Students for Instructional Purposes

Learner Classification	Functioning Level	Educational Strategy	Curriculum Selection
Developmental	Nonfunctional to low 4th grade level	Continued presentation of basic skills; mastery of basic math and language skills	Core Curriculum for math and/or language skills
Remedial	Solid 4th to 6th grade level	Remediation of gaps in knowledge and skills while boosting achievement to the integration level	Core curriculum, particular attention to pretest information, supplementary material for specific skill development—tied to specific skill sequences

SOURCE: Goodman, L., & Mann, L. *Learning disabilities in the secondary school: Issues and practices.* New York: Grune & Stratton, 1976. Used by permission of the publisher.

The second factor that clarifies the choice between attempting to remediate skills or to develop new skills is the present state of preparedness of the individual. Returning to our example of the ninth-grade student who reads on the third-grade level, the question can be asked as to whether this student is prepared or ready to develop new skills or whether unlearned skills must be fostered first. Obviously, for this particular secondary student, development of reading skills will take precedence over learning new skills that may depend on reading skills.

A third factor that can drastically influence decisions in this area is that of the pupil's previous learning history. In this case, attention is focused on the past successes as well as failures in learning. Also of concern are the types of situations in which the student learned or failed to learn, as well as the types of persons who may have enhanced or detracted from the student's learning.

Compensatory strategies.

As mentioned previously, this teaching approach tries to compensate for student weaknesses by avoiding them and using alternate procedures, or by implementing prosthetic techniques. Another way to conceptualize this orientation is to envision "a process whereby the learning environment of the student, either some of the elements or the total environment, is modified to promote learning" (Marsh, Gearheart, & Gearheart, 1978, p. 85). Remember that remedial methods focus on changing the student directly while compensatory methods are most interested in changing the situational or contextual character of the learning environment such that the adolescent acquires skills despite having learning difficulties.

On the secondary level, consideration must be given to factors such as course selection (degree of difficulty), course requirements (assignments, textbooks, tests, homework, grades), course content, and skill demands (reading, writing, etc.). In terms of compensatory intervention, these issues would be singularly analyzed and appropriate alternative strategies would be designed. The use of tape recorders, typewriters, and oral examinations are examples of compensatory intervention for students with writing problems.

Figure 4.4 illustrates one way of meshing some of the features of both remedial and compensatory strategies in order to utilize supportive services effectively (that is, the resource teacher) and to maximize the learning potential of the student.

Lastly, if compensatory strategies are to work effectively, then someone, usually the resource teacher or guidance counselor, must assume the role of consultant to the regular teachers. Good rapport and open dialogue with the regular teachers who have the exceptional student in their classes are the *sine qua non* for appropriate programs. Marsh, Gearheart, and Gearheart (1978) mention that in the secondary school there is an informal power structure that must be recognized by the special education staff, especially if members of this staff of special teachers are young and ambitious. As far as effective programming is concerned, potentially its worst enemy may very well be the alienation of regular teachers with whom the support staff must work closely and openly. As Marsh and colleagues suggest, establishing public relations is quite important for the acceptance and cooperation that is desired. We believe this prerequisite condition is mandatory regardless of the level of schooling.

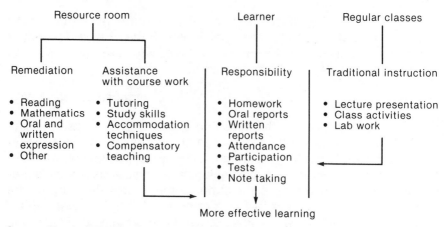

SOURCE: Marsh, G.E., Gearheart, C.K., & Gearheart, B.R. *The learning disabled adolescent: Program alternatives in the secondary school.* St. Louis: C.V. Mosby Co., 1978.

Figure 4.4
Interface of Instruction

The Remediation Process

The remedial strategy is used quite extensively in many secondary level settings and warrants further discussion. One of the first questions to be resolved in the remediation process is, What stage of learning is a student functioning at in this particular area of study? More specifically we, as teachers, would first be involved in determining where the student is generally operating as far as overall learning is concerned.

Stages of learning.

The three major stages of learning are *acquisition, maintenance,* and *generalization.* Acquisition involves the acquiring of or demonstration that the student has a certain skill in his or her repertoire. Maintenance involves demonstrating a skill above a chance level; that is, there is more than a 50% chance that the skill can or will be produced again. Generalization involves using the skill in a similar manner or in a similar situation. A good illustration of these three stages of learning follows:

- *Acquisition*—My job at the factory as described by the foreman was to take a full tray of cigarettes from the back of the machine making the cigarettes. After putting the full tray on a conveyor, I was to take an empty tray from the conveyor and put it on the "making" machine. I was instructed to work at two machines until I learned the job.

- *Maintenance*—Once I learned how to get the full tray off the "making" machine and put the empty tray on without any problems, the foreman told me to keep working at those two machines for the rest of that day.
- *Generalization*—The next day the foreman said that I was to do the same job; however, I was to work at five machines instead of two. Since I was barely able to keep up with the two machines, I wondered how this would be possible. I soon discovered that in order to take care of the five machines, I had to take the full tray from the back of the machine with one hand, and replace it with an empty tray, which I held in the other hand.

The major stages of learning are discussed in more detail in chapter 5.

Review of the assessment model.

For most of the adolescents that concern us, learning in a number of skill areas will be at the acquisition or low maintenance level. Since this is the case, and because a need for more specific information for remediation purposes will exist, the assessment process and data gathered from those efforts become very important. After assessment data has been gathered and analyzed, the assessment model depicted in Figure 4.3 indicates three different actions that should take place: (1) educational strategies based on the assessment data are developed; (2) these strategies are then implemented; and (3) once the strategies are implemented, the pupil's skills are reassessed. From this discussion, it is clear that the processes of assessment and remediation are not readily separated; where one ends, the other begins. However, for the present, the process of remediation will be treated as a discrete entity apart from the process of assessment.

Eight Principles of Remediation

Wallace and Kauffman (1973) have described eight principles concerning remediation that, when followed closely, will result in improvement of a pupil's skill mastery.

1. Proper remediation is dependent upon evaluation of the child's weaknesses, needs, and strengths.
2. Evaluative results should be directly utilized in planning remedial programs.

3. Remediation is a process of continuous evaluation, which is periodically altered to meet the changing needs of the individual.
4. Successful remediation is dependent upon use of a wide variety of materials, techniques, and methods.
5. Remediation materials must be carefully selected and tailored to individual needs.
6. Remedial instruction must be concisely organized.
7. The basic foundation upon which successful remediation is built is effective teaching.
8. Overcoming academic difficulties is a complicated process. (1973, pp. 61–78)

Principles one, two, and three again show the intricate relationship of evaluation and remediation. Principle one expressly indicates that in order for the teacher to remediate the pupil's problems, the pupil's overall abilities and needs must be examined. In other words, not only weaknesses but all abilities, disabilities, and needs are evaluated. Principle two points out that evaluation is not an end unto itself. Data gained from the evaluation is to be used in the attempts at remediation. Principle three ties together the first two points by focusing sharply on the fact that evaluation does not arbitrarily begin and end at some specified point, but that as the individual changes through teaching and learning, new assessments must be made.

Principles four and five, which are concerned mainly with materials, point out the need for matching the individual with methods and materials that will be used in remediating his or her learning problems. While "individualizing instruction" is an oft heard phrase in education, this concept is not often achieved. However, in the usual remedial situation where the pupil-teacher ratio is lower, where more and different materials are available, and where the teacher can spend a greater amount of time with each pupil, chances for individualizing instruction are greater. Yet, this elusive concept may still evade us if the teacher is not careful in matching materials and methods to each student's needs. Each time administrators or others dictate what materials must be used by whom, teacher flexibility is diminished. When teacher flexibility is lessened, the chances for true individualization are greatly diminished.

Principle six posits that concise organization is very important if remedial instruction is to be effective. In the sense that all types of instruction must be well organized or little or nothing will be accomplished, remedial instruction is no exception. However, as remedial instruction usually has more specific goals and/or objectives to be attained, it requires even more organization and planning. The subject of organization is discussed more fully in chapters 5 and 6.

Principle seven brings to the fore the relationship of teaching and remediation; that is, remediation does not exist without successful teaching. In other words, not all teachers engage in remediation efforts, but all instruction aimed at remediation involves teaching. Therefore, for remediation to be successful, teaching must be at least minimally effective. In line with this principle, teachers engaged in remediation attempts should: (1) know the materials they are working with; (2) be familiar with methods that incorporate these materials; (3) be consistent in their use of certain methods—not doing one thing today and something different tomorrow; and (4) teach skills that relate directly to the problems that were exposed through the assessment process.

Principle eight brings to mind the situation that always seems to come about in methods courses at the college level. Sooner or later, a student will ask, "What would you do if a pupil had this problem and displayed these behaviors?" Usually after some discussion, the student and the rest of the methods class are told that there really is no set answer or way that a teacher should deal with a certain problem or set of behaviors. While students sometimes feel this answer is a "cop-out," the one thing that can be said about this situation with virtual certainty is that remediation is often difficult and complicated. If it were not so complicated, then teachers would probably be able to tell pupils how to solve their particular problem.

SUMMARY

In this chapter, the two intricately tied processes of assessment and intervention were closely examined. Assessment was viewed as occurring in a number of different forms, for example, normative- and criterion-referenced forms. Also, assessment was divided into two levels, general and specific assessment. A teacher would use one or the other of these levels depending on the severity of the student's problems. That is, the more severe the student's problem, the more specific the assessment has to be. Other assessment techniques discussed included observation (a technique probably used by all educators) and the case study (a technique seldom used by educators). Since all educators will use observation as an assessment technique sooner or later, a number of suggestions were offered to increase the reliability of observational data. These suggestions involved using several methods to collect data, as well as observing the student frequently and in more than one setting. The last topic discussed in terms of assessment was the several components of the assessment process. These were seen as beginning with development of assessment objectives and ending with the reassessment of the student's skills.

In discussing intervention, the first topic explored was that of remedial, developmental, and compensatory teaching. Three factors that can help the teacher decide the type of teaching to use are age, preparation, and previous learning experience. Next, the stages of learning and their relationship to remediation were discussed; before one can decide where instruction is to begin, a determination must be made as to the student's level of learning in a given area. Lastly, eight principles of remediation were described. These eight principles involved initially evaluating the pupil, choosing materials to use, and organizing instruction so that learning is maximized.

REFERENCES

Bickman, L. Data collection I: Observational methods. In C. Selltiz, L.S. Wrightsman, & S.W. Cook (Eds.), *Research methods in social relations* (3rd ed.). New York: Holt, Rinehart, & Winston, 1976.

Bryan, T.H., & Bryan, J.H. *Understanding learning disabilities.* Port Washington, New York: Alfred, 1975.

Goodman, L. Programming for academic difficulties. In D. Cullinan & M.H. Epstein (Eds.), *Special education for adolescents: Issues and perspectives.* Columbus, Ohio: Charles E. Merrill Publishing Co., 1979.

Goodman, L., & Mann, L. *Learning disabilities in the secondary school: Issues and practices.* New York: Grune & Stratton, 1976.

Hammill, D.D., & Bartel, N.R. *Teaching children with learning and behavior problems.* Boston: Allyn & Bacon, 1975.

Hawisher, M.F., and Calhoun, M.L. *The resource room: An educational asset for children with special needs.* Columbus, Ohio: Charles E. Merrill Publishing Co., 1978.

Jastak, J.F., & Jastak, S.R. *The Wide Range Achievement Test.* Wilmington, Delaware: Guidance Assoc., 1965.

Lerner, J. *Children with learning disabilities: Theories, diagnosis, and teaching strategies* (2nd ed.). Boston: Houghton Mifflin, 1976.

Lister, J.L. Personal-Emotional-Social skills. In R.M. Smith (Ed.), *Teacher diagnosis of educational difficulties.* Columbus, Ohio: Charles E. Merrill Publishing Co., 1969.

Madden, R., & Gardner, E.F. *Stanford achievement tests.* New York: Harcourt, Brace, Jovanovich, 1972.

Marsh, G.E., Gearheart, C.K., & Gearheart, B.R. *The learning disabled adolescent: Program alternatives in the secondary school.* St. Louis: C.V. Mosby Co., 1978.

Mauser, A.J. Developing reading strategies for youths with educational handicaps. In D.A. Sabatino & A.J. Mauser (Eds.). *Intervention strategies for specialized secondary education.* Boston: Allyn & Bacon, 1978.

Payne, J.S. Psychoeducational diagnosis. In W.M. Cruickshank & D.P. Hallahan (Eds.), *Perceptual and learning disabilities in children: Psychoeducational practices,* Vol I. Syracuse: Syracuse University Press, 1975.

Proger, B.B., & Mann, L. Criterion-referenced measurement: The world of gray versus black and white. *Journal of Learning Disabilities,* 1973, *6,* 72–84.

Salvia, J., & Ysseldyke, J.E. *Assessment in special and remedial education.* Boston: Houghton Mifflin, 1978.

Scranton, T.R., & Downs, M.L. Elementary and secondary learning disabilities programs in the U.S.: A survey. *Journal of Learning Disabilities,* 1975, *8,* 394–399.

Smith, R.M. (Ed.). *Teacher diagnosis of educational difficulties.* Columbus, Ohio: Charles E. Merrill Publishing Co., 1969.

Smith, R.M., & Neisworth, J.T. Fundamentals of informal educational assessment. In R.M. Smith (Ed.), *Teacher diagnosis of educational difficulties,* Columbus, Ohio: Charles E. Merrill Publishing Co., 1969.

Wallace, G., & Kauffman, J.M. *Teaching children with learning problems.* Columbus, Ohio: Charles E. Merrill Publishing Co., 1973.

Wallace, G., & Larsen, S. *Educational assessment of learning problems: Testing for teaching.* Boston: Allyn & Bacon, 1978.

Wiederholt, J.L., & McNutt, G. Assessment and instructional planning: A conceptual framework. In D. Cullinan & M.H. Epstein (Eds.), *Special education for adolescents: Issues and perspectives.* Columbus, Ohio: Charles E. Merrill Publishing Co., 1979.

5

Structuring Academic Tasks

In the previous chapter, attention focused on determining what a student's abilities and disabilities might be and then possibly strengthening weak areas, as well as maintaining or increasing abilities in strong areas. The principle concern of this chapter involves teacher behaviors and decisions used to make choices relative to academic tasks and their presentation. Topics to be explored include: (1) the stages of learning—while the three major stages of learning were briefly mentioned in the previous chapter, these stages and certain intermediate stages are more closely examined; (2) the application of these stages of learning to the instructional procedure; (3) specialized techniques of teaching that are applicable in many settings; (4) curricular considerations—the ultimate in academic task structuring; (5) the individualized educational program on the secondary level; and (6) issues related to teaching the exceptional adolescent.

Although the following material has relevance for any setting, many of the examples involve the exceptional adolescent in a special setting. How one structures and programs the academic tasks of a student will depend largely on the nature and severity of the educational problem, as pointed out in chapter 4. Additionally, Hauser (1978) found that programs for the mildly handicapped adolescent often emphasized either academic or career/vocational philosophies, to the exclusion of the other. Without a doubt, the focus of a program will determine most of the curricular issues. We agree wholeheartedly with Hauser's belief that most programs designed for exceptional youth should incorporate both academic and career/vocational emphases.

Correspondingly, the teaching orientation (remedial, developmental, compensatory) most certainly will affect how the various academic tasks are structured. Nonetheless, the principles of learning remain fundamentally the same; merely the application of these principles varies according to the context.

Lastly, the needs and psychological characteristics of the exceptional adolescent must be considered. Adolescence is perplexing to the normal teenager; adolescence to the exceptional individual is just as perplexing and compounded by the problems and frustrations with which the individual must grapple. Acknowledging the complexities of this transition from child to adult, it is no surprise that the exceptional adolescent requires different intervention techniques. Hauser (1978) summarized this fact:

> MHA [Mildly Handicapped Adolescents] should be considered as a population of concern in its own right. Applying the educational technologies developed for younger handicapped children to handicapped adolescents is a dubious practice, and the efficacy of doing so has surely not been established. A large body of psychological research on handicapped adolescents points out repeatedly that they differ cognitively, emotionally, and socially from younger handicapped children. (p. 295)

Even though we agree with much of what Hauser has stated regarding mildly handicapped adolescents, we would argue that the basic methods used to teach exceptional adolescents are the same as those used to teach younger exceptional children and also average pupils. However, as stated in chapter 4, we believe that the *strategies* used to teach exceptional adolescents differ from those used with other students because, as Hauser has clearly pointed out, mildly handicapped adolescents are different from other learners.

STAGES OF LEARNING

In chapter 4, it was indicated that the three major stages of learning are acquisition, maintenance, and generalization. A substage of learning that occurs between acquisition and maintenance is *proficiency and fluency building*; a substage that occurs between maintenance and generalization is *application*. As an overview, we know by definition that: (1) acquisition is the initial acquiring or demonstration of a skill; (2) maintenance is the demonstration of a skill above chance level, that is, there is better than a 50% probability that the skill will be produced again; and (3) generalization refers to demonstrating the skill or a modification of the skill in response to new, different situations.

The substage of proficiency and fluency building refers to the increasing dexterity in execution and/or performance of a skill. An example of this would be the increased ability of the adolescent over the younger child to throw baseballs, footballs, and other objects in a more precise or adept manner.

Application implies using the same skill in a different setting, and/or using the same skill at a different time. If, for example, a student taking geometry learns to calculate the area of a square, then application occurs when this student uses the proper formula ($A = s^2$) and procedure for calculating the area of geometrically square figures presented at different times. Thus, after the student has learned the mechanics of calculating the area of a square, then this skill can be used in different settings and at different times.

No matter what stage of learning we are discussing, all mildly handicapped adolescents have had or presently exhibit problems at some particular stage. While most exceptional adolescents will have acquired some rudimentary skills in such areas as reading, arithmetic, or spelling, frequently these same youths will not be fluent or adept at using many of these skills. In some instances, acquisition of a certain skill will not have occurred and, therefore, instruction relative to this skill will have to begin at this stage. The above discussion does not infer that all mildly handicapped adolescents will have problems in *all* areas of learning. What we are saying is that by definition all mildly handicapped youth will have problems in at least one area or at one stage of learning.

INSTRUCTIONAL PROCEDURES

Since many mildly handicapped adolescents will exhibit problems at one or more of the various stages of learning, a major concern of the secondary teacher is to use instructional procedures that will help to correct these learning difficulties. Seemingly, the best way to develop and implement practices in this area would be simply to tie instructional procedures to the specific stage of learning that is a problem for the pupil. In other words, if the student has acquired a skill but has not actually developed some degree of proficiency in using this skill, then it may be meaningless to work on applying this skill in different settings. In the following discussion, several instructional practices that can be used to assist students in learning will be looked at closely to ascertain their possible use(s) with mildly handicapped adolescents.

Acquisition Procedures

There are numerous methods that a teacher might use to enable a student to establish a certain skill. Included in these methods are: (1) verbal instruction, (2) modeling, (3) shaping, and (4) correction procedures. Verbal instruction refers to simply "telling" the student how to accomplish a certain task. For example, if the instructional topic was keeping a checkbook accurately, then the technique of verbal instruction would involve telling the student how to accomplish this skill.

Modeling, or demonstration, would involve "showing" the student how to perform the desired act. For example, if the teacher is trying to help the student learn how to multiply a two place number by a two place number, then this process could easily be illustrated by doing several examples on the chalkboard or on paper. An assumption implicit with this type of procedure is that once the person sees the behavior demonstrated, the student will be able to reproduce it. However, this does not always occur and, as a result, other procedures must also be used to affect acquisition. Altman and Talkington (1971) have suggested that modeling has several positive features including: (1) little need to break tasks into smaller components; (2) reinforcement is inherent in the process (usually behaviors that are not reinforcing are not modeled); and (3) modeled behavior seems to be generalized more readily and seems to be more resistant to extinction than other types of behaviors. While the technique of modeling is often a powerful tool, most of the research demonstrating its usefulness has been conducted with more moderately and severely handicapped populations.

Shaping is another technique used in the acquisition of skills. In situations where shaping is employed, rudimentary forms of the desired behavior or skill are present and the teacher guides the student so that eventually the complete behavior or skill is mastered. More specifically, shaping is a technique that successively reinforces behaviors that approximate a target behavior. For instance, if a teacher wants a student to master the skill of detailed note taking, then initially this teacher may accept the ability to take a few notes during a short period of time; this behavior approximates the target behavior. The behavioral technique of shaping is closely related to the procedure of breaking down a skill into sequential, hierarchical parts known as task analysis. As this technique is quite useful, it will be presented in more detail later in this chapter.

Correction procedures at this stage of learning encompass pinpointing where an error is occurring in task performance, taking corrective actions, and preventing incorrect responses. Correction as a technique used in the acquisition procedure should not be confused with correction as a form of admonishment; rather, it should be considered a behavioral technique that provides students with feedback as to the accuracy of their responses or actions. An example may be helpful. Suppose the setting is an instructional unit on how to fill in the biographic information of an application. If the student filled in a reference's address where the reference's name should go, then the use of an active correction procedure would point out to the student that this entry was not in the appropriate position. Research has shown this technique to be effective in acquiring the mastery of skills. For a more intensive examination of this technique and those presented above, the reader is encouraged to consult *Applying behavior-analysis procedures with children and youth* (Sulzer-Azaroff & Mayer, 1977).

No matter which technique is used during the acquisition stage of learning, it is very important that the teacher consistently reinforce learner responses. At this point, reinforcement should occur each time a desired behavior is produced; continuous reinforcement strengthens the desired behavior. Frequent feedback should also accompany task performance to insure that the student knows what is right or wrong relative to the task. For many adolescents feedback itself may be a form of reinforcement.

Proficiency and Fluency Building Procedures

After the learner demonstrates that a certain behavior has been mastered, the teacher should have this student engage in activities that promote the development of a certain level of proficiency and fluency. One of the best known or most often used methods of developing proficiency and fluency is the use of drill work. At first, the drill work should be presented in a routine fashion; that is, activities used to promote skill refinement should initially be very similar. Activities that use a novel drill should follow a routine drill. A novel drill would involve the same skills or behaviors, only the learner would have to be aware that the presentation or appearance of the illiciting stimuli was different. For example, in solving a multiplication problem, the novelty method could be achieved by presenting the stimulus (the multiplication problem) on an overhead projector rather than on flash cards, if they had been the usual mode of presentation.

When students show that they can perform both routine and novel drill work, then independent practice is the next step in building proficiency and fluency. During independent practice, the learner is required to demonstrate the skill previously developed. However, in this instance feedback and reinforcement concerning performance may not be immediately forthcoming. This accentuates a very important fact concerning reinforcement during this stage of learning—reinforcement changes from a continuous schedule, as in the acquisition stage, to a more intermittent schedule. This change should be made for several reasons: (1) a leaner reinforcement schedule will strengthen the response in question, whereas a continuous schedule will cause the learner to become satiated and thus produce the desired behavior at a rate lower than expected; and (2) an intermittent schedule approximates more closely the type of reinforcement the learner will receive in a real life situation.

Maintenance Procedures

After proficiency and fluency procedures have been instituted and behaviors have been performed to the satisfaction of the teacher, activities that attempt to maintain these skills and behaviors are incorporated into the learning sequence. In other words, concern now shifts to maintaining skills and behaviors. Research has shown that once a

skill or behavior has been acquired a limited number of consequences can result: the skill or behavior can be decreased, increased, or maintained. However, if the goal is to maintain a certain skill behavior at a present level, then a number of points must be considered: (1) the skill or behavior must be periodically reinforced, and (2) the skill or behavior should have relevance to the student; that is, the person who has acquired the skill or behavior should have some meaningful use for it, or recognize its value as a prerequisite for doing something else. In the latter case, a person may not see any inherent value in performing or displaying a certain act; however, if performance of this action is required in order to do something more pleasant or to have some unpleasant actions terminated, then the person will probably be more inclined to do the first behavior (Premack, 1959). This technique can be illustrated by the following example. If a student was involved in a math unit or photography unit specifically related to the efficient use of a clock, and if photography/darkroom work was a reinforcing activity for this student, then time spent in the darkroom could be made contingent on classwork related to mastering the appropriate use of a clock. Not only are Premack's ideas being utilized, but the relevancy of knowing how to use a clock is easily recognized by the student.

Another point to be considered is that less complex acts are easier to maintain at a predetermined level than are more complex acts. For example, writing one or two simple sentences in response to certain questions is usually easier than writing an essay regarding a difficult topic that one has studied. In the following situation, a student is working on a "community living skill" unit dealing with filling in federal income tax forms. Since it is much more advantageous to structure maintenance activities that require less complex behaviors, the knowledgeable teacher would not require the student continually to fill in the entire 1040/1040S form, but rather would present maintenance activities that involve filling in only portions of this form.

In conclusion, in order to maintain certain learned skills and behaviors, these skills and behaviors

1. must be reinforced, albeit on an intermittent schedule. This reinforcement can be delivered internally by the individual, or externally by another person.
2. must have some use value for the individual.
3. must be used is as many different situations as possible.
4. must be used with a high frequency.
5. must initially be less complex.

Application Procedures

When an individual can maintain a skill or behavior at a certain predetermined level over a period of time, concern then shifts to applying that same skill or behavior in a different setting and/or applying it at a different time. Conversely, skills and behaviors that can be used in a number of different situations or that must be used frequently are more likely to endure than others. As the individual attempts to apply a previously learned skill or behavior in a different setting or at a different time, an important distinction must be made between application procedures and adaptation/generalization (discussed in the next section). Primarily, this distinction has to do with the characteristics of the stimuli related to dimensions of setting or time. At the application stage, the stimuli of the new setting must be very *similar* to the stimuli used during maintenance activities. If this condition is not adhered to, we run the risk of the student displaying an inappropriate behavior or skill.

Generalization Adaptation

The final stage of learning involves using a learned skill or behavior to respond to novel stimuli, and modifying a learned skill or behavior to respond to the same stimuli. In deference to the application procedures just presented, generalization implies that a certain skill or behavior is performed after a stimulus situation that varies discrepantly from those found in maintenance or application activities. A good illustration of this technique is a situation in which a student is required to use information that was only applied previously in an academic sense. For example, if a student proceeded through the sequence of learning as presented in this chapter, and this adolescent was placed in an agricultural work/study program, then the ability to calculate areas of various segments of land would be quite useful. This student may need this skill to determine the amount of fertilizer that must be purchased or to predict the amount of yield of a certain crop. Generalization would be demonstrated if this mathematical skill of calculating area were performed in this completely novel situation. Adaptation would occur in this context if this student found the area of the same plot of land but perhaps divided into subplots.

Ultimately, we would like to assist students through these stages of learning. Hopefully, they could then handle new situations and demands in appropriate ways and alter their behaviors or skills so as to solve new questions being asked in the same context.

INDIVIDUALIZING THE EDUCATION OF EXCEPTIONAL ADOLESCENTS

Due to legislative mandate, educators today are entrusted with the task of providing all handicapped children and adolescents with an appropriate education. Chapter 4 and the first part of this chapter should sensitize one to the complexities and intricacies of programming for maximal learning. When we consider the structuring of academic tasks for the exceptional adolescent, we are also required to address certain curricular issues, the individualization of the student's program (the Individual Educational Program: IEP), and the problems associated with educating handicapped youth on the secondary level. We are constantly reminded that, for the exceptional adolescent, there is just so much time remaining for formal schooling. As a result, we should heed Cegelka and Phillips' (1978) astute analysis of the situation:

> The imminence of the secondary student's adulthood requires that the quality of his total life adjustment be of paramount concern to those persons involved in developing the IEP and designing the educational experiences. (p. 86)

Guided by these ideas, one should be aware that selecting a particular program and its contents can have a most pronounced effect on the student's adult life. The seriousness of this fact cannot be overstressed.

Curriculum Selection and Content

Even though there are numerous differences among secondary schools in this country, certain common features can be recognized in most. Usually these schools are departmentalized into almost autonomous divisions with little accompanying integration of curricula (Marsh, Gearheart, & Gearheart, 1978). Thus, if the exceptional youth is in an academically oriented program and is having problems, then coordination and intervention must take this departmentalized factor into account. Similarly, a student in a more vocationally oriented program may also require supportive services.

The importance of these program orientations is that they involve curricula that are geared to the nonhandicapped student and taught by teachers who typically have had little preparation for working with exceptional adolescents. As a result, the type of curricula in which a student may function best is predicated on the following two main factors: (1) the nature and severity of the educational problems the student displays, and (2) the placement of the student in the secondary school.

If a student is for the most part in the regular secondary school curricula, then this individual may or may not need interventional strategies that allow for better performance in the courses being taken. When intervention is suggested, these strategies may include modification of the materials, testing procedures, or requirements, and can be effected through the efforts of the resource teacher or guidance counselor. If a student is in the academic curricula, then it can probably be assumed that this individual is not encountering major difficulties nor a plethora of problems, simultaneously.

For the student with more severe educational problems, alternative curricular decisions have to be made to maximize the effectiveness of the learning process. Resource intervention or a special class placement may be indicated for the exceptional adolescent who cannot succeed in the regular secondary level program. Figure 5.1 offers some guidelines for structuring curricula that could be used in a resource or special setting. While six major areas are listed, the focus of a student's educational program will be decided by a number of interdependent factors: (1) the placement committee's decision as to what type of intervention is needed—this occurs after the student has been evaluated; (2) the individual student's personal goals—what does this adolescent want to do after graduation; and (3) a realistic appraisal of what is possible for this student—hopefully mutual understanding on the part of the student and the teacher/guidance counselor can be achieved vis-à-vis continual, reciprocal communition.

I. Language Arts
   A. Reading
   B. Verbal expression
   C. Written expression
   D. Spelling

II. Mathematics
   A. Computation
   B. Application

III. Social, Emotional, Personal
   A. "Family life"

IV. Career/Vocational

V. Physical Education

VI. Survival Skills
   A. Consumer skills
   B. Daily living skills
   C. Leisure skills

Figure 5.1
Proposed Curriculum for the Exceptional
Adolescent

Mindful of Cegelka and Phillips's (1978) thoughts on the exceptional adolescent's approaching adulthood and commensurate demands and responsibilities, we should take great strides to assure that this exceptional student is given, at a very minimum, the skills required to function satisfactorily in contemporary society. For some exceptional students, college is certainly a possibility. However, these are not the students with whom we are most concerned about successful adaptation to adulthood because their problems, while limiting in some sense, are not as debilitating as those of other handicapped adolescents.

Program Modifications

Actually, many of the possible modifications to an exceptional adolescent's program have already been mentioned. When we refer to modifying the program, we are suggesting that changes can be made in any number of areas. Some students will require no changes; other students may need only slight alterations; and other students may need a complete customizing of their programs. Specifically, these modifications may affect: grading procedures, instructional methodology, course requirements (assignments, testing, reading), class participation, and course load. An obvious example of required program alteration for the exceptional adolescent would be that for a visually or physically impaired student taking chemistry. In order to elaborate and clarify many of the concepts encountered in this content area, a chemistry lab is part of this course. For the visually or physically impaired student, some chemistry laboratory experiments, innately dangerous for any student, become extremely hazardous. Therefore, certain modifications of the typical laboratory SOP (standard operating procedure) are warranted. For instance, these individuals could be teamed with nonhandicapped students.

Since every student or secondary school setting will pose different problems, any proposed list of possible modifications would be incomplete; nonetheless, the following suggested compensatory or prosthetic ideas highlight a few useful adaptations to be used with the exceptional adolescent. The first five suggestions are based in part on ideas posited by Marsh et al. (1978).

1. A mastery grading system rather than the standard normative system (A, B, C, D, F).
2. Remedial or supplementary classes in content areas in addition to those in reading and math (science, social studies, music, art, etc.).
3. Selection of courses based on difficulty of content, amount of abstract ability required, nature of the requirements, and number of students enrolled in the class.
4. Readjustment for the exceptional adolescent of the heavy emphasis put on reading and writing in order to maximize the efforts of the student.

5. New methods for evaluating the career potential of students who may have difficulty in a given area but otherwise have the capabilities for successful job performance.
6. Selection of teachers (regardless of whether they are regular content, vocational, or special education teachers) based on factors such as: (a) experience with exceptional learners; (b) attitude toward the student with special needs; (c) cooperativeness; (d) teaching style; (e) course requirements and organization; and (f) interest in individualizing/modifying their course.
7. Use of prosthetic strategies (a device used to compensate for or supplement skills or behaviors that are either absent or problematic). Examples of techniques used for this purpose include: tape recorders (used in conjunction with prerecorded reading assignments, the presentation of oral reports, taking lecture notes), calculators, prewritten outlines of lectures, large-print textbooks, pretyped copy of material put on the chalkboard, and the use of selected audio-visual media in lieu of reading assignments.
8. Test-taking adaptations: oral rather than written; shorter testing periods, which then may require more testing sessions; and substitution of a project for the formal test—this of course may not be appropriate if it conflicts with the guidelines for final evaluation as stated in the IEP.
9. Adjusting the course load: this may entail more years of secondary education or summer school. (Note that the identified handicapped student is entitled to receive a free, appropriate education until the age of 21, if so determined, as of September 1980).
10. Use of supplemental techniques such as peer tutoring, additional material, and outside-of-school resources (volunteers, specialized tutoring, community services, etc.).
11. Modifying the presentation of course content, most notably accomplished by: (a) presenting the material in smaller units, and (b) by varying instructional techniques to allow for many different presentations of the same material.

Although these suggestions are not exhaustive, they do represent alternative strategies that should be considered. Suggestion eleven, while briefly stated, involves a process known as task analysis that deserves further elaboration, especially for any teacher who works with exceptional students.

Task Analysis

Task analysis has been defined and described by numerous writers. For example, Bateman (1971) has indicated that task analysis is the process of isolating, describing and sequencing (as necessary) all the necessary subtasks which, when the child has mastered them, will enable him to perform the objective (instructional). (p. 33)

Bateman further stated that

task analysis is the procedure of determining all of the subskills which lead to performance of the instructional objectives. When the task analysis is complete, a checklist of test items corresponding to all the subskills can be used to determine where to begin instruction and children can be grouped according to the skills they need to learn. (p. 48)

Williams and Anandam (1973) described task analysis as including "specification of terminal objectives and delineation of the component objectives which lead to the accomplishment of each terminal objective" (p. 174). Payne, Polloway, Smith, and Payne (1977) have observed that task analysis is "the process [which] focuses on what the child *can do* and specifically where the child experiences difficulty. It sets the stage for determining actually what needs to be taught" (p. 59).

Regardless of how one describes task analysis, this concept is based on a number of closely related assumptions. One assumption is that the learner ultimately is capable of performing the required task. This means that, at present, the individual in question has not demonstrated that the terminal goal that has been set can be accomplished.

However, based on the evidence at hand it would appear that the required task can be done by the individual if very structured guidance is provided. A second assumption, closely tied to the first, is that the learner will be provided with individual instruction that will monitor the task-oriented behavior and give feedback relative to performance. Without careful monitoring and feedback to the learner, chances for successful performance of the required task are greatly diminished. A third assumption related to task analysis is that through a combination of careful observation of the pupil's present behavior and the separation of the desired task performance into several component parts, the learner will experience immediate success during the initial stages of task performance.

Two of the most positive attributes of task analysis are: (1) by separating task performance into several components, one can readily determine at any given moment what behavior actually has been demonstrated, that is, a determination can be made regarding what has been taught and/or learned; and (2) by using a task analysis approach, replication of the outcome of a particular analysis is provided for almost automatically. Two of the most often cited criticisms of task analysis are: (1) this approach is very time-consuming to use; and (2) it requires a great amount of skill to divide a terminal objective into specific subparts. These points are very relevant to teachers at the secondary level who may have 30 students in each class. While there is no getting around the time involved and the skill needed to analyze a task into its component parts, the competent secondary level teacher should be able to accomplish this procedure. Implicit in this statement, however, are the assumptions that this teacher has a firm grasp of the content area being taught and understands the sequence of skills necessary to achieve certain performance goals. Despite the criticisms mentioned, many educational practitioners continue to use task analysis because of its ability to provide truly individualized instruction.

The Individualized Educational Program (IEP)

In concluding the topic of individualizing the education of the exceptional adolescent, it is fitting that we discuss the IEP. In essence, the IEP provides a desirable specificity and form of accountability that should substantiate the basic premises of The Education of All Handicapped Children Act (PL 94–142): a free appropriate public education (FAPE) in the least restrictive environment (LRE). As an important requirement mandated by this federal legislation, the IEP can be conceptualized as:

the cornerstone of the law and the management tool that parents, teachers, and other professionals, as well as the eligible student, can refer to when questions arise concerning resources or educational goals. (Hayes & Higgins, 1978, pp. 267–268)

While we cannot overstate the significance of the IEP for the student, the teachers, or the local school system, the fact is that this concept is not new to everyone. Many states had similar plans guaranteeing an individualized education prior to the enactment of PL 94–142 in November of 1975. Moreover, as Schrag (1977) points out, other pieces of legislation have analogous individualized plans: the individualized program plan (IPP)—the 1976 Amendments to the Development Disabilities Act (PL 94–103); and the individualized rehabilitation plan (IRP)—the 1974 Amendments to the Vocational Rehabilitation Act (PL 93–112).

If we briefly analyze the concepts conveyed by the acronym IEP, we should begin to gain a minimal appreciation of the significance and complexities of this provision of the law.

Individualized: The IEP must realize the needs of the specific student.

Education: The IEP is required for students who are receiving special services; the concept of "education" can range from traditional academics to self-care training. This requirement must be executed, regardless of the agency providing the services.

Program: The IEP reflects the culmination of two forces: (1) recommendations for achieving certain goals—how do we change the individual, and (2) realities of the school setting—how do we change the environment. Both influences help establish curricular, instructional, and other interventional priorities.

The process.

Most of what has been presented in this and the previous chapter can be considered part of the overall IEP process. Cegelka and Phillips (1978) describe the IEP process as including five major stages: assessment, placement, curriculum, program management, and evaluation. Since assessment and curriculum have already been covered, let us consider the remaining facets of this program.

As soon as we consider placement, the thought of a placement committee immediately comes to mind. This committee may have other aliases, such as, the child study team, the staffing committee, the personal guidance team, or the evaluation committee (Schrag,

1978). Whatever its name, the function of this committee is: (1) to make decisions and (2) to ensure that the student is receiving an appropriate education with the commensurate procedural safeguards in operation. This committee is responsible for program management, which implies the development of the IEP and the monitoring of the program.

The final facet of this process is evaluation, which should be an ongoing activity. If this is the case, then the teachers who set the short-term goals and work with the student on a daily basis are in a position to monitor most efficiently the student's progress.

COMPONENTS OF THE WRITTEN IEP

Although many different IEP formats can be used by different school systems, all IEP forms must include the following information:

1. the student's present level of educational functioning
2. annual goals that the student is expected to achieve
3. short-term instructional objectives
4. listing of the specific services including special educational and related (e.g., speech, physical therapy) services that have been determined essential to the student
5. the amount of participation in the regular classrooms that is appropriate for the student
6. temporal data: dates for initiation of services and for expected termination of these services
7. evaluation procedures utilizing objective criteria to determine if the student is meeting the short-term instructional objectives
8. annual review: an approximate date must be set at which time the student's progress is reviewed.

Even though these components must be included in every IEP, the federal legislation does allow for variation and flexibility in terms of how the IEP is developed (Hawisher & Calhoun, 1978).

A number of suggestions have been offered to aid in designing a workable IEP format. Schrag (1977) breaks the IEP into three levels: (1) total service plan; (2) implementation/instructional plan; and (3) annual review. Completion of the total service component is the responsibility of the placement committee and basically is a general guideline for more specific planning. Figure 5.2 illustrates the key features of the total service plan. Note that the total service plan includes

Local Education Agency
Name and Number _____
School _____
Name of Student _____ Age ____ Grade ____
Date of Birth _____
Summary of Present Levels
of Student Performances:

Description of Educational Placement Recommendations:

Special Education Program Model	Hrs/Week	Regular Education	Hrs/Week	Legal Category of Exceptionality (for funding purposes only)

Program Goal(s)	Specific Special Education and/or Related Services	Person(s) Responsible For Implementation	Hours Per Week	Starting Date	Projected Ending Date	Annual Review Date (Mo-Yr)	Child Study Team Recommendations: Methods & Materials— (If appropriate)	Evaluation Criteria

CHILD STUDY TEAM MEMBERS PRESENT

Signature	Position

Agreement with IEP: Total Service Plan
(Check appropriate space)

YES ____   NO ____

Date of
Child Study
Team Meeting: _____

SOURCE: Schrag, J.A. *Individualized educational programming (I.E.P.): A child study team process. Austin, Texas: Learning Concepts, 1977.* From *Mainstreaming Series: Individualized Educational Programming (IEP)* by Judy A. Schrag, Ed.D., edited by Thomas N. Fairchild, Ph.D., illustrated by Bart I. Miller; copyright 1977 by Judy A. Schrag, Ed.D., Thomas N. Fairchild, Ph.D, and Bart I. Miller; published by Teaching Resources Corporation, 50 Pond Park Road, Hingham, Massachusetts. Reprinted by permission.

Figure 5.2 *Individualized Educational Program: Total Service Plan*

all required components of the IEP except the specific short-term instructional objectives and the evaluation criteria for monitoring these instructional objectives. Thus, we then can expect the next level to include these components.

According to Schrag, the implementation/instructional plan includes the specific teaching components tailored to the needs of the exceptional adolescent. Completion of this IEP level is the responsibility of those persons involved with executing the interventional strategies; however, ultimate responsibility for all aspects of the IEP remains with the placement committee. Figure 5.3 provides an example of this level of IEP development, and from this figure additional components are recognizable. Although supplementary components, such as, "Strategies and/or Techniques" and "Materials and/or Resources" are not required, they definitely increase the usefulness and specificity of the IEP.

Level three, annual review, as conducted by the placement committee is of paramount importance to the exceptional adolescent because it accomplishes two very significant functions: (1) this review analyzes the student's present program as to its appropriateness and (2) at this time, future educational recommendations/revisions are made. Figure 5.4 illustrates the qualities of this level of IEP development.

Although we have chosen a model of IEP development that we believe to be very adequate, we want to stress that there are many viable alternative formats that can be used to meet the mandated standards. For more information or other examples of IEP development, we recommend consulting the following sources: Hawisher and Calhoun, 1978; Marsh, Gearheart, and Gearheart, 1978; Russell, Shoemaker, McGuigan, and Bevis, 1976; and Schrag, 1977.

Issues related to the IEP.

Assuming the premise or philosophy behind the IEP is valid and acceptable, there are, nevertheless, some concerns that must be considered in maximizing its usefulness. The following list merely scratches the surface of all the possible issues, but hopefully it will introduce the reader to some of the "hot topics" as we see them.

1. Inappropriate instructional objectives: too easy or too difficult.
2. Poorly written instructional objectives: difficult to evaluate.
3. Estimation of the duration of the intervention program: specific idiosyncracies of a student may not be discernible; therefore, these estimates may be inaccurate.

Local Education
Agency
Name & No. _____

Name of Student _____ Date of Birth _____ Age _____ Grade _____ School _____

Date of Entry into Program _____ Projected Ending Date _____

(Signature of Implementor Completing this Form)

Program Goal(s)	Implementation/Instructional Objectives	Strategies and/or Techniques	Materials and/or Resources	Date Started	Date Ended	Criteria for Mastery of each Implementation/ Instructional Objective

Source: Ibid.

Figure 5.3 *Individualized Educational Program: Implementation/Instructional Plan*

Name of Student _____ Date of Birth _____ Age _____ Grade _____ School _____

Local Education Agency
Name and Number _____ Date of Annual Review _____

IEP: Total Service Plan and
Implementation/Instructional Components:

	Level of Appropriateness (Check appropriate space)		Recommended Change:
	YES	NO	
Special Education Placement	____	____	____
Regular Education Placement	____	____	____
Specific Special Education and/or Related Services	____	____	____
Program Goal(s)	____	____	____
Implementation/Instructional Short-term Objective(s)	____	____	____
Specific Materials and/or Resources	____	____	____
Specific Teaching Strategies and/or Techniques	____	____	____
Evaluation Criteria for Completion of Program Goal(s)	____	____	____
Evaluation Criteria for Completion of Implementation/Instructional Objective(s)	____	____	____

CHILD STUDY TEAM MEMBERS PRESENT

		Agreement of Annual Review (Check appropriate space)	
		YES	NO
Signature	Position		
_____	_____	____	____
_____	_____	____	____
_____	_____	____	____
_____	_____	____	____

SOURCE: Ibid.

Figure 5.4 *Individualized Educational Program: Annual Review*

4. The number of teachers that may be needed to develop a student's program on the secondary level.
5. Accountability: it is imperative that teachers be aware that the IEP is not legally binding, but should be used as a measure of accountability.
6. Time factors: the development of the IEP is a very time-consuming procedure, especially if done properly.
7. Authorship (i.e., writing responsibilities) of the IEP: the law does not specify exactly who must write the IEP; this task is not necessarily the specific responsibility of the teacher.
8. Preparation of staff for IEP participation: PL 94–142 allows for inservice training of potential participants in the EP process; however, the quality of these inservice sessions may not always be acceptable.
9. Release time: should release time be given to those teachers involved with the development of the IEP?
10. Computerized IEPs: is this a prostitution of or a revolutionary technological advance in programming for individual needs?
11. Time of annual review: is the end of the school year the best time to review a student's progress? Perhaps this review should take place in late September or October in order to monitor changes that occurred during the summer; thus, any recommendations would reflect the current state of affairs.
12. IEPs for all students: if we constantly emphasize individual needs, then why not have written plans for all students, handicapped or not?

Obviously, there are a number of issues central to the IEP process. Throughout this process, we must strive to be constantly mindful of what is best for the adolescent, disregarding any personal biases, logistical factors, or administrative hurdles that could inhibit this consciousness.

THE RESOURCE TEACHER AT THE SECONDARY LEVEL

This chapter would be incomplete without mention of the resource teacher who works in the secondary school. We feel this is necessary since this specialist often provides a number of supplementary services to both secondary teachers and students. The resource teacher is often called on to: (1) assist regular teachers in developing IEPs that specifically meet the educational needs of an exceptional youth rather than trying to fit that particular pupil into a set curriculum; (2) work directly with some students in such academic areas as math or history to help these students grasp the concepts being taught and help them meet certain graduation requirements; and (3) work with both teachers and students in areas where the materials related to daily lessons need to be scaled down or completely revised—in vocational programs it may be necessary to simplify the language of some manuals. In these supplemental roles, the resource teacher often must display a broad knowledge of the entire secondary school. Additionally, this specialist must know how the various units in the secondary school interface.

SUMMARY

This chapter has highlighted a variety of topics directly related to the structuring of academic tasks. The first major part of this chapter presented and then integrated the principal stages of learning (acquisition, proficiency and fluency, maintenance, application, and generalization/adaptation) with instructional procedures that have proved useful with exceptional students. The second major part of this chapter elaborated on individualizing the educational programs of exceptional adolescents. Curricular concerns (selection and content), possible modifications of the educational program, the technique of task analysis, and the characteristics of the individualized educational program (IEP) were considered at length as being intricately related to programming specific academic tasks.

In reviewing this chapter, the reader will notice that classroom management techniques were not addressed. While we believe that this topic must be considered simultaneously with curriculum and specific instructional objectives, classroom management is important enough to deserve an entire chapter. Up to this point, an adequate amount of information concerning content and process has been presented in order to investigate additional procedural techniques that are extremely useful to teachers on the secondary level.

REFERENCES

Altman, R., & Talkington, L.W., Modeling: An alternative behavior modification approach for retardates. *Mental Retardation*, 1971, 9(3), 20–23.

Bateman, B. *The essentials of teaching.* San Rafael, California: Dimensions Publishing, 1971.

Cegelka, P.T., & Phillips, M.W. Individualized education programming at the secondary level. *Teaching Exceptional Children*, 1978, *10*, 84–87.

Hauser, C. Education for mildly handicapped adolescents: Structure and quality of published information from the past decade. *Journal of Special Education*, 1978, *12*, 285–301.

Hawisher, M.F., & Calhoun, M.L. *The resource room: An educational asset for children with special needs.* Columbus, Ohio: Charles E. Merrill Publishing Co., 1978.

Hayes, J., & Higgins, S.T. Issues regarding the IEP: Teachers on the front line. *Exceptional Children*, 1978, *44*, 267–273.

Marsh, G.E., Gearheart, C.K., & Gearheart, B.R. *The learning disabled adolescent: Program alternatives in the secondary school.* St. Louis: C.V. Mosby Co., 1978.

Payne, J.S., Polloway, E.A., Smith, J.E., & Payne, R.A. *Strategies for teaching the mentally retarded.* Columbus, Ohio: Charles E. Merrill Publishing Co., 1977.

Premack, D. Toward empirical behavior laws: I. Positive reinforcement. *Psychological Review*, 1959, *66*, 219–233.

Russell, F., Shoemaker, S., McGuigan, C., & Bevis, D. *I.E.P.: Individual education programming.* Boise, Indiana: State Department of Public Instruction, 1976.

Schrag, J.A. *Individualized educational programming (I.E.P.): A child study team process.* Austin, Texas: Learning Concepts, 1977.

Sulzer-Azaroff, B., & Mayer, G.R. *Applying behavior-analysis procedures with children and youth.* New York: Holt, Rinehart, & Winston, 1977.

Williams, R.L., & Anandam, K. *Cooperative classroom management.* Columbus, Ohio: Charles E. Merrill Publishing Co., 1973.

6

Classroom Management

Many positive things can happen in the school environment; for example, the teacher can possess a tremendous array of teaching skills, pupils can be highly motivated to learn, and the best equipment that money can buy can be present. And yet, students still may fail to learn. If this is the case, the teacher is in need of something more than teaching skills, motivated students, and good equipment. There must exist in the teacher's mind, or perhaps on paper, a plan for managing all of these elements so that order is achieved in the classroom. Achieving order is more than having a neat looking room where pupils sit in seats placed in straight and even rows. Achieving order is the overall structuring of the environment so that all types of learning are facilitated. Obviously, there are numerous ways to accomplish this general goal. For example, developing, planning, and scheduling activities, arranging work and nonwork areas in the classroom, and providing for nonacademic activities all contribute to the classroom structure. The question to be considered at this point is, What are the basic elements in the classroom that the teacher must consider in attempting to manage this environment effectively? The primary aim of this chapter is to examine a number of factors that lead to good classroom management.

EFFECTIVE CLASSROOM MANAGEMENT TECHNIQUES

Regardless of the reason that a particular mildly handicapped adolescent may perform poorly in the classroom, two of our broad goals as their teachers are to: (1) improve academic performance and (2) increase or maintain positive behavior in the classroom. Unquestionably, there are numerous ways that these general goals can be accomplished. Reports in the professional literature have demonstrated that many systematic techniques, based on behavior management principles, have been used successfully in managing academic as well as nonacademic behaviors in the school environment.

Behavior Modification

In recent years, a number of persons associated with the field of education have attempted to control systematically behaviors that take place in and out of the classroom. Generally, these individuals are known as behaviorists, or behavior modifiers, and the system they use to control behaviors is known as behaviorism or behavior modification. Behavior modification has been used to control academic behaviors of adolescents (Nolen, Kunselmann, & Haring, 1967; Staats & Butterfield, 1965; Tyler, 1967), as well as voice problems (Jackson & Wallace, 1974), work performance (O'Hara, 1970), and disruptive behaviors (Broden, Hall, Dunlap, & Clark, 1970). Behavior modification techniques have also been used by many teachers to gain efficiency in the use of certain teaching strategies (Lindsley, 1971; Skinner, 1968).
    Before citing a number of examples of how behavior modification works in different settings, certain terms closely connected with behavior modification will be defined and described. Behavior modification itself can be defined as the systematic control of antecedents to and consequences of behavior in order to change one or several behaviors. In general, behavior modifiers manipulate behaviors in order to do at least one of three things: (1) increase appropriate behavior, (2) maintain appropriate behavior, or (3) decrease inappropriate behavior. A behavior is manipulated by contingently applying reinforcement; that is, when a behavior is performed, it is reinforced or rewarded in some positive or negative way.

Definition of terms.

In order to acquire some understanding of this often technical jargon, we have compiled the following brief list of behavioral terminology. It will make the reading of this chapter more meaningful and more comfortable.

Behavior—the measurable, observable, definable act performed by an individual.

Behavioral contract—an agreement made by the behavioral modifier and the student stating the goals and guidelines of a particular program.

Chaining—a procedure whereby behaviors that a student can already perform are reinforced sequentially in order to establish more complex behaviors.

Contingencies—"the specified dependencies between behavior and its antecedents and consequences" (Sulzer-Azaroff & Mayer, 1977, p. 514).

Deprivation—a procedure that discontinues the use of a reinforcer for a set period of time in order to maximize the value of the reinforcer.

Extinction—the procedure in which a certain behavior is no longer reinforced with the ultimate effect of a decrease in the frequency of the behavior (e.g., ignoring an undesirable behavior).

Fading—the systematic removal of any number of cues or prompts so that a certain behavior occurs without any auxiliary assistance.

Imitation—the situation where a student simply replicates or imitates the behavior of another person or model.

Probe—a mini-evaluation technique used to assess a given portion of a behavioral problem.

Prompt—an auxiliary cue or additional assistance used to maximize the elicitation of a desired behavior; typically the prompt is faded from the program.

Punishment—a procedure where an unpleasant event or consequence is presented immediately after a behavior in order to decrease the strength of this response (i.e., decrease its reoccurrence).

Reinforcement—an event that follows a response and tends to increase or maintain this behavior. The reinforcing event must be of value to the student and can be of two types: positive (the presentation of an event that is reinforcing) or negative (the removal of an aversive event).

Response—often having the same meaning as behavior; it can be considered a measurable, observable, definable unit of behavior.

Satiation—a phenomenon whereby a reinforcer loses its effectiveness, as noted by a decrease in performance, due to its repeated use or excessive administration.

Schedule of reinforcement—the specific criteria that determine when reinforcement is presented. There are four basic types: interval (fixed and variable) and ratio (fixed and variable).

Self-management—a technique whereby students monitor and change some component of their behavior; the recording process serves as the reinforcing event.

Stimulus—anything to which a student responds; however, the stimulus may or may not affect the student's behavior.

Stimulus control—simply the process in which a differential relationship has been established between a specific stimulus or set of stimuli and a response.

Time-out (TO)—a procedure in which the opportunity of receiving the reinforcement is removed contingent on the occurrence of a certain response; usually a specified amount of time in TO is prescribed.

Token economy—a system built on economic principles in which tokens are used as reinforcers contingent on desired behaviors; the token acquires value because of its exchange value (i.e., the tokens can be traded at a later time for reinforcing materials or activities).

While we hope that these terms have been described clearly and adequately, it is important to elaborate on the concept of punishment. There is much debate today in regard to the appropriate use of punishment in the school system or, for that matter, even in the home. As a result, a few cautions are in order. Though punishment decreases a behavior, many educators caution that it should be used sparingly. MacMillan, Forness, and Trumbull (1973) have suggested the following guideline be used when considering the use of punishment.

1. A prior positive relationship with the recipient renders punishment more effective.
2. Punishment, if it must be used, should be early in the sequence of misbehavior and consistently applied.
3. A relatively intense aversive at the onset may be more effective than having to gradually escalate the intensity, but at the same time one must guard against "punishment overkill."
4. Whenever possible, punishment should be paired with cognitive structure, i.e., specification of the behavior being punished.
5. Punishment is more effective if an alternative is available to the punished behavior and if incompatible behavior is positively reinforced.
6. The same aversive should not be used over and over, e.g., the wording of a reprimand should be changed.
7. Soft reprimands, i.e., reprimands directed only at the recipient, are probably more effective. (p. 95)

The application of various behavioral strategies.

Perhaps the best way to describe the dynamics of a behavioral management orientation is to relate the concepts to reality. Today, there are a number of strategies available to the secondary teacher including: token systems, modeling, peer tutoring, behavioral contracting, group contingency programs, and self-management techniques.

A strategy that has been used widely for a number of years is a *token economy system.* Rather than describing a token system, the following two case studies introduce and illustrate how such a system can be implemented. As in Jerry's situation, it is frequently necessary to reassess the nature of a token system to adapt various components and achieve an effective management system.

Another strategy that can be used with exceptional adolescents is *modeling.* This technique uses the principle of imitation described earlier in this chapter. Madsen and Madsen (1974) define modeling as

a technique whereby the behavior which is to be taught is demonstrated for the learner and any semblance of the goal behavior is initially rewarded. The criterion for reinforcement is then gradually increased until the goal behavior is obtained. (p. 207)

According to Payne et al. (1977), modeling possesses a number of advantages over other techniques used to foster learning and/or control certain behaviors. Included in the advantages are the fact that

less concern [is] needed over the breaking of tasks into small steps; reinforcers need not be determined since reinforcement is inherent in the modeling process; and, behavior acquired in this manner is more resistant to extinction and more likely to generalize to other behaviors. (p. 25)

The above discussion leads one to conclude that modeling can be a powerful tool with which teachers can effect learning as well as control behaviors. In this respect, the teacher can model many of the behaviors that the student is supposed to imitate, or the teacher can cause a student to acquire such a revered status that other students will model the behavior of the "star." However, since a person can model both positive and negative behaviors, the teacher must exercise a great deal of forethought when using this technique.

One area in which peers have been used successfully as models is that of *peer tutoring.* Williams and Anandam (1973) have stated that "there are few educational endeavors which have generated more reports of success than the use of student tutors" (p. 98). In this situation, a number of very positive things can happen to the exceptional adolescent who needs remediation or who needs to develop skills usually associated with much younger children. There are a number of ways that peer tutoring can take place. First, a peer of the student who needs help can tutor that person and assist in increasing the student's level of achievement. Wagner (1974) reported the occurrence of such a

Anecdote 6.1
Ben

Ben was a loud and generally obnoxious person in class. He constantly made negative statements about his classmates during the day. Ben could often be heard saying something like, "You're the dumbest guy that I've ever seen," or "You're a pretty ugly girl, you know that?". Even when he referred to himself he often used a negative tone.

Because he demonstrated a low achievement level, as well as a low opinion of himself and others, it was decided that Ben, and several other junior high school students, would be placed in a program to help these students develop the basic academic skills they were lacking. Even after being enrolled in the program for sometime, Ben continued to display the same negative behaviors and low achievement level. If anything, his general behavior took a turn for the worse.

At this point, a conference was held because almost everyone connected with the program felt that Ben's behavior was such a disruptive influence on his classes that something would have to be done to change the situation. After much discussion, the assembled group agreed that a token economy would be instituted in Ben's reading resource class. The general aim was to improve the academic work of all pupils, and specifically to decrease the number of occurrences of Ben's disruptive acts.

The first step in the initiation procedure involved explaining the token economy and how a student could earn money by:

1. coming to class on time;
2. picking up work materials when they arrived in class;
3. starting to work, if the day's schedule called for it, or waiting for their turn with the teacher; and
4. finishing work at an agreed on level of accuracy (about 90%).

Ben had a lot of questions about the whole operation, but finally consented to try the system out by mumbling under his breath. Things went well for a few days. However, Ben's behavior began gradually to reach his old level after he found out that items in our store did not appeal to him. Lest the system collapse, we asked Ben what he would want to buy. He stated that he wanted to buy a trip to a nearby town to visit a relative. We explained that this trip might be possible, but it would take some time to work out the details and Ben would have to start saving immediately if he was going to have enough money for the trip. Needless to say, after this discusion Ben became all business. He would come in and work hard each day with little or no disruptive problems. Finally, after saving for several months, Ben got his trip.

Anecdote 6.2
Jerry

For some reason, after repeated tries, I was unable to motivate Jerry to do his work during class each day. Even after a token economy was established, Jerry's performance was erratic at best. This was very surprising in light of the fact that he was earning a large amount of money each day via the token system. Since the backup reinforcers that we were using did not seem to work with Jerry, I asked him why he was not spending his money and what he would want to buy. As usual, he did not have an answer to either question, so we continued to "hold" at square two.

Later that same afternoon, I noted that Jerry was playing cards with some of the other boys. He seemed to be highly interested in the game that was being played. Toward the end of the next few days, I noted that Jerry exhibited the same behavior during the card playing sessions. Jerry's behavior indicated to me that he was very much interested in competing against the older pupils. After making these observations, I asked him if he would like to play the same game with me. He said yes, he would like to play.

During that same afternoon, we played our first game. The rules for playing the game were pretty simple: (1) Jerry or anyone else who wanted to play me, "the champ," would have to buy my time for $15 per game; (2) if the student won the game he or she received the money back; and (3) no betting was allowed on the games. After we had played on several occasions, Jerry had to buy my time quite a few times. Since he wanted to continue to play the card games in the afternoon, and since he was spending a lot of his money, Jerry began to be more consistent in his work performance in order to earn a greater amount of money.

situation in a high school tutorial program in Portland, Oregon. In this particular program, about 500 of the 2,000 students agreed to work as student tutors. Evaluative findings from this project indicated that results of one student tutoring another student were positive. In the second situation, the tutor, who may or may not initially possess the certain skills that are to be taught or demonstrated, works with younger children to help them acquire the skills in question. Again, Wagner (1974) has reported several cases where this situation has taken place. For example, in Baltimore, Maryland, high school students worked with elementary aged children, and in Santa Rosa, California, older children tutored first graders to improve their basic skills. Usually, as the result of a peer-tutoring program, two positive things happen to the person being tutored: (1) the student receives a great deal of individual attention, and (2) the student receives help in needed areas. At the same time, the tutor

> in the process of teaching another person . . . reviews material already learned, giving him a more comprehensive grasp of the subject matter. Tutors achieve such benefits as a consequence of increased motivation, stemming from their need to learn (or relearn) such basic skills as primary mathematics and reading comprehension in order to become tutors. (Wagner, 1974, p. 53)

Teachers, however, should be sensitive to the fact that not every secondary student wants nor will benefit from peer-tutoring. Some students will react negatively to such a program due to the stigmatizing effects of this arrangement. Therefore, we suggest that caution be exercised prior to instituting a peer-tutoring program.

Recently, interest has focused on a technique known as *behavioral contracting.* Marsh et al. (1978) describe behavioral contracts as mutual agreements between a student and a teacher aimed at accomplishing some stated objective. In this situation, the student is actively involved in determining how the task will be accomplished, as well as what immediate reward or reinforcement will be gained from the accomplishment. These same authors offer a set of ten guidelines, which they have adapted from material originally developed by Homme (1970):

1. The contingency (reward) should be immediate.
2. Initial contracts should call for and reward small approximations.
3. Reward frequently with small amounts.
4. The contract should call for and reward accomplishment rather than obedience.
5. Reward the performance *after* it occurs.
6. The contract must be fair.
7. The terms of the contract must be clear.
8. The contract must be honest.
9. The contract must be positive.
10. Contracting as a method must be used systematically. (pp. 130–132)

Even though all of these guidelines are important, guideline number seven cannot be overstressed. Clarity as to what the contract specifically implies behaviorally is a must! The fact that this strategy allows for a certain amount of confidentiality, complete individuality, and student input makes it a very desirable technique if done properly.

Although used effectively on the elementary level, another strategy that can be applied on the secondary level is *group-* or *peer-reinforcing contingencies.* This technique incorporates reinforcement on

a group level in which a whole class or group of students are rewarded for the appropriate or desired behavior of one or a number of fellow students. This system will frequently encourage peer cooperation, assistance (peer tutoring), and group togetherness. At first glance, this strategy may seem ideal; however, it may not actually be so easy to implement on the secondary level where the students in various classes may seem socially distant from one another. Additionally, this technique is susceptible to peer backlash, if criteria are not met, or to pressure from other students in the form of threats. As a result, caution again is recommended.

The final behavioral strategy that has been found effective is referred to as *self-management.* As mentioned earlier, this technique requires that a student become intimately involved in the monitoring and change process of the program. Sulzer-Azaroff and Mayer (1977) consider the student's responsibility to include part or all of the following:

1. selection of their own goals
2. monitoring their own behavior
3. selection of procedures for behavioral change
4. implementation of the procedures
5. evaluation of the effectiveness of the procedures. (p. 78)

In many situations where this technique could be used on the secondary level, a certain sophistication or maturity on the part of the student is required for it to be effective. Nonetheless, many exceptional adolescents are capable of self-managing a program that embodies these five components.

The previous discussion has been limited to concerns related primarily to techniques that place a heavy reliance on positive gestures

toward the student and on efficiency of operation. However, even though positiveness and efficiency should be stressed, we realize that this is not always possible. Let us face the fact that sometimes behaviors cannot be ignored, they must be punished. Also, efficiency is not always possible due to extenuating circumstances. Yet, the condition of accentuating positiveness and efficiency is preferable.

General problems encountered with the
behavioral management paradigm.

Before we conclude this section on the use of behavioral strategies, a few concluding points need to be emphasized.

1. The culture of the classroom in which a specific behavioral strategy is to be instituted: certain settings just are not conducive to various behavioral techniques!
2. The skills required of the teachers or staff in order for a program to be effective: Deno, Gutman, and Fullmer (1977) stress that the success of a behavioral education program depends on the skills of those who administer it and that any sophisticated behavioral program demands many teacher competencies!

3. The predisposition of an education setting to a behavioral intervention: many teachers do not believe in this system and it would be fruitless to wage a lengthy battle to convince them because it is usually the student who suffers the aftereffects of such a confrontation.
4. Suitable reinforcers: locating events, activities, or materials that are reinforcing or suitable for the secondary level student could be quite exhausting, yet are indispensible.
5. Concern for the attitudes of the student and his or her family: ethically, this is obligatory.
6. The development of self-esteem: while this concept may be difficult to define in the first place, there has been concern that behavioral strategies ignore the development of self-esteem. Krumboltz and Krumboltz (1972) very simply address this issue:

> How do you develop a child's self-esteem? You make sure that he is learning to master the tasks in his environment, that he is praised and rewarded for his accomplishments, and that he is loved and respected by those around him. The end result of these behaviors is the development of a feeling in a child which we label "self-esteem." (p. 248)

If behavioral techniques attempt to assist a student in the mastery of certain tasks then, using these criteria, they most certainly consider the development of self-esteem.

Without an intensive scrutiny of these potential problems, the success of any behavioral management program is seriously jeopardized. As a result, we strongly urge that these points be kept in mind prior to initiating behavioral strategies.

Issues Associated with Managing the Exceptional Adolescent in the Classroom

In addition to the issues just presented with regard to the behavioral paradigm, there are other important concerns when we consider the exceptional youth in the classroom. Some of these issues have been raised in other contexts in previous chapters. In this chapter, a number of classroom and program-related topics are discussed.

Motivation.

If we want to maximize the learning potential of the exceptional adolescent, then we certainly want this student to realize that there is a purpose to his or her efforts. Unfortunately, this type of student historically has probably experienced much frustration in educational endeavors. There are a number of methods for instilling motivation into most normal-achieving students, namely quizzes, tests, strict absence policies, and ultimately grades. But for the exceptional student these motivators often don't work. We have already suggested that mastery grading would be more appropriate for this student. More importantly, however, in terms of motivating the exceptional adolescent we want to instill an intrinsic relevancy. Ideally, the student will see meaning in school. How this adolescent is managed in class, as well as what is presented, must be programmed so that this student acknowledges its value and usefulness.

The climate of the classroom.

Just as exceptional adolescents are a heterogeneous group, so classrooms vary widely as to internal dynamics. Rules, tolerances of certain behaviors, classroom freedom, use of punishment, expectations of classwork, ad nauseam, all vary from class to class. All of these factors have a great impact on how to manage the exceptional adolescent. For instance, if rules are vague or unfamiliar, the mildly handicapped adolescent may react like the character that appeared in a cartoon in *The Wall Street Journal.* In this cartoon, a boy who was sitting in a corner stated to a girl standing nearby that he could not "tell the rules from the guidelines." This example clearly points out that it is very important that teachers in all classrooms be as consistent as possible in dealing with students at this level. Additionally, the climate of each classroom should be as positive and as open as possible so that both students and teacher can work cooperatively.

Management in the Regular Classroom

All of the previous discussion has a bearing on any type of classroom that includes an exceptional adolescent. Yet, some mention should be made at this point of specific strategies the regular classroom teacher should use in conjunction with those already mentioned. There are several suggestions that can dramatically aid the regular classroom teacher in managing a secondary level classroom composed of average and exceptional youth.

Do	*Do Not*
• realize that the exceptional youth has special needs that must be met so that he or she will be able to learn.	• call undue attention to the exceptional youth by constantly dwelling on his or her learning problems.

Do

- individualize instruction, working through common areas at the beginning of a lesson, and then moving to instruction with individuals and small groups.

- individualize assignments. Since all pupils will not be able to do the same amount or quality of work, inclass as well as out-of-class assignments must be made on the basis of what reasonably can be expected from each student.

- have specific teaching/learning objectives in mind for each period of instruction. Develop specific subobjectives for the exceptional pupil when and if necessary.

- be positive and firm in working with exceptional youths.

- promote success by making initial classwork and assignments at a level below the known capabilities of the student.

- require completion of classroom assignments before the student moves to a new task. If a student is not expected to complete an assignment, then he or she should not be assigned that work.

Do Not

- assume that all students in a class learn or can be instructed in the same manner.

DEVELOPING AND PLANNING ACTIVITIES

Although this discussion will not reiterate the facts presented in the previous chapter, the topic of developing and planning activities is presented again to show the heavy constraints that these two ele-

ments place on management and control in the classroom. Without careful development of activities geared to meet the specific needs of each pupil, and without a well-thought-out plan for using the developed activities, the battle is lost before it is begun; the teacher has no tools to work with or, if the teacher does possess some small amount of tools, there may be no systematic plan for using them.

It seems apparent, then, that at least three major considerations must be accounted for in developing and planning activities at this level. These considerations include: (1) instructional objectives—both short- and long-term; (2) time constraints; and (3) student characteristics.

In considering these three topics, it seems safe to say that one major concern is what instructional objectives have been developed for a given student or group of students. Initially, our concern should focus on instructional objectives because these short- and long-term objectives will provide us with a road map. Secondly, an acute awareness must be maintained regarding schedules, or the amount of time in which we have to accomplish certain activities. This matter is discussed in greater detail below. Lastly, student characteristics must be considered in deciding exactly what instructional activities will be developed and implemented in the classroom.

SCHEDULING

In chapter 2, a brief examination was made of a typical schedule for a secondary student and of scheduling at this level. Now we are going to inspect more closely the inner workings of scheduling in secondary educational programs. This inspection will show the relationship of scheduling and classroom management, that is, how the total school schedule and its numerous subparts set up many of the time and space parameters within which the teacher and other school personnel must work.

The framework that pulls together the various component activities of the secondary school is the general schedule. Therefore, our initial discussion focuses on various matters related to the general schedule. Subsequent discussion is concerned with the different enabling activities that take place under the broad umbrella of the general schedule, for example, daily, weekly, and yearly activities.

The General Schedule

Most secondary schools use a general or daily schedule composed of six to eight time periods. These various time periods are usually 40 to 50 minutes each, with a short time space between periods to change classes. Some of these blocks of time are exclusively devoted to academic matters; others are devoted to independent study or extraclass activities. Approximately three-fourths of each student's daily schedule is made up of academic classes. The remaining portion of the student's schedule usually involves such extraclass activities as band, athletics, and/or school clubs, as well as time for lunch or inschool study. On certain short days—days in which the normal time frame of school operations is shortened or restricted—many secondary schools use an "activity schedule." An activity schedule involves shortening all periods of the days by a specified amount of time, for example, 15 minutes. Thus, the activity schedule results in the same number of periods during the day, but less time is available for use in these periods. Some students who are in special programs, such as a vocational preparation program, follow a general schedule that is slightly different from that of the majority of students. Students in special programs may attend school for a half-day session, where they engage in academic work, and spend the other half of the school day away from the school, where they receive other types of training.

Individual Periods

The individual period is the pivotal unit in the overall secondary school schedule. During the individual periods of the general schedule, most daily instruction as well as other activities takes place. Just as the general schedule may be separated into several individual periods, an individual period may be composed of several components, namely, daily activities, weekly activities, and activities that require more than one or two weeks to accomplish.

Depending on the particular objectives of a given teacher, daily instructional activities usually begin by introducing daily, weekly, or unit concerns that are to be attended to during this specific day. Following the introductory portion, there are activities aimed at fostering different types of learning. For example, new activities that might occur during this period would probably be aimed at acquisition learning, whereas review activities might be geared to maintenance or generalization learning. At the end of each period would come a number of closing activities. Usually, these closing activities represent an attempt to bring together in a fairly cohesive manner all the different things that have taken place during this one daily period.

Often, a certain objective cannot be accomplished in one day or during a single period; therefore, activities to accomplish this objective may take place during several days of the week or even one or two complete weeks. Thus, it can be surmised that weekly activities focus on the coordination of several ongoing daily activities. Also, since the goals and objectives of weekly activities are somewhat broader than those associated with daily endeavors, it is easier to integrate these weekly goals and objectives with similar and related concerns taking place elsewhere in the school. In some instances, even one or two weeks is not enough time to cover certain objectives or certain amounts of material. Schools usually attempt to provide for such cases by dividing the school calendar year into very large blocks of time (semesters, quarters, or six-week periods).

Further Considerations

While the above comments provide us with several general ideas as to how the individual or daily class schedule works, this topic needs to be examined further to ascertain how a teacher might make the maximum use of each period. The point to be stressed is that teacher flexibility in this area is very crucial. Flexibility, in this case, means that instead of using only one type of daily schedule, several types or combinations need to be utilized. A teacher who seldom deviates from a fixed daily schedule invites boredom, apathy, and resistance on the part of students. On the other hand, by employing a variable daily schedule, the teacher evokes renewed interest and active participation on the part of students.

Flexibility in the daily schedule can be enhanced in a number of ways. Probably the best way to achieve this goal is to vary the daily schedule so that: (1) on some days the teacher lectures regarding some previously selected topic; (2) on other days the teacher may lead student discussions of a particular topic, or have students actually conduct the discussions; and (3) on other days the teacher may have students work on group or individual projects in the classroom. These examples of teacher lectures, class discussions, and student projects provide different activities during several individual periods. Since several kinds of activities are used, different blocks of time have to be organized within the individual period. Several examples of schedules will further clarify these points.

A teacher who used a lecture method would probably set up a daily schedule similar to the following.

Schedule 1

Class Lecture—History
Topic: The War of 1812
Activity: Introduction   9:00
            Lecture   9:10
            Conclusion   9:45
            Dismiss Class   9:55

During this particular class session, most of the time would be spent acquainting students with various facts related to the War of 1812. In this situation, instructor output would be high whereas student output would be much lower.

A second teaching approach is that of class discussion—either teacher or student led. A typical schedule would probably look like the following example.

Schedule 2

Class Discussion—History
Topic: The War of 1812
Activity: Introduction   9:00
            Discussion—Group I   9:05
            Discussion—Group II   9:25
            Summary of Discussion   9:45
            Dismiss Class   9:55

This type of arrangement allows for much more input/output by class members than the previous one.

The last type of schedule devotes the class period to student projects. An example of this arrangement follows.

Schedule 3

Class—History
Topic: The War of 1812
Activity: Development of Student Projects   9:00
            Dismiss Class   9:55

Of all the examples of scheduling arrangements mentioned, this last one allows for the greatest amount of student participation.

The overriding fact about all three of the sample schedules is that they can be used alone or in various combinations. It should also be apparent that, depending on the objectives that have been developed for the course and for the students in the course, each instructor will or should vary the times and amounts of direct and indirect class participation. Lastly, we have not exhausted the possible number of scheduling opportunities with these three illustrations. Teachers who work in different areas of the secondary curriculum should be able to cite many other examples that would enhance and/or increase flexibility.

ARRANGEMENT OF THE CLASSROOM

Although classroom arrangement may at first glance appear to be quite simple, the following case clearly illustrates what can happen if a teacher does not effectively use the time and space at his or her disposal. For the sake of anonymity let us call this teacher, Helen.

It seems that Helen's main complaint at the end of each day was that she could "barely make it" because she was so tired. A consultation with a medical specialist determined that there was nothing physically wrong with her. At this point, we (as consultants to this project) began to observe Helen's daily teaching behaviors to ascertain whether she was becoming overly tired from too much work. Our observations, along with Helen's confirmations, revealed that:

1. Helen was unable to control students effectively in the classroom, even though there were usually no more than six or seven students in the room at one time;
2. in a large number of instances she could not find materials or equipment when she wanted or needed them; and
3. students did not seem motivated to do their inclass work or to do it well.

The major concern in this example was not how to teach a given activity; an assumption was made that the teacher knew how to teach. The primary concern was *when* and *where* to teach a specific activity. More precisely, the question that involved was, What facts must a teacher take into consideration when scheduling activities and setting up the classroom environment? In line with this question, Premack (1959) has concluded that certain objects or events have more value than other objects or events, and the acquisition of these valued entities can be used to motivate an individual. Moreover, certain classroom activities and certain areas of the classroom would have more appeal or value than others because of an association with positive consequences or reinforcement. A classroom is more than just a classroom; it is a conglomerate of stimuli with which a student (and teacher) must interact—stimuli that can be positive or negative. Thus, according to Homme (1970), a teacher who is concerned with effectively managing the classroom environment and motivating students will not overexpose the student to either positive or negative consequences in the classroom.

In the attempt to resolve the numerous problems in Helen's classroom, a currency-based token economy was implemented whereby students could earn money for doing classwork correctly and for exhibiting appropriate behaviors. Other recommendations that were made included: (1) placing the token economy store and bank in one corner of the room and setting up an area to sell games and other fun activities, thus decreasing the major work area by approximately one-fourth; (2) placing infrequently used materials in the corner opposite the token economy, thus providing a teacher work and storage area and reducing the academic portion of the room by another one-fourth; and (3) providing students with learning centers for independent maintenance activities.

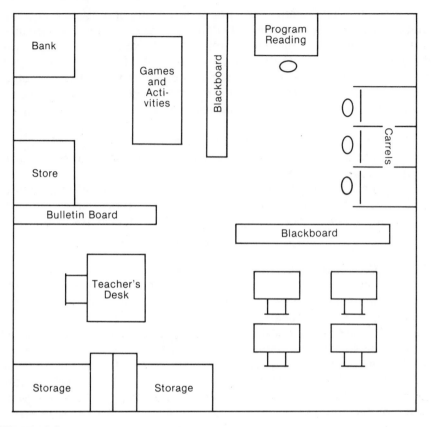

Figure 6.1
A Well-Designed Instructional Environment

Figure 6.1 shows the results of the several recommendations made to this teacher. In this classroom, the arrangement:

1. provided definite work and nonwork areas;
2. provided a clear demarcation between high and low probability areas;
3. placed infrequently used materials in specific areas for quick and easy retrieval;
4. decreased the total amount of space that the teacher had to control overtly in order to keep the class running smoothly; and
5. increased the total amount of time that the teacher could use for instructional purposes.

Clearly, one of the natural enemies of the classroom teacher is inefficient use of classroom time and space. To make good use of time and space, the teacher needs to conduct lessons and other activities in an area that provides opportunities for several types of ongoing activities at one time (independent work, one-to-one activities by students and/or teacher, or small and large group instruction). The classroom teacher must also be aware of and take advantage of certain high and low probability areas in the classroom. This can be done by making entrance to high probability areas dependent on adequate performance in low probability areas. By logically and systematically observing the natural consequences in the classroom, the teacher is in a good position to structure academic and nonacademic tasks for effective learning.

NONACADEMIC ACTIVITIES

In every classroom, a number of activities occur that are not directly related to instruction or academic activities. These nonacademic activities can include sitting around doing nothing, engaging in pleasant conversation, straightening up the classroom, or having a birthday party for a student. Teachers are often afraid and embarrassed to mention these activities to outsiders, or even to other teachers, feeling that they will be looked down on or viewed as "duty shirkers." However, this need not be the case since these activities take place in all kinds of work environments and, more importantly, they can be used productively. For instance, any worker who has worked on a certain task for a period of time will tire. If this person continues to perform this task when fatigued, then performance will suffer. On the other hand, by introducing short rest or nonwork periods into the daily routine, the teacher can reduce the likelihood of fatigue seriously affecting the student's work.

The observant teacher also takes advantage of nonacademic activities by noting differences in student behaviors during these periods. The teacher can also obtain valuable information from or about the student because this is a more relaxed time and students and teacher can interact more informally.

Three important points should be considered as the teacher endeavors to make positive use of nonacademic activities. First, these activities should be of *short duration.* If these activities extend beyond a certain time limit, little or no academic work will be accomplished and the nonacademic period will become counterproductive. Second, since nonactivities will take up only short periods of time, these activities or periods should be *used as breather or transition activities.* For example, after students have worked hard on the day's reading exercises, they probably should not go directly to another such activity, but should be allowed to pause momentarily. Third, nonacademic activities should be made *contingent on completion of daily work.*

SUMMARY

The primary concern of this chapter was to delineate a number of factors that can help the teacher achieve order in the classroom. A brief overview of the behavioral management paradigm was presented that included a discussion of behavioral strategies, such as, modeling, peer tutoring, behavioral contracting, group-reinforcing contingencies, and self-management. Some problems encountered with this paradigm were also explained. The next section considered some of the issues inherent in the process of managing the exceptional adolescent in the classroom.

The topics of scheduling, arrangement of the classroom, and nonacademic activities were also discussed in detail. Scheduling was viewed in terms of the general schedule and the individual periods that make up this schedule. The general schedule provides the overall framework for the total school operation; the individual periods provide the parameters for each teacher's work. Arrangement of the classroom considered the controlling of positive and negative stimuli that interact in all classrooms. We contend that unless the teacher exercises a good deal of control over these positive and negative stimuli, control over the class will be weakened. Lastly, the topic of nonacademic activities that occur in all classrooms was discussed. It was concluded that these types of activities should be used in transitional situations.

REFERENCES

Broden, M., Hall, R.V., Dunlap, A., & Clark, R. Effects of teacher attention and a token reinforcement system in a junior high school special education class. *Exceptional Children,* 1970, *36,* 341–349.

Deno, S.L., Gutman, A.J., & Fullmer, W. Educational programs for retarded individuals. In T. Thompson & J. Grabowski (Eds.), *Behavior modification of the mentally retarded* (2nd ed.). New York: Oxford University Press, 1977.

Homme, L. *How to use contingency contracting in the classroom.* Champaign, Illinois: Research Press, 1970.

Jackson, D.A., & Wallace, R.F. The modification and generalization of voice loudness in a fifteen-year-old retarded girl. *Journal of Applied Behavior Analysis*, 1974, *4,* 461–471.

Krumboltz, J.D., & Krumboltz, H.B. *Changing children's behavior.* Englewood Cliffs, New Jersey: Prentice-Hall, 1972.

Lindsley, O.R. Precision teaching in perspective: An interview with Ogdon R. Lindsley. *Teaching Exceptional Children,* 1971, *3,* 114–119.

MacMillan, D.L., Forness, S.R., & Trumbull, B.M. The role of punishment in the classroom. *Exceptional Children,* 1973, *40,* 85–96.

Madsen, S.H., & Madsen, C.K. *Teaching/Discipline: A positive approach for educational development.* Boston: Allyn & Bacon, 1974.

Marsh, G.E., Gearheart, C.K., & Gearheart, B.R. *The learning disabled adolescent: Program alternatives in the secondary school.* St. Louis: C.V. Mosby CO., 1978.

Nolen, P.A., Kunzelmann, H.P., & Haring, N.G. Behavioral modification in a junior high learning disabilities classroom. *Exceptional Children,* 1967, *34,* 163–168.

O'Hara, E.A. Using pay to change mentally retarded students' work behavior. *Teaching Exceptional Children,* 1970, *2,* 163–169.

Payne, J.S., Polloway, E.A., Smith, J.E., & Payne, R.A. *Strategies for teaching the mentally retarded.* Columbus, Ohio: Charles E. Merrill Publishing Co., 1977.

Premack, D. Toward empirical behavior laws: I. Positive reinforcement. *Psychological Review,* 1959, *66,* 219–233.

Skinner, B.F. *The technology of teaching.* New York: Appleton-Century-Crofts, 1968.

Staats, A.W., & Butterfield, W.H. Treatment of non-reading in a culturally deprived juvenile delinquent: An application of reinforcement principles. *Child Development,* 1965, *36,* 925–942.

Sulzer-Azaroff, B., & Mayer, G.R. *Applying behavior-analysis procedures with children and youth.* New York: Holt, Rinehart & Winston, 1977.

Tyler, V.O. Application of operant token reinforcement to academic performance of an institutionalized delinquent. *Psychological Reports,* 1967, *21,* 249–260.

Wagner, P. Children tutoring children. *Mental Retardation,* 1974, *12*(5) 52–55.

Williams, R.L., & Anandam, K. *Cooperative classroom management.* Columbus, Ohio: Charles E. Merrill Publishing Co., 1973.

part three

Career Provisions

The four chapters in this section of the book take a close look at how the secondary school prepares the mildly handicapped adolescent for a career in our society. In chapter 7, career education, vocational education, and the high school work/study program are discussed in terms of how each can aid the career preparation of the special needs youth. Chapter 8 discusses counseling techniques that are aimed at providing sound advice to these youths in the areas of personal adjustment and career preparation. Chapter 9 discusses in detail how to place mildly handicapped youths on different job sites and how to begin working with community employers. In chapter 10, program evaluation and follow-up procedures for determining program effectiveness and client adjustment are discussed.

7

Career Preparation

Even though some mildly handicapped adolescents will be able to leave their respective high schools and move on to compete successfully in a college or university, most of the youth who comprise this heterogeneous population will enter the job market after graduation. Thus, a major goal for many mildly handicapped youth is to prepare for a career while still in high school. A first step in preparing this group of youth for a career is to develop a set of career program objectives.

An adequate career preparation program for the mildly handicapped would include the following broad objectives:

1. increase the occupational awareness and aspirations of each student through career counseling;
2. develop a preliminary assessment of each student's vocational skills and interest;
3. provide each student with direct or "hands-on" job-related experiences and activities;

4. aid each student in the development of entry level job skills; and

5. provide a job placement service for students who complete the career preparation program.

In the ongoing attempt to foster a career preparation program that meets the needs of all students, school personnel must successfully manipulate a large number of diverse elements. This chapter closely scrutinizes a number of these factors, for example, the concepts of career and vocational education, career personnel, and the high school work/study program, to determine how these elements can be combined to produce students who are able to find and hold jobs successfully in their respective communities.

CAREER EDUCATION

Kolstoe (1976) defined *career* as the totality of work a person does in a lifetime; he defined *vocation* as the primary work role a person has at any given point in time. He went on to define education as "all those activities and experiences through which one learns" and career education as "all activities and experiences through which one learns about work" (p. 199).

The concept of career education was conceived by Dr. Sidney Marland, Commissioner of Education, in 1971. Marland (1971) described career education as encompassing three main ideas. First, career education was perceived as being for all students, including the handicapped, whether they would go to college, technical school, or a sheltered workshop. Second, career education not only occurs at the secondary level; it begins in kindergarten and goes beyond grade 12 and into adulthood. Third, Marland emphasized that as a result of the first two ideas, career education would give the student a start in earning a living. He did not say it would be a successful start or that all of the skills a student might need would be acquired at that point. He did, however, maintain that some of the skills required for a chosen career would and should be learned before a student left high school.

In an attempt to clarify the difference between career education and vocational education, Pollard (1977) firmly stated that the two concepts are not the same. Further, Pollard indicated that vocational education is only one of the many components of career education, and that it deals mainly with the development of occupational skills. Much of the confusion that arises about these two concepts has to do with the fact that at the secondary level a strong emphasis is placed on the development of occupational skills to prepare the student for employment.

Career Preparation from Childhood to Adulthood

Payne, Mercer, and Epstein (1974) have suggested that career education at the junior high school level should include orientation to and exploration of different occupations through various classroom work experiences and field trips into the work world. At the senior high school level, simulated work experiences and job tryouts for the student are recommended in conjunction with a close evaluation of progress and follow-up of the student in the training phase on the job, and after the job has become permanent. Career education for the student, whether handicapped or not, will evolve through five stages of development. Those stages are awareness, orientation, exploration, preparation, and skill refinement. Figure 7.1 depicts the grade level at which each of these broad stages should begin.

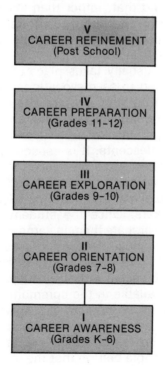

Figure 7.1
Career Education Objectives by Grade Level

During the early school years (K–6) career awareness should be emphasized. Students at this stage are developing positive attitudes toward the world of work and about themselves as future employees or workers. At this stage, the child begins to self-assess his or her interests and preferences for certain types of careers. However, no attempt should be made to train a student for any particular career at this early stage. The main objective of this stage and the next one is to expose the students to the world of work (Pollard, 1977). This is to be accomplished by such activities as showing pictures or filmstrips and playing games with the theme of people at work. Also plays or skits that call for the student to dress like a worker in a certain occupation can be used. For example, having the class put on hard hats and carry hammers or shovels may give them some idea of how a construction worker looks and feels.

Once the students become interested in and knowledgeable about a large number of different occupations, they should move to the career orientation stage. During this stage (grades 7–8), the student is introduced to more specific information concerning different potential careers. For example, the student learns that all medical doctors are not alike and that, rather than knowing every single job title, certain jobs can be grouped into categories that have a number of common characteristics (clerical personnel would include clerks, clerk-typists, secretaries, and related jobs).

Career exploration usually takes place at the secondary school level and is often referred to as prevocational training. At this time, students are exposed to a vast array of occupations, their specific vocational skills and interests are assessed, and they try out a limited number of these occupations for a short period of time. For many mildly handicapped adolescents, it is especially important to have a hands-on experience when being introduced to the many jobs in the work world. This objective can be accomplished by taking field trips to various job sites, role playing, and handling basic equipment used by different types of workers. Once the students' interests are determined, then it is time to prepare them in earnest for a career.

Career preparation usually moves into fully swing during the junior or senior year. At this stage, we try to match the abilities and competencies of the adolescent with the local jobs available and those predicted to become available in the community. Vocational training for a specific occupation is initiated. Job surveys, job tryouts, and part-time employment are emphasized. Later, many students are placed on permanent job sites. Once the student is placed in a permanent job, many people believe that the matter of career preparation is closed. However, even though a student may be able to perform a certain job successfully, he or she may want to develop other vocational skills, or may not like this particular job and want to move to another. An analogous situation would be the process that many of us

go through to become teachers. Most of us held permanent jobs
sometime during that process, yet our ultimate goal was to enter the
teaching profession.

Career skill refinement is accomplished through such post-school
activities as providing routine follow-up to the students to determine
how they are progressing on their jobs. The intent of follow-up services is at least twofold. First, the school, and perhaps other
agencies, is interested in determining how well it has prepared all students for current work conditions. Second, no matter how well each
student has been prepared for a job, certain adjustments have to be
made. By providing periodic follow-up services, the school insures
that these adjustments are made with a minimum of effort. Additionally, rehabilitation agencies, special vocational schools, and citizen
advocates are services that some students may need after formal
school training. All of these groups should continue to monitor and
train the student to refine certain vocational skills. For instance, after
the student has secured a first job, he or she should be able to go
through the job-hunting process more smoothly at a later time.
Another example of career skill refinement would be the situation in
which an automobile plant worker is laid off. In this situation, the
worker must find a new job shortly, or learn to use the services of
agencies, such as the unemployment commission, to help during the
time of unemployment and perhaps provide the means for new job
training.

History of Career Education

The comprehensiveness of the career education concept necessitates
a broad historical review to capture the various integral parts that have
emerged from several disciplines and that have contributed to the

development of this concept. The histories of vocational education and special education reflect a number of components of the career education movement that have implications for mildly handicapped youth.

Some highlights of the vocational education movement, which possess identifiable components of the career education concept, are exemplified by the Ford Foundation Sponsored Projects over the last decade, the Manpower Development Training Act of 1962, and the Vocational Education Act of 1963. The 1969–1972 recommendations of the National Advisory Council on Vocational Education are also congruent with the career education concept being emphasized by the United States Office of Education (Wolfe, 1973). Several events in the history of vocational education have particular significance for the mildly handicapped learner. For instance, Olympus Research Corporation (1972) reported that the "zero reject" concept employed in San Mateo, California, schools focuses on providing salable skills to all students. The Manpower Development and Training Act of 1962 emphasized remedial training and extended services to disadvantaged persons. The Job Corps was established in 1964 to provide vocational education for school dropouts without salable skills. The 1968 amendments to the Vocational Education Act of 1963 included a directive mandating that 10% of the federal funds allocated for vocational education must be used to provide vocational education to the handicapped.

The history of special education also reflects a broadening scope of services directed toward handicapped persons. In referring specifically to the retarded, Goldstein (1964) acknowledged the expansion of services over the years by indicating that initially services for this group were within state-operated institutions, then in public schools, and recently in public and private rehabilitation agencies and clinics. In terms of the career education concept for the retarded, Dunn (1961) credited Hungerford and his associates with emphasizing the need for occupational information in public school classes. Although an occupational core curriculum was suggested by Hungerford in 1948, it was not until 1965 that major legislation was passed that supported a joint vocational rehabilitation-special education effort toward preparing the retarded for employment. Dunn (1973) has claimed that even today, work/study programs have been one of the most innovative features of secondary curricula to occur over the last decade. At the present time, the stage is set for vocational education, vocational rehabilitation, and special education to pool efforts to effect career education and consequently achieve even greater acceptance and integration for exceptional children and youth. Although it is apparent that the thinking of modern times reflects an attitude of helpfulness and responsibility (Younie & Rusalem, 1971), the career education concept offers the philosophy and the impetus needed to achieve acceptance and integration for handicapped persons. Complementing this growth of the various disciplines toward occupational preparation of the handicapped has been the USOE's very timely emphasis on career education. Career education depends on all these related disciplines mutually planning and working together to achieve the goals of the movement.

During the mid to late 1970s, the career education movement made rapid strides in its attempt to expand the career potential of all persons moving through the educational system. A number of specific events were: the passage of PL 93–112 and the accompanying Section 504 (1973), which is essentially a civil rights bill for all handicapped persons (Ballard & Zettel, 1977); the sponsoring of national conferences on the topic of career education by such groups as CEC (St. Louis, Winter-1979); and the large volume of literature that has been written since Commissioner Marland first discussed this concept in the early 1970s. The interested reader should consult the following sources for additional information: Brolin, D.E. (Ed.), *Life centered career education: A competency based approach* (1978) published by CEC; and Brolin and Kokaska, *Career education for handicapped children and youth* (1979) published by Charles E. Merrill Publishing Company. In addition, interested persons may want to peruse the following publications: *An introduction to career education: A policy paper of the U.S. Office of Education* (1975), the 1977 winter issue of *Career Education Quarterly* that explores the topic of career education for the disabled student, and Clark's (1974) paper on career education for the mildly handicapped in *Focus on Exceptional Children.*

Rationale for Career Education

The raison d'etre of career education is illustrated by a brief review of some statistics. Marland (1972) reported that for every ten students in high school, two receive vocational training and three go to college (although one drops out). These figures do not include youngsters who drop out before reaching high school. This means that over one-half of all high school students (1,500,000) need more attractive options as they prepare for various careers. Marland continued by acknowledging that in the 1970–71 school year a total of 2,450,000 pupils left school unprepared to enter the job market. He reported that these 2,450,000 pupils cost about one-third (28 billion dollars) of the entire educational expenditure for the nation. Finally, Marland stated that an emphasis on career education is more realistic than continued overemphasis on academic programs, since the labor department indicates that for now and the foreseeable future 80% of the nation's jobs will require less than a baccalaureate degree. Although many jobs now require less than a baccalaureate degree, the number of unskilled positions is diminishing (Wolfe, 1973; Dunn, 1973).

For exceptional children and young adults this increasing demand for salable skills comes as disheartening news. Their education has unfortunately left many exceptional youths unemployable or underemployed due to a lack of adequate vocational preparation. As Martin (1972) noted, only 21% of the handicapped youth presently leaving school are fully employed or continue on to a higher education. This report underscores the need for mildly handicapped youth to receive adequate career preparation and vocational training to improve their position in the competitive job market. Career education at the secondary level affords the exceptional student an opportunity to prepare for a career, as well as job entry, and it is also an effective vehicle for preparing all students for the job market. In summary, the justification for increasing and improving career education programs for handicapped youth is fully documented. What remains is to implement quality programs.

RELATIONSHIP OF VOCATIONAL EDUCATION AND SPECIAL EDUCATION

Vocational education is one of the main components of career education for the mildly handicapped student at the secondary level. A student can progress through all the many direct and indirect aspects of career education, but if the student is not vocationally trained with at least some minimal skills, then the whole career education process will have failed to produce an employable individual. Thus, a major goal of vocational education is to provide an individual with entry level skills for at least one or two jobs. Another goal is to teach each student how personally to develop certain work skills or attitudes. Obviously both of the above goals will only be accomplished at a minimal level when the student leaves high school. However, if adequate follow-up is provided by the school or vocational rehabilitation or some other agency, then the student will have a much greater chance of succeeding at a chosen occupation.

In general, vocational education has not been aimed at specifically meeting the needs of mildly handicapped adolescents. For this reason, special educators in the past either developed parallel vocational training programs for the mildly handicapped—mainly for the

EMR group—or they attempted to convince vocational educators that these special needs adolescents also needed and deserved vocational training. One of the foremost persons to push for increased vocational training for the retarded was John Duncan of England. Duncan (1943) felt that there was a distinct need to emphasize the practical arts in a realistic curriculum that trained the retarded in a program of woodworking, homemaking, beekeeping, and many other tasks common to the English lower-class style of living. However, according to Kolstoe and Frey (1965), one of the main problems with Duncan's program was that no generalizing or modifiable skills were taught. Therefore, these skills could not be applied to other working situations. The program trained the individual only on certain very specific vocational tasks. Certainly frustration could result if these tasks were changed, or the environment or working conditions were altered.

Special educators struggled with this problem for a number of years. One of the most positive results of this struggle was the development of the high school work/study program (Capobianco & Jacoby, 1966; Kolstoe & Frey, 1965). Although this type of program is mainly associated with education and training of the mildly retarded, in reality the work/study program (and/or many of its components) have been used quite extensively with other mildly handicapped youth. Additionally, a trend that developed concurrently with the work/study program attempted to provide all mildly handicapped youth with vocational training that met their specific needs. Thus, many vocational and special educators came to the conclusion that we could: change the job to fit the client's needs; change the client to fit the job; or do both to insure that ultimately the client was successful.

CAREER PERSONNEL

During the previous discussion, we alluded to the duties and responsibilities of people who would ultimately be responsible for operating a comprehensive career education program at the secondary level. Most programs at this level will include: a career counselor, numerous teachers, employers, civic clubs, and parents. During the career exploration and preparation phases of the high school program, these persons are vital to the adolescent's successful entry into the community and the world of work.

Career counselor.

Career counselors, sometimes referred to as vocational counselors, help each student make decisions concerning what type of post-secondary school, occupational choices, and work can be found in the community. There has to be some compromise between what kind of work the client is interested in or can perform and what is available in the community (Salomone, 1971). Many times in the high school setting, career counselors are the guidance counselors assigned to the students. They may give aptitude tests, orient the student to filling out job applications, and also help the school find part-time employment for students under special funds provided by the state. These counselors also perform similar services for the college bound student, that is, the student is helped to select an appropriate college, determine a potential major, and line up funds to pay for the college education. The high school counselor can complement the work of the vocational instruction teacher and work coordinator by relaying any information pertaining to the employability of the student. The counselor can, in addition, assume some of the responsibilities of the other professionals, such as, acquiring parental permission for the student to participate in a job tryout, contacting rehabilitation counselors, and arranging special meetings with administrators and employers involved with the client. The matter of counseling and different types of counselors is discussed extensively in chapter 8.

Rehabilitation counselor.

Rehabilitation counselors, sometimes referred to as vocational rehabilitation counselors, are often employed by the local rehabilitation agency and are assigned to work with high school personnel. Their purpose is to act as a liaison between employers, the school, and other agencies in supplying appropriate and adequate training for the handicapped. The rehabilitation counselor may present career exploration material to the student. Basically, the rehabilitation counselor follows the student's progress throughout high school and coordinates the services, available from the rehabilitation agency, that fit into the student's total career plans or needs. The rehabilitation counselor should initially contact the student during the freshman year or the first year of the work/study program. Some sort of orientation as to available rehabilitation services should be given to students and their parents as well. During the course of the student's program, the vocational rehabilitation counselor should become familiar with the student's progress and coordinate special services needed with school programs available. It is imperative that rehabilitation counselors and teachers work together to provide the best services for the mildly handicapped student.

Due to the changes in the rehabilitation and vocational laws, students who exhibit severe potential vocational problems are included in the case load of the vocational rehabilitation counselor. It is necessary, therefore, that the special education teacher and the rehabilitation counselor work cooperatively. The rehabilitation counselor needs to orient the special education teacher and other concerned educational personnel to the rehabilitation services available. This can often be accomplished by setting up conferences with special education teachers, supervisors, and administrators during in service days at schools.

Special education teachers.

The role of the special education teacher at the secondary level is more of a teacher-advisor or coordinator of services for most of the mildly handicapped students. It is the function of the special education teacher to integrate the services and contributions of the school, home, community, and other service agencies to complete a career education plan for the student who is expected to have some vocational difficulties. Also, if the student is mainstreamed in regular classes the special education teacher will have to advise the regular teacher and monitor the student's progress as it pertains to the student's academic and career development plan (Brolin, 1976). Other roles of the secondary special educator were discussed in chapter 3.

Work coordinator.

The work coordinator (Kolstoe & Frey, 1965) is responsible for evaluating the student's progress in each job in which he or she is placed. The progress report is an excellent evaluation tool at the prevocational level as well as in an actual job situation. Moreover, the progress report provides information on the social and emotional adjustment of the student, which can be of great help in determining future job placement (see Table 7.1). The work coordinator must also be in constant contact with the employer to determine how the student is doing on the job as work experience time increases. In addition, the work coordinator is primarily responsible for surveying the community to determine what jobs are available. After job availability is established, each job must be analyzed as to its requirements. This can be done frequently through the use of a job analysis summary sheet that has been mass produced (see Table 7.2). Another critical duty of the work coordinator is to insure that all students have a number of different work experiences. The work coordinator also must insure that the student moves smoothly from one job to the next.

Table 7.1
Sample Student Progress Report

A. Name _____
B. Employer_____
   Address _____
   _____
C. Job Title _____
   Description_____
   _____
D. Immediate Supervisor _____
E. Length of Employment _____
F. Ratings of Employee:
   1. Reports to work _____ on time _____ late (seldom)
                                    _____ late (frequently)
   2. Work produced _____ poor quality
                     _____ fair quality
                     _____ good quality
   3. Initiative   _____ poor
                     _____ fair
                     _____ good
   4. Reliability   _____ poor
                     _____ fair
                     _____ good
   5. Working with others (relationships)   _____ poor
                                            _____ fair
                                            _____ good

Employers.

The employer's role is critical in the comprehensive career preparation program. The work coordinator must work as closely as possible with the employer, since the latter provides the actual job and work experiences that are necessary for a valid evaluation of the student's capabilities and potential. An ideal employer should be willing to hire the student on a half-day basis and to switch students every two or three months so that others can have job tryouts. This periodic rotation allows for flexibility in the program in that all of the class members can gain work experience with a minimum number of participating employers (Kolstoe & Frey, 1965).

Employers in the local community can also participate in the career education program by providing presentations of their businesses and the jobs that are available, or by inviting the students to the place of business on a field trip. In the business presentation, students should be shown the actual product or service of the company, be allowed to try on any special equipment employees are required to wear,

Table 7.2
Sample Job Analysis Summary

A. Title _____

B. Description_____

_____

_____

C. Category
   Sales   _____
   Office Work   _____
   Service   _____
   Factory/Industrial   _____
   Nonindustrial   _____
   Other (describe)   _____
D. Level
   Unskilled   _____
   Semiskilled   _____
   Skilled   _____
E. Requirements
   High School Diploma   _____
   No Diploma   _____
   Past Experience
      Required   _____

and be shown how jobs at the plant or office are performed. A field trip should follow the presentation so that the students can see firsthand how the equipment they have been shown is utilized by plant employees, how products they have held or seen are manufactured or assembled, or how specific operations are performed.

Civic clubs.

Civic clubs and organizations can also aid the career program by volunteering their services to help students in their career development, by making donations, and by providing volunteers to promote program-related activities. Civic or community groups could also help sponsor field trips to business locations, thereby helping to expand employment opportunities for all students. Since employers in the community often are members of these civic groups, contacts with civic organizations may help to increase job opportunities.

Parents.

Parents should be involved in the career education program in several different ways. Initially, the youth should be made aware of the occupations of their parents and other relatives. Secondly, parents should take an active role in designing the individual education plan (IEP) to insure that career education concepts and activities are being included. The parent can assist professionals by seeking information about various programs for their child and volunteering to assist other personnel in the career education of their child.

In closing, it should be clear that since a large number of persons are involved in preparing any given student for successful entry into the job market, much cooperation must be evidenced by these groups and individuals. The preceding discussion focused on how these different career personnel can work together in a cooperative manner.

WORK/STUDY PROGRAMS

It is generally agreed that the program most used to teach vocational and occupational skills to mildly handicapped youth is the high school work/study program. While this program was discussed in chapter 3 in relation to the mildly retarded, we will now discuss the significance of this program to all mildly handicapped learners. According to Kolstoe (1976), the high school work/study program usually runs over a three-year period that encompasses the 10th, 11th, and 12th grades. The first year of the program includes such units as transportation (including driver education), banking skills, budgeting, peer relationships, personal hygiene, and measurement. These kinds of units are usually associated with the academic portion of the program. In mathematics class, for example, one or two units that stress measurement might be developed. These units would probably include linear and liquid measurements, the proper reading of scales, and other related matters. During this time, the student spends approximately one-half day in the formal classroom setting and one-half day (out of a seven- or eight-period day) in a vocationally oriented program. In the vocational part of the program, job analysis and job exploration, as well as specific assessment of the student's vocational skills, would begin during this time.

During the second year of the program, the student refines his or her skills by learning how to fill out various job applications, how to take job interviews, or perhaps set up an appointment for a job interview. Succinctly stated, the second year of the program is designed to facilitate job-hunting skills as well as help the student develop some specific job-related skills (for example, rudimentary skills in the area of carpentry, automobile repair, or food service).

For the third year of the work/study program, Kolstoe (1976) recommended a continued emphasis on units in such areas as family liv-

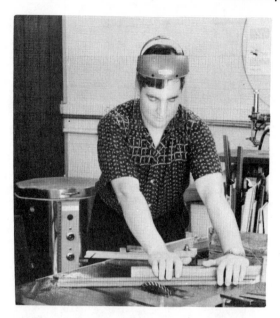

ing, maintenance of the home, the use of charge accounts, and installment buying. Developing financial skills, such as, keeping medical and dental receipts, understanding life insurance, filling out tax forms, and household budgeting should be stressed. Many students also need help in learning to use their leisure time wisely. In the vocational class, actual job interviewing takes place at this time, with the student calling and making appointments for interviews, filling out job applications, and attending simulated interviews. During the latter portion of this period, the student will begin work on an actual job for part of the day and spend the rest of the day in school. In addition to the units already mentioned, other classes in the school will include curriculum units in single living, marriage and its responsibilities, and coping with job problems, such as, being fired, laid off, or transferred to a lower paying job.

Developing Prevocational Competencies and Skills

Another way of looking at a work/study program is to divide the program into two major stages, prevocational and vocational. In this manner, it is easy to see that the different courses and activities that the student participates in are intricately related and that these elements are developed to foster some common objectives.

During the prevocational stage of the work/study or vocational preparation program, the special needs student has basically the same class schedule as students in the academic or general program.

Included in the vocational preparation part of the program would be several periods of occupational exploration. At this time, the student can volunteer or be encouraged to work at different jobs located throughout the school, such as: office helper, teacher's aide, library assistant, stockroom attendant, or school maintenance worker.

At the prevocational level a heavy emphasis is placed on evaluation: evaluation of the student as well as analysis of potential jobs the student may perform in the future. Lawry (1972) defines job analysis as "a systematic way of observing jobs; determining the significant worker requirements, physical demand, and environmental conditions; and reporting this information in a concise format" (p. 27). As Brolin (1976) has stated, a job analysis is concerned with "what, why, and how" a client fulfills the requirements of the job. Thus, by evaluating the student's vocational skills and interests we know what that person's capabilities are and what type of jobs he or she may be interested in; and by analyzing local and regional job requirements and availability, we are in a position to match a student with a specific job or type of job.

Assessment of local job requirements and availability will often lead to the development of a work sample or job simulation. The purpose of this type of student assessment is to evaluate each student's

rate of production and general job-related behaviors. However, several difficulties may be encountered in setting up a work sample/job simulation. Such problems include the lack of proper tools or equipment, limited or unavailable space, and lack of funds. Another major problem associated with a work sample/job simulation is that it may become rapidly outdated. Despite these potential problems, there are many positive features associated with a work sample/job simulation. Brolin (1976) offers the following suggestions for making the most of this procedure. He has indicated that the job sample or work sample should be written up and organized so that the job tasks required are arranged sequentially, from the least difficult or demanding to the most difficult. The student should be allowed to practice each task and master it completely before proceeding to the next task. In this way, the student can be taught to master all the job tasks necessary to produce a particular product or service.

Developing Vocational Competencies and Skills

Immediately following the development of prevocational competencies and skills comes the stage of vocational development. The element that clearly separates these two stages is the directness of the approach used in developing student skills. During the prevocational stage, the student is exposed to many general facts, concepts, and types of jobs; during the vocational stage, more specificity is required in all of these areas. Actual job tryouts (outside of the school), permanent placement, and program follow-up and evaluation characterize this stage of career preparation. The client's adjustment to the work environment is one of the many factors evaluated at this time. For example, attitude, punctuality, and relationships with other workers are assessed.

Job tryouts begin the first phase of the more formal vocational preparation, which follows prevocational development. During this time, the student must be exposed to several job situations so that the teacher or work coordinator can obtain an overall view of the student's strong and weak attributes on the job. By moving the student to several jobs (about three or four), it is possible to determine the situations in which the student is most or least effective. This procedure also allows the student to make some important decisions concerning the type of job he or she likes best, or would like to continue working on without being forced to make a premature decision. After the student has worked on several jobs for an extended period of time, permanent employment is sought. Hopefully, the student, the employer, and the school personnel have made a good decision in choosing a particular placement. However, by providing follow-up services to the student and employer, it is possible to rectify problems that may ensue.

Since many of the points just discussed have a tremendous impact on the vocational and career preparation of the special needs learner at the secondary level, a number of these factors, for example, counseling, placement, and follow-up services, will be discussed in following chapters. Additionally, a number of mildly handicapped learners will be able to enter trade or commercial schools, community colleges, and other technical schools after receiving preliminary training in the high school work/study program. Thus, it is important that the work coordinator and other program personnel refrain from automatically assuming that each work/study program student should be placed in a permanent job following graduation.

SUMMARY

The major concern of this chapter was preparing the mildly handicapped adolescent for entry into the world of work. Five broad goals of a career preparation program were discussed. Included in these goals were (1) the development of career awareness by each student, and (2) the development of entry level job skills by each student. In this chapter, a *career* was defined as a person's lifetime work, whereas a *vocation* was defined as work in which a person is presently engaged.

The concept of career education espoused by Sidney Marland, Commissioner of Education, was postulated to: (1) be for all students;

(2) begin at the elementary school level and continue into adulthood; and (3) give a student a start on the road to making a living. Career education was viewed as existing in five stages: (1) awareness, (2) orientation, (3) exploration, (4) preparation, and (5) skill refinement. The career education concept has developed through the passage of several vocational education acts during recent years, as well as through the broadening provision of services by special educators, rehabilitation specialists, and vocational educators.

Numerous roles and functions of various career personnel were also described in this chapter. Some of these personnel are: the career counselor, who advises the student concerning career possibilities and often assesses the vocational skills and interest of the student; the employer, who may be requested to present his or her program to a number of students; and the work coordinator, who surveys the community for potential job sites and works to place as well as follow-up the student.

Lastly, we took a look at the work/study program in two ways. One way examined the many activities that take place during the several years (usually three) of the program: the first year usually involves initial hands-on job experiences with a great deal of vocational assessment done at this time; the second year continues these initial experiences; and, during the third year, the student is placed on a number of job sites. Another way to conceptualize the work/study program is to divide it into two primary stages, the prevocational and vocational stages. During the prevocational stage, the individual explores many possible jobs and has vocational skills and interests assessed to arrive at a potential match. During the vocational stage, each student is actively involved in on-the-job training.

REFERENCES

An introduction to career education: A policy paper of the U.S. Office of Education. U.S. Government Printing Office, Washington, D.C., 1975.

Ballard, J., & Zettel, J. Public Law 94–142 and Section 504: What they say about rights and protections. *Exceptional Children*, 1977, *44*, 177–184.

Brolin, D.E. *Vocational preparation of retarded citizens.* Columbus, Ohio: Charles E. Merrill Publishing Co., 1976.

Brolin, D.E. (Ed.) *Life centered career education: A competency based approach.* Reston, Virginia: CEC, 1978.

Brolin, D.E., & Kokaska, C.J. *Career education for handicapped children and youth.* Columbus, Ohio: Charles E. Merrill Publishing Co., 1979.

Capobianco, R.J., & Jacoby, H.B. The Fairfax plan: A high school program for mildly retarded youth. *Mental Retardation,* 1966, *4*(3), 15–20.

Career Education Quarterly, Winter 1977, 2(1).

Clark, G., Career education for the mildly handicapped. *Focus on Exceptional Children,* 1974, *5*, 1–10.

Duncan, J.S. *Education of the ordinary child.* New York: Ronald Press, 1943.

Dunn, L.M. A historical review of the treatment of the retarded. In J.H. Rothstein (Ed.), *Mental retardation: Readings and resources.* New York: Holt, Rinehart & Winston, 1961.

Dunn, L.M. Children with mild general learning disabilities. In L.M. Dunn (Ed.), *Exceptional children in the schools: Special education in transition* (2nd ed.). New York: Holt, Rinehart & Winston, 1973.

Goldstein, H. Special and occupational adjustment. In H.A. Stevens & R. Heber (Eds.), *Mental retardation: Review of research.* Chicago: University of Chicago Press, 1964.

Kostoe, O.P. *Teaching educable mentally retarded children* (2nd ed.). New York: Holt, Rinehart & Winston, 1976.

Kolstoe, O.P., & Frey, R.M. *A high school work-study program for mentally subnormal students.* Carbondale, Illinois: Southern Illinois University Press, 1965.

Lawry, G. Matching students with gaps: A real challenge. In *Vocational evaluation and curriculum modification.* Des Moines: Department of Public Instruction, 1972.

Marland, S.P. Career education. *Today's Education,* 1971, *60*, 22–25.

Marland, S.P. Career education: Every student headed for a goal. *American Vocational Journal,* 1972, *47*(3), 34–36.

Martin, E.W. Individualism and behaviorism as future trends in educating handicapped children. *Exceptional Children,* 1972, *38*, 517–525.

Olympus Research Corporation. *Career education: A handbook for implementation.* Salt Lake City, Utah: Olympus Research Corporation; and Baltimore, Maryland: State Department of Education, February 1972.

Payne, J.S., Mercer, C.D., & Epstein, M.H. *Education and rehabilitation techniques*. New York: Behavioral Publications, 1974.

Pollard, N. Career education in the classroom. In R.L. Carpenter (Director), *Colloquium series on career education for handicapped adolescents*, West Lafayette, Indiana: Purdue University, 1977.

Salomone, P.A. A client-centered approach to job placement. *Vocational Guidance Quarterly*, 1971, *19*, 266–270.

Wolfe, H.E. Career education: A new dimension in education for living. *The New Outlook for the Blind*, 1973, *67*, 193–199.

Younie, W.J., & Rusalem, H. *The world of rehabilitation: An atlas for special educators*. New York: John Day, 1971.

8

Counseling the Mildly Handicapped

In order for the mildly handicapped, secondary school adolescent to make wise decisions concerning the future, he or she has to receive good advice about the many personal and career concerns that arise at this time. Often this advice comes from school personnel who have had little or no formal training in the area of counseling. These advisors are chosen by the student for many different reasons; for example, a student may seek advice from a teacher because the student sees the teacher as fair, honest, or knowledgeable, or because this particular teacher also coaches a team on which the student plays. Regardless of why a student chooses a particular advisor, the student is seeking the best advice and information available. Hence, a major purpose of this chapter is to acquaint all teachers with counseling techniques that will enable them to provide sound advice to students. Conversely, the intent *is not* to train professional counselors, but to provide the means for educators to do a better job of counseling and/or advising students. In subsequent portions of this chapter, we will specifically define counseling, discuss some characteristics of a good counselor, and discuss two types of counseling—personal counseling and career counseling. Lastly, other roles and functions of the school counselor will be discussed.

DEFINING COUNSELING

The concept of counseling can be defined or described in numerous ways. Following are several definitions and/or descriptions of the term. Thompson and Poppen (1972) have stated that " . . . it offers an opportunity to explore alternative plans of action and decisions which are helpful to the client in overcoming blocks to his personal development" (p. 11). These authors further described

> the counseling relationship as being a person-to-person relationship where one person helps another resolve a conflict or problem that he has not been able to handle by himself. In the case of actual counseling, the helper is, by virtue of his training and experience, a counselor who attempts to assist his client in becoming an independent person capable of meeting life's challenges on his own. (p. 51)

Cottle and Downie (1970) defined counseling as "the process by which a counselor assists a client to face, understand, and accept information about himself and his interaction with others, so that he can make effective decisions about various life choices" (p. 1). In the preface to their book, Hansen, Stevic, and Warner (1972) defined the concept of counseling as

> a process that assists an individual in learning about himself, his environment, and methods for handling his roles and relationships. Although individuals experience problems, counseling is not necessarily remedial. The counselor may assist an individual with the decision-making process in educational and vocational matters as well as resolving interpersonal concerns. (p. vii)

As one considers the above definitions of counseling and continues to reflect on this matter, a number of general statements describing counseling come to the fore. These general statements can be summarized as follows: (1) a major goal of the counseling process is to help the client become more independent—the counselor assists the client in achieving this goal by showing him or her that the environment can be controlled in many instances; (2) one specific role of the counselor in this process is to help the individual develop and explore alternative ways and means for dealing with his or her problems or conflicts; (3) a second role of the counselor is to help the client overcome blocks or obstacles that impede progress in any area; (4) the client is helped to overcome these heretofore undefined blocks or obstacles through an information-gathering and sorting process; and (5) as a result of information derived from the counseling process, the client is better able to make decisions that will lead to a resolution of present uncertainties and conflicts. An important point is that ultimately the individual who comes to the counseling environment, not the counselor, is responsible for solving his or her problems or conflicts. The counselor can provide information, console the client, and assist in solving these problems; the counselor cannot solve the client's problems. In this instance, the counselor is in much the same situation as the teacher. The teacher can prepare a conducive learning environment, know the particular subject matter well, and present it equally as well, yet it is the student alone who learns or fails to learn.

CHARACTERISTICS OF A GOOD COUNSELOR

Usually when a youth approaches a counselor with a specific problem or dilemma, this matter is only the tip of the iceberg. In a large number of cases, the client frequently has more than one problem or dilemma to solve. Since this is the case, the counselor must refrain from offering premature advice and must pause and reflect on the matter for some time in order to make a reasoned response. Clearly, two qualities often distinguish the effective counselor from a less effective counterpart. Availability is the first distinguishing quality. An effective counselor is available to students even when they manifest no problems. We do not mean that the counselor always drops other matters to converse with or advise students, or that the counselor always has the door open to students. These actions are often impractical since overavailability could easily prevent the counselor from getting anything done. However, the opposite condition is just as negative. The counselor can be so preoccupied with tasks that there is little or no time to deal with the client outside of formal and prearranged sessions. The point is that an effective counselor works with students in formal and informal settings so that they can know the counselor as a person and the counselor can know each student as an individual. The good counselor also knows when to drop routine matters and show a genuine openness to students. In this case openness implies structure with flexibility.

A second quality of the effective counselor is the ability to refrain from giving "man on the street" advice (Poppen & Thompson, 1974).

Frequently in the "man on the street" situation, little thought is given to what one is saying, or the effect or implication of one's statement. As just indicated (see also chapter 3), the mildly handicapped adolescents with whom the counselor or teacher will be working do not come to the counseling session with just one problem; they frequently exhibit more than one problem or problems in several areas. Thus, to tell a youth with a severe reading problem that all he or she needs to do to solve that problem is to "learn to crack the code" is to provide simplistic and often false advice.

As we move from the general to the specific in determining the characteristics of an effective counselor, the following list seems especially pertinent. Often the effective counselor can be distinguished from contemporaries by the following behaviors:

1. *builds rapport* with the client by engaging in frank discussions of matters that may be tangential to the client's problems. The counselor may start off a discussion with the client about a matter known to interest the client. The important fact is that the counselor works up to a point where it is deemed most appropriate to discuss problems of the client.

2. *listens* (pays attention) to what the client is saying without un-
necessarily projecting personal values and/or style of living on
the client. In other words, the counselor not only physically
hears what the client says, but attaches some type of
meaning to the client's statements.
3. *is accepting* of behaviors and beliefs of the client that may differ from his or her own. For example, the counselor may
choose to wear a certain style of clothing while the client
wears a different style. In this case, the counselor is obligated
to accept the client's clothing habits unless the style or type
of clothing has some direct bearing on the present problem(s)
of the client.
4. *helps the client to identify personal problem(s)*. In many
cases, the client will be aware that a problem exists, but will
be unable to focus directly on the specific problem due to any
number of intervening variables. The counselor attempts to
help the client develop the necessary focusing skills.
5. *helps the client to identify alternative ways and means of solving personal problems*. After the client has identifed the problem, the next step is to identify different potential methods of
solving the problem. At this point, the concern is not whether
the client's problem-solving behaviors are appropriate; this
will come later after the client has in fact developed several
problem-solving strategies.
6. *sets goals and limits.* Unless certain goals and limits are set,
the client will remain in the same position. By developing certain short- and long-term goals, which are agreeable to the
client and the counselor, the counselor helps the client to perceive where he or she is and is going.

Hansen et al. (1972) have summed up this matter of counselor effectiveness very concisely. They stated that

> studies of the relationship between counselor effectiveness and per-
> sonal characteristics indicate that effective counselors may be distin-
> guished from less effective counselors in terms of having more expe-
> rience, higher affiliation and greater tolerance of ambiguity. . . . The
> largest amount of data and most consistent findings show the more
> effective counselor as being able to provide a meaningful relationship
> with the client. Is the counselor's ability to be congruent and to com-
> municate positive regard and empathy a personality characteristic, or
> is it learned in a training program? Possibly both. The counselor must
> have a life style that permits him to behave in a facilitating manner,
> and it may be possible for the training program to assist in this pro-
> cess. (p. 172)

PERSONAL COUNSELING

It has been noted throughout this book that the mildly handicapped youth with whom we are concerned will experience a number of difficulties during their secondary school years. Consequently, one can reasonably conclude that many of these youth will be in need of personal and social counseling. The greatest portion of the counseling services required by exceptional adolescents will be provided by the school counselor. However, teachers and other school personnel will often supplement these direct services, especially as these services relate to personal and social concerns. Thus, this section of the chapter is divided into three principle parts: the first two examine techniques and approaches that the trained counselor would use to help an individual resolve problems and conflict; the third part of this discussion focuses on strategies that a teacher can use to do the same types of things, or accomplish the same goals.

Counseling Tasks

When a student comes to the counseling situation, the counselor is immediately put in the position of having to perform certain tasks to help the student progress smoothly in attempts to reorganize the behaviors that occasioned the counseling. Cottle and Downie (1970) have indicated that in the first meeting of the counselor and the student, the immediate counseling needs of the student should be identified. At the same time, the structure within which counseling will take place should also be described to the student. After these general duties are taken care of, the counselor then moves to more specific tasks that hopefully will help the concerned youth to resolve or alleviate the problem. These specific tasks are: (1) listening, (2) examining, (3) specifying alternatives, (4) drawing conclusions, and (5) developing new behaviors. Before discussing these tasks, it should be pointed out that the described approach to counseling is an eclectic one. Rather than centering the discussion around specific kinds of counseling, such as, "rational-emotive therapy" (Ellis, 1973), or "behavioral counseling" (Krasner & Ullman, 1965), or even "client-centered counseling" (Rogers, 1951), a conscientious attempt has been made to describe the approach that most counselors seem to use, that is, an eclectic one (Cottle & Downie, 1970).

Listening.

When the troubled youth begins to talk to the school counselor, the counselor should attempt to gain an accurate view of the student's problem. This can only be done through active listening, not talking. As previously mentioned, premature advice is to be avoided at this time. The primary goal of this counseling is to achieve a match between what the client says is the problem and what the counselor hears the client say is the problem. This is not a play on words. The statement describes a situation all of us have experienced; that is, we heard someone say one thing when in actuality they meant something else.

Examining.

After the counselor and the student have arrived at a consensus as to the specifics of the student's problems, the process of examining the behaviors and actions that led to this dilemma should begin in earnest. Often the counselor will have to ask the student exactly what or which behaviors are causing the conflict or prohibiting the resolution of the conflict. In some cases, the individual cannot avoid conflict. In fact, in certain instances, conflict is good because it motivates one to take action rather than to think about what should be done. For example, in writing this book we often engaged in avoidance behaviors that caused us to manifest a great deal of anxiety. Ultimately, however, this anxiety and the resulting conflict were reduced by our finishing either a part of or the whole manuscript. When the counselor talks with the student, the same type of action must take place. The student must attempt to specify as closely as possible what is causing the problem or conflict. Frequently, the student will explain "why" he or she thinks there is a problem. However, these "why" explanations are usually unproductive because they do not lead directly to the solution.

Specifying alternatives.

Once the student can describe in some fashion what the problem is, and also identify the factors contributing to the permanence of the conflict, then the next step initiated by either the counselor or the student is to specify alternative behaviors or actions that may lead to a solution. At the beginning of this step, it is not imperative that all the alternatives the student develops be realistic or that these alternatives be especially good ones. What is important is that the youth realizes that there is at least one other means of resolving the problem than the one (s)he is presently using. Poppen and Thompson (1974) recommmended that once several alternatives have been articulated, the student should then write these alternatives down. By developing such a list, the student will be in a position where known alternatives are not constantly rediscovered.

Drawing conclusions.

After a list of alternatives has been drawn up by the student, the next step is for the student to narrow the list to one or two alternatives that seem the most reasonable. The counselor can often help the student to reduce the number of possibilities by asking such questions as: "What will happen if you do this?" or "How will this action change the present situation?" During this process the counselor probes the student's answers to make sure that he or she understands their implications. In some cases the student will draw conclusions that are reasonable, but unappealing to the predilections of the counselor. When this takes place, the counselor must show restraint and not impose conclusions on the troubled youth. To illustrate this point, let us say that a student comes to the school counselor and states that he believes that a number of students in his class are cheating on exams. After the student and counselor explore this problem, the student decides that the best thing to do would be to confront the suspected cheaters personally rather than going to the instructor. Whether the counselor believes this is the best approach or not should not be a consideration because, under the circumstances described, this is a reasonable way to handle the problem.

Developing new behaviors.

The last step in the counseling process calls for the student to adopt a certain alternative or solution and to adhere to that decision until the problem is resolved or the particular alternative or solution proves inappropriate. During this time, the counselor should support the student by using positive reinforcement, such as, "I like the way you are sticking to your guns" or "Keep going. You're putting up a good fight." Obviously, finding the solution to one problem does not mean that the student has solved all of his or her problems. In some cases, the student and counselor will have to return to some of the previous steps just outlined so that other facets of the overall problem can be resolved.

When the school counselor and the student have gone through this general process on several occasions, the student will probably be able to carry through many of these procedures alone, or certainly with less help from the counselor. The student now will have realized one of the primary goals of counseling—to have the student become more of a self-governing individual.

Counseling Techniques

In the prior discussion, counseling tasks provided the focal point for many of the comments. We now turn our attention to a few of the many techniques counselors use to move through the steps just described. Three of the most well-known counseling techniques used to help students solve their problems are role playing, behavioral counting, and rehearsal. *Role playing* involves the portrayal of a role that the student or the counselor has previously talked about or described. In this situation, the counselor may ask the student actually to assume for a short time the role of the teacher, parent, or administrator with whom he or she is having a conflict. One purpose of this exercise is to have the student feel what the person being portrayed feels like in the conflicting situation, or to have the student understand that he or she can predict some of the actions and reactions of this other person. Once the student understands that some of the person's behavior is predictable, then the student can modify certain personal behaviors to lessen that person's negative behaviors toward him or her. For example, after a student tells the counselor that a teacher has been embarrassing her in class for several weeks by saying that her work is sloppy, the counselor requests that the student play the role of the teacher in the situation just described. The student then acts out the role of the teacher and does what she thinks the teacher is doing when the embarrassing moments occur. Since the student actually becomes the other person, she has more of an idea as to what that person is thinking about when the negative behaviors occur. The counselor further helps the student to clarify her perceptions of the other individual's role by asking questions, such as, "What did you feel as the teacher when you were saying to Mary that her work in class has been very poor during the last few weeks?"

Behavioral counting is another technique frequently used by the counselor to specify what behaviors are causing conflict maintenance. Behavioral counting requires the studlent (or someone else) to record the behaviors being displayed by this individual. There are numerous ways to do the recording. Let us say, for example, that the student believes his talking out in class is causing him to have problems with fellow students and the teacher. The student relates this belief to the counselor who, in turn, comes to the classroom, observes, and records certain predetermined behaviors of the student. Behaviors to be checked in this instance might be:

Negative Behavior
1. Talking out in class without raising hand or waiting for turn.
2. Chewing gum or eating food during work period.
3. Arriving late for class.

Positive Behavior
1. Raises hand to signal wanting to talk; waits turn to talk.
2. Completes class work during work period.
3. Arrives on time for class.

Using the following design, these behaviors can easily be recorded by an observer.

In this illustration, observed behaviors could be coded *X*, signifying positive behaviors, and *O*, signifying negative behaviors. Additionally, each rectangular area represents a 10-second interval during which the recorder observes and records the individual's behavior. Thus, on a typical day, the student's behavioral rating may look like the following:

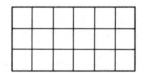

X	X	O	O	X	O
O	O	X	O	O	O
X	O	O	O	X	O

Results of this particular rating show that the student displayed twice as many negative behaviors as positive behaviors. If this same procedure were followed for several successive days, then it would be possible to specify further exactly what negative behaviors are causing the student's problem in the classroom. Even though this illustration concentrated on the use of an outside observer/recorder, the student can also record self-behavior by checking a card or punching out holes on a card every time a certain behavior occurs.

The *rehearsal* technique used in counseling involves having a youth who has selected a certain alternative as a possible problem solution to practice or rehearse the strategy before putting it into effect. Baseball, football, and other teams go through a similar procedure when preparing a new game play or planning to execute a special play, such as the "onside kick" in football. The purpose of the rehearsal procedure is to familiarize the student with reactions that will probably occur once the new strategy is put into effect.

Other counseling techniques frequently used by school counselors include: (1) modeling—this technique calls for the student to do certain behaviors that a model demonstrates; and (2) listening dyads—this consists of the counselor listening and writing down what the student says and then checking with the student to make sure that the recorded information is correct. The purpose of this activity is to make sure that the counselor and the student are communicating directly with each other. If the information the counselor writes down is the same as what the student said, then it can be assumed communication is adequate. However, if the reverse is true, and the written report of the counselor does not agree with the student's perceptions of the discussion, then good communication is evidently lacking and better communications have to be fostered.

Throughout this discussion, our attention has centered on one-to-one counseling techniques since these are the types of techniques teachers are most likely to use. However, there are also a number of group counseling techniques that would be appropriate for working with many mildly handicapped adolescents, for example, the common problem group technique (Blocher, 1966) where members of a group share a common problem such as a mild learning problem. The members of such a group usually talk about past approaches to their problem(s) that have or have not been successful for them. Members of this type of group also try to support each other in solving a specific problem. Another technique that fits this category is the case-centered group (Foreman, Poppen, & Frost, 1967). Members of this type of group follow many of the same steps mentioned in connection with one-to-one counseling procedures (listening, deriving alternatives, etc.). However, the group also engages in the actual counseling of one of its members during an entire session.

Counseling Strategies for Teachers

Even though many of the teachers who ultimately read this book will have no formal training in the area of counseling, all teachers can help the mildly handicapped student in a number of ways. First, a teacher can help in a general way by being a good role model. Secondly, a teacher can actively listen to a student's problems or dilemma and accept student behaviors with which he or she may not agree. Finally, each teacher can help students with problems by assisting them in identifying alternative solutions to the problems.

In addition, the following suggestions and activities for dealing with specific personal and social adjustment problems should prove helpful to the teacher.

1. Ask the student to write a short autobiographical sketch. Tell the student to emphasize the positive aspects of his or her life. This type of activity will promote the firm establishment of a healthy self-concept and self-awareness.

2. Redl (1971) and Morse (1971) advocate the use of life space interview (LSI) techniques to probe emotions of individuals who are experiencing conflict. The LSI technique is a structured way of listening to a person. Thus, it would be useful in resolving problems having to do with personal relationships.

3. Many mildly handicapped youth do not feel part of the total school society. One procedure for increasing the feeling of belonging is to train the student to care for and set up pieces of audio-visual equipment in the school. When school personnel need this equipment, the student will be able to provide a valuable service.

4. The technique of sociodrama can be used by the teacher and student to identify certain social problems and to evaluate alternative solutions to these problems. In this situation, the student or group of students can role play the individuals involved and gain knowledge of what these persons feel about this particular situation.

5. Encourage youth who display physically aggressive behaviors to enroll in a martial arts program. The dogmaticism associated with this type of training will show the student that aggression can be channeled into productive activities (Portuondo, 1974; Ross, 1975).

6. Make highly desired activities (such as leaving school early or coming late) contingent on the student avoiding a troublesome behavior (Premack, 1959).

7. Make students aware of the clues that others give us about our behavior through facial and gestural expressions. This can be done by presenting pictures showing different emotions and expressions, such as, love, pain, anger, or surprise.

8. Use "rap sessions" to find out what problems students are having and what they perceive as solutions to these problems.

At the conclusion of the discussion, have the students choose one problem and a solution to it.

Obviously, the above are only general strategies for helping students with problems. However, the resourceful teacher will modify and build on these suggestions to help students solve their problems.

The question arises, Who owns the counseling process? or, more specifically, When does teaching stop and counseling begin? It can be said that teachers are trained to teach and counselors are trained to counsel. However, these two sets of school personnel share a number of common goals; both groups are interested in seeing that all secondary youth continue to acquire and refine educational, social, emotional, and career-related skills. On the other hand, a major difference between the two is that the counselor's primary job is to help the student resolve present and future dilemmas and evolve into an independent person. Analogously, we could say that the classroom teacher can apply a Bandaid to minor problems of the student. But when major problems arise for the student, the counselor is the person who should help resolve these problems.

CAREER COUNSELING

The past few pages explored the topic of personal counseling. The fundamental goal of this process was to enable the individual receiving counseling to become more self-sufficient and independent. Interestingly enough, when we talk about career and vocational counseling the process is pretty much the same. The major difference is that the center of attention now shifts to making realistic career and vocational choices. Thus, it can be reasonably stated that the focus of counseling at this time is to identify the student's abilities, needs, and interests as they relate to a work environment satisfying to this particular individual (Brolin, 1976).

In order for the counselor to determine what the student's abilities, needs, and interests are, he or she will have to obtain relevant personal information concerning the student's social, psychological, medical, educational, and work history. Much of this information can be gained from school and medical records. Other information can be secured by observing the student, and interviewing the student, the family, and other people in the school and community. Another, more formal means of gathering information would be to use such instruments as aptitude tests, vocational interest inventories, and work samples. Before discussing these devices and how they work, we wish to reiterate our position that counseling at this time should be geared toward career and vocational development so that the student gains more confidence in his or her ability to work in some capacity in society and to direct various aspects of his or her life.

Assessment of Career and Vocational Potential

It has already been mentioned that career and vocational information can be derived from aptitude tests, vocational interest inventories, and work samples. Each of these types of evaluation are discussed briefly.

Aptitude tests.

This type of test measures the abilities and traits of an individual in a certain area. For example, an individual who can easily do various jobs with his or her hands is said to have high manual dexterity. By using an aptitude test that measures this ability, the results should indicate that the person has a high ability in the area of manual dexterity, whether or not it has been demonstrated before. Results from these tests are often used to predict an individual's chances for success in a certain field. Examples of aptitude tests that measure career-related skills are the *General Aptitude Test Battery* (U.S. Department of Labor, 1970) and the *Nonreading Aptitude Test Battery* (U.S. Department of Labor, 1970). Additional examples of this and other types of assessment devices are discussed in Table 8.1, and in Wallace and Larsen's (1979) book *Educational assessment of learning problems: Testing for teaching.*

Interest inventories.

The student's feelings and preferences about certain types of occupations are assessed by this instrument. While aptitude tests show probable abilities, interest inventories show individual preferences or wants. Examples of test devices in this category are the *Gordon Occupational Checklist* (Gordon, 1967) and the *Minnesota Vocational Interest Inventory* (Clark & Campbell, 1966). (See also Table 8.1.)

Work samples.

The last type of formal evaluation to be discussed is the work sample. A work sample is a testing procedure done through the use of a large portion of a specific job or in some cases the entire job. For example, in a work sample dealing with printing, part of the sample may call for the student to operate a heavy duty paper cutter. On the other hand, in a work sample related to the placing of materials in packages, the

---

Table 8.1
Descriptions of Career and Vocational Assessment Instruments

Aptitude

1. *Differential Aptitude Test* (DAT) (Bennett, Seashore, & Wesman, 1969). This test, which is to be used with students in grades 8–12, is composed of seven subtests that yield separate scores in the areas of: verbal reasoning, numerical ability, abstract reasoning, space relations, clerical speed and accuracy, mechanical reasoning, and language usage. Reliability and validity data gathered concerning the test seems to be quite appropriate. The test takes at least three hours to administer.

Interest Inventory

2. *Reading-Free Vocational Interest Inventory* (R-FVII) (Becker, 1975). This test is composed of pictorial triads from which the individual must choose one picture that shows an activity he or she would like to do most. There are 55 male triads and 40 female triads (not included in the same booklet). The triads provide scores relating to 11 male and 8 female interest areas such as, food service, clerical, and laundry service areas. The test takes less that an hour to administer. This test, and other similar ones, is especially appropriate for use with individuals who have low verbal and reading skills.

Work Sample

3. *Jewish and Employment Vocational Service Work Samples* (JEVS). Brolin (1976) describes these work samples as being composed of 28 tasks that measure worker skills in 14 general industrial categories. During the evaluation, which covers a two-week period, the person being evaluated is required to perform work-related tasks that vary from the simple (lettering signs) to the complex (disassembling and reassembling equipment). Since the worker is under constant scrutiny during this time, a great deal of valuable information can be obtained regarding this person's ability to do certain types of work.

student may be required to perform the entire job. Work samples are extremely useful since they allow for a comprehensive evaluation of all the areas previously mentioned, that is, aptitude, interests, and skills. Since this is a comprehensive evaluation, it requires an extended period of time, possibly from one to two weeks. (See Table 8.1 for an example of a work sample.)

Criticisms of Assessment Instruments and Procedures

While the foregoing instruments and procedures do yield valuable information about the student's vocational capabilities, they have been criticized. It has been shown that as far as many aptitude tests and interest inventories are concerned: (1) the reading level is probably too high for many mildly handicapped students (reading levels for these instruments are usually at or around a 6th-grade level); (2) there are a low number of or no items relating directly to females; (3) socioeconomic differences in the society at large are not accounted for (a preponderance of items reflect a middle-class orientation); and (4) the racial and cultural diversity of the population of this country is not reflected in the items that make up the test.

Criticisms usually directed at work samples include: (1) work sample evaluations are expensive to obtain; (2) the individual to be evaluated must be able to spend a large amount of time going through the process; and (3) extensive travel to and from the site of the work sample may be required, thereby adding more time and expense to the factors already mentioned.

Using the Career and Vocational Assessment Data

Once the abilities, needs, and wants of the student have been assessed, the question that must be resolved is, How will this information be used? At this point, it is the counselor's job, or the teacher's if there is no counselor, to help the student organize the information so that some realistic decisions can be made relative to present and future career choices. As stated before, the counselor and/or the teacher helps the student to perceive the alternatives that exist. Once a number of alternatives are clearly defined, one or more will have to be eliminated by the student. After the choices are reduced to the best one, the student often has to be reinforced and reminded why this was a good choice if he or she is to stick with this option. During this time, the counselor and/or the teacher should be available to advise the student and help clarify any other problems he or she might be experiencing.

Vocational and Rehabilitation Personnel and the Counseling Process

In many instances, the high school counselor and teacher will work closely with vocational educators and rehabilitation personnel during the counseling process. Since several different roles of the counselor and teacher have already been discussed, we will now take a closer look at the roles these other people play in this process.

As the mildly handicapped adolescent attempts to make wise decisions concerning future career choices, vocational educators and rehabilitation personnel, who may work directly in a school or be closely associated with certain school programs, are called on to provide certain counseling services to the student. Frequently, the vocational educator acts as a catalyst in helping the student explore different occupational possibilities, develop positive work habits and skills necessary for competitive employment, and develop a salable, entry level occupational skill (Brolin & Brolin, 1979). At the same time, the rehabilitation specialist may work with school personnel in an advisory capacity, or directly with the student in any one of the areas previously mentioned.

Other roles performed by vocational and rehabilitation personnel that relate more directly to the counseling process include: (1) selecting and administering appropriate career and vocational assessment instruments; (2) interpreting the data derived from these instruments for the student and other interested individuals; (3) serving as a resource person between the school and vocational agencies, such as, evaluation and work adjustment facilities; and (4) providing follow-up services to the student who completes a specific vocational preparatory program. Many of these services enable the student to identify clearly any vocational problems that he or she may be having, and also to choose suitable solutions to these problems.

OTHER FUNCTIONS OF SCHOOL COUNSELORS

In the previous discussions, two of the primary functions of school counselors, personal and career counseling, were described. The following discussion describes other roles or functions of the school counselor. Poppen and Thompson (1974) have stated that one function of the counselor, aside from working directly with students, is to be a humanizing influence in the total school environment. This means that the school counselor will often engage in activities with other school personnel and students aimed at preventing certain mental health problems. For example, most adolescents are concerned about gaining specific information regarding different sexual matters; yet they are often stymied in their attempts to get this information and unhealthy conflicts frequently ensue. In this particular instance, the perceptive counselor will realize that some of the above conflicts can be prevented by having student concerns brought out in small and large group discussions, or by having knowledgeable speakers provide students with the information they are seeking. The point is that not only is the school counselor responsible for helping students solve problems once they occur, but in some cases the counselor is called on to prevent certain mental health problems from occurring.

Another function of the school counselor is to educate parents. In this role, the counselor is frequently called on to explain certain school programs to parents and other adults in the community. For example, the school counselor may be asked to explain to a local parents' organization the types of counseling services the school offers to different levels of students. In other instances, the counselor may be asked to work directly with parents who have unrealistically high or low expectations regarding their child's achievement. McCowan (1968) has reported that in this type of situation, where the counselor works directly with parents instead of students, positive results can be shown in the achievement of underachieving students. Additionally, the principal may request that the school counselor work with parents on some school-related project, such as a dance or play.

Counselors also work frequently with teachers in certain in-service projects. The counselor in this situation acts as a consultant, or brings in consultants to interact with the teachers concerning issues about which they wish to know more. An example would be a request from a group of teachers to the counselor to receive some in-service training in the area of drug abuse. A counselor having some expertise in this area might conduct this in service training. However, if the counselor feels inadequately prepared to instruct others concerning drug-related problems, then he or she may arrange for others to conduct a limited number of sessions on this topic. This example also highlights another function that counselors perform. Frequently counselors act as referral agents. When school conselors are not equipped to handle matters that come to their attention, they must refer these matters to more appropriate individuals, who are directly in charge of or handle the matter with the cooperation of the counselor.

In summary, school counselors often are called on to perform functions in the school other than those of personal and career counseling. Frequently, these counselors serve as mental health catalysts in the schools where they work, as in service educators, as parent educators, and as referral agents.

SUMMARY

A major purpose of this chapter was to acquaint all teachers with counseling techniques that would enable them to provide sound advice to their students. Prior to discussing characteristics of a good counselor, the concept of counseling was defined. In general, the definitions of counseling that were cited indicated that counseling is a process that helps the individual explore alternative ways and means of dealing with problems and overcoming blocks or obstacles that impede progress. The good or effective counselor was seen as one who builds rapport with the client, listens to what the client actually says, accepts behaviors and beliefs of the client, helps the client to identify his or her problem as well as strategies for dealing with that problem, and sets goals and limits to deal with present and future behaviors. The next topic discussed was personal counseling. Tasks associated with this type of counseling include listening attentively, examining present behaviors and actions of the student that may have led to the present situation, specifying alternatives to the problem, drawing conclusions, and developing new behaviors. Counseling techniques discussed relative to these tasks were role playing, behavioral counting, and rehearsal.

Following this discussion, it was noted that a teacher would follow the same general procedures as the counselor in working with a student who had a problem, albeit in a less formal manner. It was also stated that many of the tasks of career counseling were the same as those of personal counseling. However, the central theme of career counseling was the identification of the student variables as the related to the work world. Although material in the chapter concentrated on the personal and career-related problems of the student, other functions of the counselor (such as being a humanizing influence in the school) were also discussed.

REFERENCES

Becker, R.L. *Reading-free vocational interest inventory.* Washington, D.C.: American Association on Mental Deficiency, 1975.

Bennett, H., Seashore, G., & Wesman, A.G. *Differential aptitude tests.* New York: Psychological Corporation, 1969.

Blocher, D. *Developmental counseling.* New York: Ronald Press, 1966.

Brolin, D.E. *Vocational preparation of retarded citizens.* Columbus, Ohio: Charles E. Merrill Publishing Co., 1976.

Brolin, J.C., & Brolin, D.E. Vocational education for special students. In D. Cullinan & M.H. Epstein (Eds.), *Special education for adolescents: Issues and perspectives.* Columbus, Ohio: Charles E. Merrill Publishing Co., 1979.

Clark, K.E., & Campbell, D.P. *Minnesota vocational interest inventory.* New York: Psychological Corporation, 1966.

Cottle, W.C., & Downie, N.M. *Preparation for counseling.* Englewood Cliffs, New Jersey: Prentice-Hall, 1970.

Ellis, A. The no cop-out therapy. *Psychology Today,* 1973, *7,* 56–62.

Foreman, M., Poppen, W., & Frost, J. Case groups: An inservice education technique. *Personnel and Guidance Journal,* 1967, *46,* 388–392.

Gordon, L.V. *Gordon occupational checklist.* New York: Harcourt, Brace, Jovanovich, 1967.

Hansen, J.C., Stevic, R.R., & Warner, R.W. *Counseling: Theory and process.* Boston: Allyn & Bacon, 1972.

Krasner, L., & Ullmann, L. *Research in behavior modification.* New York: Holt, Rinehart & Winston, 1965.

McCowan, R. Group counseling with underachievers and their parents. *School Counselor,* 1968, *16,* 30–35.

Morse, W.C. Worksheet on life space interviewing for teachers. In N.J. Long, W.C. Morse, & R.G. Newman (Eds.), *Conflict in the classroom.* Belmont, California: Wadsworth Publishing Co., 1971.

Poppen, W.A., & Thompson, C.L. *School counseling: Theories and concepts.* Lincoln, Nebraska: Professional Educators, Publications, 1974.

Portuondo, J. Judo as an activity for disturbed children in a state hospital. *Hospital and Community Psychiatry,* 1974, *25,* 651.

Premack, D. Toward empirical behavior laws: I. Positive reinforcement. *Psychological Review,* 1959, *66,* 219–233.

Redl, F. The concept of the life space interview. In N.J. Long, W.C. Morse, & R.G. Newman (Eds.), *Conflict in the classroom.* Belmont, California: Wadsworth Publishing Co., 1971.

Rogers, C. *Client-centered therapy: Its current practice, implications, and theory.* Cambridge, Massachusetts: Riverside Press, 1951.

Ross, B.K. Martial arts for the handicapped. *Recreation and Fitness for the Mentally Retarded,* 1975, *10*(1), 3–5.

Thompson, C., & Poppen, W. *For those who care: Ways of relating to youth.* Columbus, Ohio: Charles E. Merrill Publishing Co., 1972.

U.S. Department of Labor. *Manual for USES nonreading aptitude test battery.* Washington, D.C.: U.S. Government Printing Office, 1970.

Wallace, G., & Larsen, S. *Educational assessment of learning problems: Testing for teaching.* Boston: Allyn & Bacon, 1978.

9

Placement

In chapters 7 and 8 we looked at the career education process from the perspective of exploration, preparation, and counseling concerns. Although this chapter touches briefly on preparing the student for a career, the primary focus is on vocational placement, whether semi-permanent, permanent, part-time, or full-time.

Throughout the history of vocational preparation or work/study programs in the United States, one of the most important aspects has been that of vocational placement. In more recent years, economic conditions have made this phase even more intricate in its daily as well as long-term operations. Thus, many public schools and other agencies have become motivated to create job classifications for "placement specialists," or some similar title. However, if one discusses the responsibilities of such a position with the school placement specialist, we usually find that this person has had very little (if any) specialized training in placement, usually functions within poorly defined limits, and may be suspect to colleagues. Placement specialists may be employees of the local school system, or the Division of Vocational Rehabilitation, or possibly both. But regardless of where the salary comes from, the task is simple and straightforward—place students on jobs.

Most school persons who have had any success in the placement process will readily admit that their modus operandi is largely the result of trial-and-error. In fact, a person who has worked in the area of vocational placement for a year or two would be lucky to develop *one* good approach for dealing with different employees. In contrast, professional salespeople in most industries are taught their profession in three distinct stages. First, they are given all the available *information regarding their product*, be it encyclopedias, insurance, waterless cookware, or vacuum cleaners. Second, they are taught the most effective method of *presenting the product* to the potential buyer. Third, these salespeople are taught how to sell the product to the consumer, that is, how to overcome those who say, "I can't afford it" or "I don't need it." Most school placement specialists would be hard pressed to cite similar preparation and/or training backgrounds. Thus, a main concern of this chapter is to show a school placement coordinator how to move through these three stages: gathering information about clients, presenting this information and the clients to community employers, and selling the program and the clients to these employers. The topics of preparatory stages for student placement, approaching employers, and job sites will be discussed extensively. Following these topics are a number of conclusions and recommendations to enhance placement.

PREPARATORY STAGES FOR PLACING STUDENTS

As already mentioned, there are a number of preparatory stages before the placement person is ready to enlist the aid of employers in providing either temporary or permanent job sites. However, these preparatory stages do not exist independently of later stages in the placement process. There is a good deal of overlap in the transition from one stage to the next. Regardless, we will describe some general techniques that will be helpful to a placement person in putting the student on a suitable job site.

Gathering Information About the Program and Its Clients

At this stage, the placement coordinator should be primarily concerned with acquiring a basic knowledge of the characteristics of the client population. Information such as the characteristics of the mildly handicapped, which were discussed in chapter 2, should help the counselor greatly. Additionally, a great deal of information can be gleaned from each student's individual education plan or program (IEP) (Cegelka & Phillips, 1978). For example, in Figure 9.1 one can easily see that this particular student is not ready to be placed on a permanent job in September. Therefore, the placement specialist, and other educators, would be more concerned with helping this particular student learn how to search and apply for a job. Once these skills are attained, then the student will be ready for actual placement.

In acquiring other information about clients and the program, the placement specialist should seek answers to the following questions. In what types of jobs have similar persons been successful or unsuccessful in the past? In what kinds of jobs are these students interested? What jobs are available in the community? Many of the answers to such questions will be easy to find if good record-keeping procedures have been followed during program development. For example, by consulting the results of vocational surveys, such as the *AAMD-Becker Reading Free Vocational Interest Inventory* (1975), the placement person will be able to determine what specific jobs or categories of jobs interest students. Data from job survey forms, similar to the one mentioned in chapter 7 will also provide a large amount of information on the availability of jobs in the community or region, types of hiring practices in the area, and the number of companies that offer general or specific job training.

Interestingly, a source of information that is frequently overlooked or only minimally dealt with in the past is the families, and especially parents, of the youth participating in the vocational program. With the passage of PL 94–142 and the subsequent involvement of parents in the planning of their child's IEP (Ballard & Zettel, 1977), more parents will become directly involved in the placement part of the program. Since parents will be more actively involved in the entire process, their input should be sought regarding the matter of their child's vocational interests. Parents may be asked what jobs the youngster does at home, or seems to like to do (Brolin & Kokaska, 1979). Often parents have pertinent information about availability of job sites in the community, or places for permanent jobs. They may collect such information through business contacts, informally scouting about for jobs for their son or daughter, or membership in social organizations.

Presenting the Program to Employers

The matter of how to present the vocational program to the potential employer will be discussed extensively in the next section of this chapter. However, at this juncture, there are two important points to

Student __Joe Dokes__

Period of individualized education program

__9/15/xx__ to __12/15/xx__

Curriculum areas requiring special education and related services	Present level(s) of performance	Annual goals	Short term objectives	Time required	Objectives attained (dates)
Area: Occupational	Not Competent	Seek, secure and maintain employment	1) search for job 2) apply for job 3) interview	1) 9/15 to 10/8 2) 10/10 to 11/11 3) 11/11 to 12/15	1) 10/6 2) 10/30 3) 12/14

A. List any special instructional material or media necessary to implement this individualized education program.

1) Job search exercises, job application forms, video-tapes of job interviews.

B. List the criteria, evaluating procedures, and schedule for determining whether the short term objectives are met.

Short-term objectives	Objective criteria	Education procedures	Schedule
1) Search for job	Competency Rating Scale	Administer CRS	10/6/xx
2) Apply for job	same	Same	10/30/xx
3) Interview for job	same	same	12/14/xx

ADAPTED FROM: Brolin, D.E., & Kokaska, C.J. Career education for handicapped children and youth. Columbus: Charles E. Merrill Publishing Co., 1979. Reprinted by permission of the publisher.

Figure 9.1   An abbreviated IEP

consider relating to the future development of the entire vocational preparation program. The first point is that the placement person should initially develop employer interest in the program, and then move the employer to develop specific interest in individual clients; secondly, the positive attributes of the prospective client(s) must be stressed. According to Payne, Polloway, Smith, and Payne (1977), by first developing the employer's interest in the program, and not the client, the employer will feel like a member of "the team"—the team that is attempting to insure that its clients are successful on the job. These writers have further indicated that by following such a procedure, the employer becomes *program-oriented* rather than *product* (*client*)-*oriented*. Therefore, if a certain client fails to meet expectations on the job, the employer will not feel that the entire program has failed. In the second instance, the placement counselor should actively present the positive facts about the clients so that any misconceptions the employer has about mildly handicapped persons will be dispelled and the employer will realize that the students employed do have numerous positive attributes (Payne & Chaffin, 1968). For example, the employer should be told about past successes of the client on trial work sites in the school, eagerness to learn, ability to cooperate with fellow workers, et cetera. However, the placement specialist should not lie or purposely distort the truth so that a client will look better. Again, the counselor's aim at this point is to present positive facts about clients to counter any negative misconceptions the potential employer might hold and to set the stage for the employer to try out at least one or two clients.

Selling the Program

Payne et al. (1977) have indicated that there are a number of general strategies a placement counselor can use to sell the vocational preparation or work/study program to community employers. These methods include: (1) leading with a winner—maximizing the initial chances of job success for the client and the employer by placing someone who has a more than average chance of doing well; (2) reporting the positive changes of the client to the employer—the placement person should make the employer aware of positive ways that this job has helped this particular client; (3) assisting employers in developing training skills—showing the employer how systematically to observe the trainee's initial work-related skills, and then how to direct the trainee in refining these skills or developing new skills; and (4) sponsoring employer conferences to let employers show their "successes" and learn what other employers in different areas are doing. While these strategies are general in nature, the following discussion focuses on the kind of placement approach that one might use with certain types of employers.

APPROACHING EMPLOYERS

After the student has gained a number of work-related skills, and is ready for either temporary (more training is necessary) or permanent placement on a job, employers have to be contacted before placements can be made. Since some information about community employers will already be available to the placement person, the question now is, Where do we go from here? Does the placement person simply contact several employers and ask them to place a student? The answer is a qualified no. Before employers are contacted, the placement person should consider the type of participation sought from a certain employer. In this regard, an employer can become involved in a vocational preparation program in at least five different ways. An employer can: (1) provide the worker with a job; (2) provide training for the worker; (3) advise program personnel concerning technical aspects of the program; (4) aid in securing other employers to work with the program; and (5) assist in public relations efforts. In many instances, the first two roles are the most desirable. However, when an employer assumes any of the last three roles, it does allow other program personnel to be released from these tasks.

Since the first two roles of the employer are of greatest concern to the placement specialist, our attention now moves to developing a systematic approach for effective and efficient placement of students on jobs. One approach that has worked consistently for a number of placement specialists is that based on a theoretical model developed by Dr. Clare W. Graves of Union College in Schenectady, New York. Dr. Graves has devoted approximately 20 years to the development of his *Open System Theory of Values* (Graves, 1970), often referred to as *Graves' Psychological Levels of Existence* (Payne, Mercer, & Epstein, 1974). The theory holds that all people develop through a series of psychological levels in which their needs, value systems, and motivators differ, and hence they respond differently to their environments at these several levels. The descriptions of the levels include enough basic information so that people can be identified at specific stages in their developmental processes. Additionally, ideas and suggestions emerge from these descriptions as to how to deal with individuals differentially. By applying the theoretical model to the placement process, a systematic approach can be learned and used for placement purposes. Using this model, employers can usually be grouped into three categories: (1) saintly conformist, (2) materialistic, and (3) sociocentric.

These three types of employers can be described briefly in the following manner: (1) saintly conformist employers tend to be autocratic in management style and conservative in many respects; (2) materialistic employers are "result" oriented and will use any management style deemed necessary to get the result or product they desire; and (3) sociocentric employers are people oriented, viewing the existence of harmony in their business operation as equal to the end product. They believe a good product can only be produced by a happy worker in a harmonious environment. Obviously, much of this information about an employer will not be available to the placement specialist prior to the first contact. Therefore, when making the first visit to a particular place of business, the placement person has to search for clues to determine with what kind of employer he or she is dealing. For instance, if the employer comes out to greet the placement person, introduces him or her to workers who are nearby, and wears soft, comfortable clothing (as opposed to formal business attire), then this employer is probably sociocentric and should be treated accordingly.

Whether one chooses to interact with employers using Graves' theory or not, it is important to remember that, in general, all approaches to community employers follow a three-phase cycle consisting of initiation, development, and continuance. Initiation refers to the first approach or contact (i.e., getting one's foot in the door to present one's program); development is getting the employer to try a mildly handicapped person on the job; and continuance refers to the actual hiring of a client on a paid, full-time basis, or the employer's willingness to continue on-site job training.

A Three-Phase Placement Approach

Initiation.

As with any introductory relationship, the first order of business is what is known in the field of education as the establishment of rapport (Brolin & Kokaska, 1979). This phrase probably strikes a chord with most readers since it is used extensively in courses in counseling, special education, and psychological testing. Yet, few professors explain *how* to establish rapport. It is assumed that one *knows* how, just as it is assumed that people know how to exchange a handshake properly. If you have shaken hands with someone who did not know how to perform that act, then you are fully aware that people do not innately know how to do many relatively simple tasks often taken for granted. Establishing rapport falls into this neglected category.

Initially, many people are at a loss for words and/or ideas in talking with people they do not know. Therefore, the presentation of useful tips on establishing rapport with employers is important at this point. As you enter the office of the employer, ask how the person got into this business, or what he or she did previously. Another way to establish rapport would be to talk about the employer's office. For instance, comments on the neatness of the office, the pictures on the wall, or the furnishing would certainly be appropriate. The important point is to get the other person to talk about himself or herself or about the business. This makes a person feel that you are interested in them. More importantly, this situation increases your knowledge base.

After rapport has been established, the placement person should present information about the vocational preparation program and the youth it serves. According to Brolin and Kokaska (1979), during this time the placement specialist must resist the urge to tell the employer everything about the program. The initial presentation should be simple and concise. In the initial presentation, briefly describe the program, the youth who benefit from it, and the benefits that the employer will derive from participating in the program. Near the end of this first discussion with an employer, the matter of pupil follow-up should be mentioned. This makes the employer aware that the school continues to assume some responsibility for the student placed on this particular job or at this work station. Furthermore, by mentioning that follow-up services are routinely provided, the employer is assured that an important program goal is to insure the student receives training of high quality, or that support services will be provided if something goes wrong at the placement site. Finally, the placement specialist should leave the initial meeting with some type of commitment from the employer, even if it is only a commitment for a second meeting. This action assures the vocational representative a better chance of getting an employer to participate in the program in at least one of the five ways described at the beginning of this discussion.

Development.

Once the employer has agreed to place one or a number of students in the business, the development part of the cycle begins. During this phase, the placement person's efforts are directed toward fostering the employer's confidence in working with the clients placed at this site. It is important that the employer does not feel that this person has been dropped on the doorstep, and that he or she alone must deal with the situation. Rather, the placement person should be supportive, constantly reassuring the employer that this is a joint endeavor.

The techniques involved in the development phase, while simple to master, are rather difficult to implement because of the time required for continual contact. Many secondary programs have excellent initial placement procedures, but fail to provide the supportive services necessary to assure ongoing employer involvement. Thus, the placement counselor must view the development phase as a partnership with the employer.

Throughout this particular phase of the vocational preparation program, the following points are important in working with all types of employers. The placement person should: (1) help the employer to perceive his or her continued importance to the program, thus demonstrating that client placement on this site is not in most cases a terminal goal, but rather a means to an end; (2) develop and refine his or her own observational skills to ensure knowing what is actually transpiring in the ongoing job process; (3) provide feedback to the employer about his or her performance as well as that of the client/employee, thus allowing the employer to refine personal skills for dealing with old and new clients; and (4) provide supportive assistance when problems ensue. This can be accomplished in different ways for different employers; some employers are helped by a "standard operating procedure" for dealing with problems, whereas other employers can be shown through diagrams that such problems have occurred before and were solved in a certain fashion.

Continuance.

As mentioned previously, during the continuance phase an employer agrees to hire the client on a full-time basis or to work with more students in the near future. At this time, it may be appropriate to move employers who have had successful experiences with clients from the vocational preparation program to another level of participation. This successful employer could provide consultative services to program personnel, serve in a public relations role, or bring other community employers into the program. By using this procedure, no one employer becomes "stale" or bored with his or her part in the program.

Conclusions

Obviously, the placement process is complex. Yet, we feel there are definite skills and techniques that can be learned by the vocational placement practitioner. It is important for the placement person to: know as much as possible about specific jobs; develop a thorough understanding of clients; cultivate skills relative to the presentation of materials and information about clients; develop techniques concerning the selling of client skills; and know as much as possible about the behavioral and management characteristics of employers. Thus, a good placement specialist is aware of the employer's needs, knows how to establish rapport with a variety of employers, and can carry out the placement process from initiation through continuance.

JOB SITES

As a placement specialist develops skills in approaching employers and in actual job placement, attention must be given to the sequence of activities leading to employment. As mentioned in chapter 7, the entire career preparation process begins at the elementary level and proceeds through the secondary level. Near the end of this process, the student usually attempts the first real job. Often job tryouts occur within the school at the end of the junior year or the beginning of the senior year. Depending on the size of the school environs and the school system, the student may be placed in such jobs as grounds person, stockroom clerk, or garage worker at the school system's motor pool.

School Job Sites

School job sites, sometimes referred to as on-campus sites, provide many opportunities for the student to learn various general and specific job-related skills. School job sites are usually easy to obtain and allow for close supervision; at the same time, these sites provide realistic first work experiences. In such a situation, academic concepts that are being learned can be related to the job being performed.

The vocational objectives set for school job sites are usually global in nature and seldom require more than minimum skill development. For instance, when a student is placed with a school custodian, the vocational objectives may include more than specific skills such as mopping, scrubbing, or general types of cleaning. These skills may be attained, and in fact may be highly desirable, but major vocational objectives for most students at this point center around reporting to work on time, completion of a work task, responsiveness to supervision, following instructions, and other similar concerns. At this time, the young worker should learn to evaluate personal work performance based on the job requirements (Phelps & Lutz, 1977).

Successful completion of the requirements at a school work site can be a very valuable step in a student's vocational training. To get the most out of a school work site, opportunities for immediate and accurate feedback must be available and provided to the student. The student should know what to do, be taught exactly how to do it, and receive immediate feedback regarding work performance on a regular basis. The attitude of the supervisor is of paramount importance; the supervisor sets the tone for good work performance and provides the above mentioned feedback. Smith (1974) has indicated that students must also realize that a serious and concentrated effort is required of them during the work period in the school environment.

Overall, the strength of the school work site lies in its flexibility. It may or may not be highly structured. It may provide close supervision or allow a great deal of independent responsibility. It may be very strenuous and demanding or extremely simple. The value of school work sites depends on how they are used, that is, whether they are used as places to keep students busy, or as a place to teach skills.

Out-of-School Job Sites

Out-of-school experiences, sometimes referred to as community job sites, are extensions beyond the school job site. The vocational objectives at these sites are similar to those of on-campus jobs, yet the setting is less sheltered. Initially, in both school job sites and community job sites, evaluation and training are emphasized. However, as the student moves into the community for short periods of time, the opportunities within the community setting take on more of the flavor of real work. This does not mean that school job sites do not require real work but, to most students, community work stations are "real."

The major point to remember about these temporary job sites is that their purpose is evaluation and training, not actual employment. If and when the site fails to provide evaluation and training opportunities, it should be discontinued. Each student should have an opportunity to participate on several community work sites so that a feel for working in different environments and under different conditions is gained. Then, the student and the placement specialist will have a more accurate perception of the true capabilities of this individual. At this time, the placement specialist should resist the temptation to leave a student on a particular site because he or she is doing well.

Because of the heterogeneity of communities in which out-of-school work sites are sought, recommending specific procedures for

selecting these sites is somewhat difficult. However, there are some general guidelines for selection. First, consider the variety as well as the quantity of community stations that exist within the immediate locale. To eliminate transportation problems, work stations often need to be within walking distance from the school. However, if other forms of transportation are available, longer distances can be traveled and more diverse sites can be used. Regardless of travel arrangements, the contact person (teacher, placement specialists, etc.) should become familiar with the immediate area by talking to school personnel, friends, parents, and community leaders, and/or driving around the community to obtain a general overview of sites that do exist. The telephone directory, and especially the yellow pages, are helpful in this respect. Also, if the area under consideration is fairly large, a business directory may be available. This type of directory lists the names of companies, types of businesses, and locations.

After obtaining an overview of potential out-of-school work sites, and before any initial employer contacts are made, standardized survey forms for collecting information regarding businesses and a system of filing them should be carefully developed. In general, employer survey forms should contain the following information: date(s) of community contacts, name and type of business, address and distance from the school, telephone number of business, name of informant, preferred training hours, preferred interview (contact or follow-up) time, and a place for additional comments. Next, thought should be given to a system of cross-filing the information obtained from a community job site search. There are many ways of filing this information, but the following example will suffice in most cases. Information gathered from the job search should be filed by the name of the business, the name of the employer, the location from the school, and the type of work training provided. Although this may seem like unnecessary duplication, it could become a valuable time-saver as a program progresses and a large number of employers are accumulated. Once the potential of community sites is determined, actual contacts must then be made.

Permanent Sites

After students have gone through a number of in-school and community placements, many will be ready to seek employment on a permanent job site. Obviously the prospective worker must largely decide where to work or what to do. Of course this decision will be affected by the worker's previous training and availability of jobs in the community. However, if the vocational program staff has done a thorough job, then the chances for a close match between the worker's skills and available jobs will be very high. Follow-up services for the program graduate should also begin at this time to aid the above determination. Phelps and Lutz (1977) have suggested that these services should be provided to the client for at least three years following termination from the program. If other agencies are involved, this length of time for follow-up services may be quite reasonable. However, if only school personnel are involved, then a one-year provision of follow-up services is more reasonable.

Pay Versus Non-Pay

A problem often discussed regarding both school sites and community sites centers around financial remuneration. Should a student participating on a work site for evaluation and training purposes be paid? There are many obvious advantages to paying the student. Two most cited are: (1) money provides excellent motivational opportunities, and (2) students earning money can engage in additional curricular activities, for example, counting change, minor bookkeeping, consumer spending, or saving at a bank.

A case can also be made for non-paying work sites, both in and out of school. At the high school level, vocational training programs may be viewed as educational in nature, similar to English, science, and social studies classes. Usually students do not receive pay in such classes. Another problem with paying a student is the difficulty of rotating the student from work sample to work sample. When pay is involved, some employers are reluctant to change students as often as

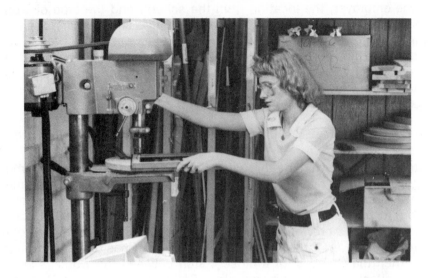

recommended. If an employer is paying a student who is in training, it is reasonable for the employer to want the client to continue working after training, rather than invest more time and money in a new client. It is also difficult sometimes to explain to a parent that their child will be getting paid on a job site during school hours while other students not involved in work programs do not get paid. However, many parents seem to understand non-paying work sites, providing these sites are used for educational purposes.

The issue of paying versus non-paying work placements is complex and each school program must determine the best approach for the particular situation. Additionally, it should be stated that when a student develops the skills for competitive employment, then without question the student should be paid, and paid comparably to what other workers receive for a certain job. Work sites both in school and out of school are provided as part of an educational program; when the purposes of evaluation and training are overshadowed by competitive employment problems, it is important that the student be moved to a different site for further evaluation and training. The major issue is exploitation, that is, whether students should provide services or make products without receiving pay for these tasks. It is the school's responsibility to determine the fine line that separates beneficial educational services from actual competitive work production.

PLACEMENT PROCEDURES—A SUMMARY

The placement process was taken apart and examined in a number of ways in this chapter. The following list of ideas and suggestions to enhance the flow of the entire placement process evolved from the previous discussions, as well as from placement personnel active in work-training programs for handicapped youth. No attempt has been made to rank or categorize items for the list.

1. *Use outside organizations as much as possible.* Service clubs such as Lions, Kiwanis, and Rotary are excellent contacts for securing information about possible placement sites.
2. *Personal contact with employers is imperative.* Although appointments initially may be determined by phone, personal contact is essential in enlisting employer support for the vocational preparation program.
3. *Use business cards and other printed material whenever possible.* Business cards and brochures explaining your program are expected by most employers.
4. *Leads can be found many times through the want ads section in the local newspaper and through staff acquaintances.* When searching for work sites do not overlook the most obvious sources of information, such as, want ads or the telephone directory.
5. *Business persons like the idea of working with public schools and local service agencies.* When talking to prospective employers, mention the vocational program's sponsors. Many business persons identify with agencies within the immediate community.
6. *Use testimonials and successful employer references.* Individuals who support a training program may want to tell others. Invite them to become a part of the recruitment team.
7. *As the program grows, become more selective and secure jobs that best meet the objectives of the program.* As sites are accumulated, it will be possible to select work situations on the basis of suitability rather than availability.
8. *To date, there are no guaranteed ways to predict employability; therefore do not predict success.* Placement specialists must realize they cannot predict to any reliable degree whether a student will succeed on a job site; therefore, they should avoid telling employers that a certain client is guaranteed to be successful.
9. *Do not get depressed if things start off slowly.* It is difficult to get started, but after the first few employer commitments are made to the program others seem to come easier.
10. *Placement is a two-way proposition.* It must be recognized that, in asking business persons to give of themselves, school personnel will also be required to give of themselves.
11. *Placement is time-consuming hard work.* Allow adequate time for locating and securing job sites and proceed syste-

matically and enthusiastically in the provision of follow-up and support services.

12. *The employer must be considered a part of the program, but not in charge of it.* At all times, the employer must keep in mind the programs' goals and objectives to understand his or her place on the team.   .

13. *Civic responsibility is the business person's Achilles' heel.* In many communities, employers have responded in a spirit of civic responsibility when informed of the problems and cost of educating and training all students.

14. *Employers can be used time and time again.* Since there are different levels of participation for employers in the vocational preparation program, they should be moved systematically from one level to another.

REFERENCES

Ballard, J., & Zettel, J. Public Law 94–142 and Section 504: What they say about rights and protections. *Exceptional Children,* 1977, *44,* 177–184.

Becker, R.L. *Reading—free vocational interest inventory.* Washington, D.C.: American Association on Mental Deficiency, 1975.

Brolin, D.E., & Kokaska, C.J. *Career education for handicapped children and youth.* Columbus, Ohio: Charles E. Merrill Publishing Co., 1979.

Cegelka, P.T., & Phillips, M.W. Individualized programming at the secondary level. *Teaching Exceptional Children,* 1978, *10,* 84–87.

Graves, C.W. Levels of existence: An open theory of values. *Journal of Humanistic Psychology,* 1970, *10,* 131–155.

Payne, J.S., & Chaffin, J.D. Developing employer relations in a work study program for the educable mentally retarded. *Education and Training of the Mentally Retarded,* 1968, *3,* 127–133.

Payne, J.S., Mercer, C.D., & Epstein, M.H. *Education and rehabilitation techniques.* New York: Behavioral Publications, 1974.

Payne, J.S., Polloway, E.A., Smith, J.E., & Payne, R.A. *Strategies for teaching the mentally retarded.* Columbus, Ohio: Charles E. Merrill Publishing Co., 1977.

Phelps, L.A., & Lutz, R.J. *Career exploration and preparation for the special needs learner.* Boston: Allyn & Bacon, 1977.

Smith, R.M. *Clinical teaching: Methods of instruction for the retarded* (2nd ed.). New York: McGraw-Hill, 1974.

10

Follow-up and Evaluation Procedures

In this chapter, the two related concerns of follow-up and evaluation procedures will be discussed. These two sets of procedures are closely related because the follow-up services provided to the employer and former program participants allow one to evaluate roughly how effective the training program has been for these individuals. Moreover, since one goal of the career preparation program is to provide services to mildly handicapped adolescents that will better equip them to adjust to the world of work and society at large, then another goal must be to determine the extent of that adjustment. Therefore, it seems only logical that the career preparation program should have or develop a number of procedures for assessing its overall effectiveness: program effectiveness is determined in most cases through various evaluation techniques.

In the 1970s, an era the U.S. Department of Health, Education, and Welfare (1972) has dubbed the "decade of accountability," an ever increasing number of working professionals cringed in fear at the mention of the term *evaluation*. This negative connotation acquired by the process is not without validity because of the increasing politicization of evaluation (Weiss, 1970, 1973). The point is, however, that evaluation is a common practice, one in which we engage daily without consciously labelling it evaluation. Every reader who has been unable to start a car on a winter morning, or who has cheerfully greeted a colleague who responds negatively or not at all, has performed evaluation at some level of sophistication. It is the purpose of evaluation that gives the process its meaning and the resulting emotional overlay. That is, assessing a program, by gathering documentary evidence, for the purpose of improving or changing it implies that some positions, roles, or duties in the program may be changed or lost, and that certain program goals and objectives may be changed as well. Unfortunately, many people view these possibilities in a negative light. Yet this need not be the case since evaluation can just as easily lead to positive changes and improvements in a program. In fact, that is the main reason that follow-up and evaluation procedures are being discussed in the same chapter—they both can lead directly to program improvement.

In the sections that follow, we first take a broad look at the topic of evaluation. Next, follow-up services for participants in the career preparation program (described in the last several chapters) will be discussed. Lastly, the process of total program evaluation will be examined.

EVALUATION—AN OVERVIEW

Worthen and Sanders (1973) have defined evaluation as "the determination of the worth of a thing. It includes obtaining information for use in judging the worth of a program, product, procedure, or objective, or the potential utility of alternative approaches designed to attain specified objectives" (p. 19). These writers further stated that evaluation is characterized by the fact that it

1. is used to determine the solution to practical problems.
2. leads to the formulation of decisions.
3. describes an entity in respect to some value scale.
4. can be used directly to assess social utility of a certain entity. And
5. is directly related to questions of the value of a certain thing or program.

The following comments regarding these five characteristics are offered to aid the reader in understanding the process of evaluation.

The first point we wish to make is that evaluation usually is not undertaken as an end in itself. That is, evaluation is most often used as a means to a *better* end. Better may be viewed as increased ouput, more pleasant interpersonal relationships on the job, a decrease in waste associated with a product or service, or in any way one chooses to define it. Secondly, once a person or group decides that some problem or concern needs to be resolved, evidence that leads to decision making has to be gathered. Lastly, the entity under consideration, whether a product or service, is compared to some value scale during the evaluation process. The objective of the comparison is to determine the relative worth of this entity.

According to proponents of the discrepancy evaluation model, evaluation is defined "as the comparison of what is, a performance (P), to an expectation of what should be, a standard (S). If a difference is found to exist between the standard and the performance, this difference is known as a discrepancy (D)" (Yavorsky, 1976, p. 3). If a negative discrepancy is found between the performance and the standard, then some corrective action must be taken. This corrective action can occur in one of three ways: termination, exerting greater control over performance, or adjusting the standard in some way.

Both of the previous definitions of evaluation clearly point out that when something is being evaluated it is compared to another entity or standard. Usually the comparison is being made so that a decision can be reached about performance or the worth of the entity being evaluated. Once performance or worth is actually determined, decisions concerning what to do about this entity are then made. It should be mentioned that further actions are usually taken in the event that negative results are obtained from the comparison. That is, when performance is less than the standard used for comparison, a negative performance result will be observed and consequently some type of corrective action is deemed appropriate. However, in some instances when the comparison results are positive, adjustments are still made. For example, companies that engage in large-scale production efforts frequently compare their present production record with past performance. In many cases, the present production rate will be higher. Yet, company officials may decide that an even higher rate of production could be achieved if certain facets of the production process were changed. In such an instance, results of a comparison would be viewed as positive but not positive enough.

Purpose of Evaluation

In general, evaluation is used to provide information or data for decision makers relative to the value or benefits of the thing being evaluated. Evaluation information is also useful to other persons interested in a certain program or project. These individuals may want to know how this program or project compares to similar ones as far as design, costs, and benefits are concerned. Thus, they are interested in the evaluation of the entity because it will provide them with needed information. Often, the purpose of an evaluation effort is to provide information that can be used in developing programs that will meet the needs of unique individuals or groups. Such would be the case in the development of an instructional program or career preparation program for mildly handicapped youth.

According to Walker (1972) another specific purpose of evaluation is to account for what is going on in the program. Once it is known what each member of the program staff is contributing to program development, then consequences can be differentially applied to each staff member. Since this is the case, Walker recommends that staff members be involved directly in the process of setting goals. Once goals are set, each one should receive some rating as to its value in the program. By following this procedure, the results of the program can be determined easily. Additionally, each staff member can be judged as having contributed or not to the attainment of program goals, and thus be rewarded equitably.

Types of Evaluation

Evaluation, like a great many other processes, can be looked at in several different ways. For example, evaluation can take two basic forms: *internal* or *external* evaluation. Internal evaluation would be an integral part of the entire program and would probably be done by one or several members of the ongoing staff. While this type of evaluation can be very good for purposes of self-appraisal, there is the constant danger that the evaluator(s) could be forced or lured into making the outcome of the evaluation more positive than it is. In this situation, management can give rewards or withhold them from the evaluator(s), based on its perceptions of what the outcome of the evaluation process should be. This potential co-opting by management may be more damaging in the case of internal evaluations because this may be the only evaluative endeavor that will be undertaken. However, the same problem may occur in other types of evaluation.

External evaluation, on the other hand, is performed by persons outside of the program. This type of evaluation would be done by adjunct staff, through independent contract, or on a consultant basis. In any case, the external evaluator interacts with program administrators and staff, as well as program recipients, to understand why the evaluation effort is being undertaken, what the program goals are, and how each of these groups (and the overall group) defines program effectiveness. Lastly, the evaluator reports the evaluative findings, derived from the review and analysis, to program members and attempts to interpret these findings in relation to the present structure and goals of the program.

Rather than comparing or contrasting different types of evaluation, Provus (1969) has indicated that evaluation can be grouped into five stages: (1) design, (2) installation, (3) process, (4) product, and (5) cost. During the design stage, the formulation of the program's plans are rigorously examined to determine whether they are adequate for whatever purpose they were developed. Installation and process evaluation refer to determinations made at some point as to whether the program is set up as planned and whether improvements can be made in program operation. During these two stages, comparisons are made to determine internal conditions of the program. Product or output evaluation compares the product to the original goals of the program. Evaluation during this stage centers around the effectiveness of the program in meeting its terminal objectives. Lastly, during the cost evaluation stage, the program presently under consideration and at least one other are compared as to differences in costs and/or benefits produced by each.

In summary, evaluation is the process of comparing something to a standard in order to determine its worth. Evaluations are frequently used to provide information to decision makers and others regarding program development and cost. Program evaluation can also be used to assess the effectiveness of the entire staff for the purpose of providing differential treatment of staff members. Regarding types of evaluation, the above discussion focused on internal and external evaluation, as well as the five-stage model of evaluation advocated by Provus (1969). Obviously, there are many other ways of looking at evaluation and the interested reader is encouraged to consult the following sources for additional information: Brolin (1976), especially chapter 14, and Worthen and Sanders (1973), especially pages 209–217.

FOLLOW-UP SERVICES

At this point, our attention shifts momentarily to the provision of follow-up services to former program participants and employers. One purpose of providing these follow-up services is to minimize on-the-job problems of the new worker. A second purpose is to evaluate the effects of the career preparation program on the recipient, as well as its projected effects on future program participants. A third purpose emanates from the evaluative data gathered that will be used to make recommendations for changing the program. In addition, Brolin (1976) has outlined several reasons for emphasizing the provision of these important services. According to him, the provision of follow-up services

1. helps to validate the results of training and evaluation attempts.
2. aids in keeping the program up to date. By providing these follow-up service efforts, program modification can be made at the most appropriate times.
3. allows the placement specialist to quickly provide needed services to either the employer, to the worker, or both when job-related problems come about.
4. shows that the school program staff and the placement worker are concerned about the new employee and that this same attitude would be manifested when other individuals from the program are placed at this site. Thus a successful placement with good follow-up services increases the likelihood of other clients being placed at a certain site.
5. gives the individual who has been placed on the job a chance to use the placement specialist as an advisor regarding job-related problems and concerns.
6. reduces the chances of the new worker being fired because of interpersonal conflicts. (Brolin, 1976)

The preceding discussion alluded to several roles that would be performed by the school placement specialist, the employer, or the new worker as follow-up services are provided. In the following discussion, the different roles of these persons are described more fully.

Role of the Placement Specialist

The primary role of the placement specialist, after the training stage is completed, is to provide periodic contacts with the employer and the new employee. Brolin (1976) has suggested the following procedure for conducting these periodic follow-up contacts:

1. First follow-up _____ first day of job.
2. Second follow-up _____ end of first week.
3. Third follow-up _____ end of second week.
4. Fourth follow-up _____ end of third week.
5. Fifth follow-up _____ end of first month.
6. Monthly follow-up until six months have passed on job.
7. Continue with mail follow-up for two years. (p. 185)

Whether one uses the procedure suggested by Brolin or a slightly different approach for checking working conditions and employee job adjustment, the most important point to be considered is that the first contact should be made as soon as possible after the new worker begins the job. Certainly this first contact should be made within two days after job commencement. Subsequent follow-up sessions should take place on a regularly scheduled basis. These latter sessions should be set up on the basis of perceived employer and employee needs.

During these follow-up sessions, the placement specialist should systematically observe the work environment, as well as the behavior of the employee and employer, to determine what factors may be causing the worker to fail or to succeed on the job. Since a great deal of activity usually goes on at the job site while the placement specialist is there, a good procedure for gathering information would be the use of a checklist. By using a checklist that has space for additional comments, the placement person can check off items as they are discussed and record other relevant information. Tables 10.1 and 10.2 present two examples of such checklists.

Two other roles that the placement specialist performs in this situation are those of counseling the new worker about work-related problems or conflicts and reinforcing appropriate behaviors of the workers. Many of the counseling strategies and techniques mentioned in chapter 8 will be appropriate to use at this time. The checklist forms mentioned previously can also assist the placement person in quickly determining the job strengths and weaknesses of the new employee. Comments relating to these strengths and weaknesses can then be integrated into the individual follow-up sessions held with the employee. For example, if the placement person determines that the employee shows up for work on time, cooperates with fellow employees, produces high quality work, but fails to complete work on time, then all of these points have to be conveyed to the worker. We stress conveying *all* of this information—the worker will be able to make adjustments better if he or she knows which job behaviors are correct and which need some correction.

The following specific suggestions are intended to delineate further the duties and responsibilities of the placement person.

- *Make initial follow-up contacts in person.* By making initial follow-up contacts in person with the employer and employee, the placement specialist shows a willingness to give of his or her time to insure that all goes well as the new employee is integrated on the job. Personal contacts also imply that the placement specialist does not regard the placement and follow-up process as simply a mechanistic endeavor. Rather, this type

Table 10.1
Checklist Evaluation (1)

Trainee _____ Date _____

	Always	Usually	Sometimes	Seldom	Never
Understands directions					
Sustains an appropriate routine					
Accepts pressure					
Accepts criticism					
Gets along with supervisors and co-workers					
Appears motivated					
Works without supervision					
Observes regulations					
Appearance is appropriate					
Meets production schedule					
Is a steady worker					
Does satisfactory work					
Good attention span on job					
Appears trustworthy					
Uses tools correctly					
Expresses self appropriately					

of contact clearly demonstrates that the placement specialist views this as a process where a number of persons must interact in a job setting, and that his or her job is to make this interaction as humane as possible.

- *Keep communication lines open.* Once the new worker is placed on a job and one or two follow-up sessions have taken place, the placement specialist should endeavor to keep communications open between all the people involved in this process. If the placement specialist has an extensive case load, it will be nearly impossible to visit constantly each site that has a client. Therefore, such things as follow-up letters and telephone contacts become very important.
- *Use a positive approach.* In dealing with both the new worker and the employer, the placement specialist should constantly strive to be as positive as possible. While this statement seems

Table 10.2
A Checklist Evaluation (2)

Trainee's Name _____   Employer's Name _____
Address _____
Date Started _____   Job Title _____
Time on Job _____   Supervisor _____

| Factors | AVERAGE EMPLOYEE | | | Comments |
	Less Than	Same As	More Than	
Self-confidence				
Cheerful				
Cooperates with supervisor				
Respects supervisor				
Cooperates with other employees				
Minds own business				
Accepts criticism				
Mixes socially with other employees				
Neat and clean				
On time				
Safety conscious				
Careful with materials and property				
Completes work on time				
Quality of work				
Understands work				
Shows initiative				
Other				

Would you be as willing to hire this individual as you would your average applicant if a job were available?

Yes _____ Probably _____ Probably Not _____ No _____

If the above answer is "Probably Not" or "No" please answer the following:

Would hire IF . . . (State Conditions):

very simple, people in charge of placement, like others, often seem to forget what it means. The statement implies that, in a given situation, where a goodly number of things are positive and yet one or two negative factors exist at the same time, one should not concentrate solely on the negative portions. For in-

stance, in the earlier example concerning the worker who displayed several positive job-related behaviors, but who also failed to complete work on time, both the worker and employer may need to be reminded that there are several positive things going on.

- *Actively involve the new worker in follow-up and evaluative efforts.* The worker should be an integral part of the process rather than a passive recipient. To accomplish this goal, the placement person should seek to promote, as well as reinforce, client behaviors that move the client toward independence on the job and in other spheres.
- *Seek specific information from the employer about client behaviors.* Payne, Polloway, Smith, and Payne (1977) have reported that frequently employers do not report specific behaviors of the client when they are referring to the job performance of that individual. For example, a typical employer might say when asked how Mary is doing on the job, "Mary is doing fine," or "Mary is doing a lousy job." In both instances, the placement person needs to ask further questions to find out which specific client behaviors are causing the client to do a good or lousy job. Hopefully, after the placement person and the employer go through this type of exchange on a number of occasions, the employer will realize that statements about client work adjustment should be as specific as possible.

Role of the Employer

Although the employer will receive a number of follow-up services from the placement specialist, it is critical that he or she perform certain concurrent duties. During this particular time, the employer should take at least three actions to insure that the newly placed worker succeeds. These three actions are: (1) avoid too much or too little contact with the new worker so that he or she neither expects the employer always to be physically present nor fears the presence of the employer (who perhaps was only seen during the period of hiring); (2) keep adequate records of the new employee's behaviors on the job— this could be done by using one of the checklists already mentioned (see Tables 10.1 and 10.2); and (3) call in the placement specialist at unscheduled times if the situation warrants, that is, when a specific problem has taken place or is expected to occur in the near future.

In the first situation mentioned, the employer greatly promotes the work adjustment of the client by showing that he or she is available for helpful suggestions about the employee's job. However, the employer should make it clear, by staying in the background much of the time, that he or she is no more or less concerned with this worker than with other workers. Also, by neither avoiding nor becoming unduly concerned with the mildly handicapped worker, the employer avoids calling unwanted attention to this person.

The second necessary action of the employer is record keeping. It has already been suggested that the placement specialist and the employer use the same form or type of form for recording job-related behaviors of the employee. By using this procedure, these two individuals can compare their ratings of the worker and arrive at a consensus relative to the employee's job performance.

Since the placement specialist is available to the employer for advice and consultation, the employer should take advantage of these services, especially in situations where a number of minor problems have occurred. By calling in the placement specialist before these minor problems become exacerbating, the employer avoids the position where the only option is to terminate the employee.

Role of the New Worker

A new worker who accepts a position with a business must begin immediately to take steps to adjust to this new environment. The worker may be concerned with such matters as getting to and from work, having enough money for lunch, and saving some of the money that is earned. Even though this person is no longer in school (or training), school personnel should stress that a placement specialist will be following his or her progress very closely. The worker should be told specifically to seek advice from this person regarding any work-related concerns. In addition, the former student should seek advice from both the immediate supervisor and other responsible persons on the job. Lastly, if conditions on the job become so restrictive that the employee anticipates being fired or having to quit, then the placement specialist should be sought out immediately to determine whether this dilemma can be resolved in a positive fashion.

PROGRAM EVALUATION

As indicated at the beginning of this chapter, evaluation is often used to solve a problem. The problem which concerns us now and which will concern persons who work directly with career and vocational preparation programs is how to determine the effectiveness of such a program. Brolin (1976) developed a framework for answering this question via his program evaluation formula (see Figure 10.1). This formula indicates that to assess the effectiveness of career and vocational preparation programs, a program evaluator has to determine first what community needs brought about this program. Next, the specific objectives of the program should be looked at to determine how these community needs are being met. Following this, the methods used to accomplish the objectives should be scrutinized. Lastly, the outcome or product of the previous steps should also be checked to see how it conforms to or achieves the conditions set out in the stated objectives.

Source: Brolin, D.E. *Vocational preparation of retarded citizens.* Columbus, Ohio: Charles E. Merrill Publishing Co., 1976. Reprinted by permission of the publisher.

Figure 10.1
Program Evaluation Formula

Since the last four chapters of this book dealt with the general topic of career provisions, we will draw from this material in order to illustrate further the ideas just briefly described. Referring again to Brolin's formula, our first concern would be what community needs brought this matter to our attention. Before elaborating on this point, we should describe how we perceive the term *community.* In this instance, community is equated with the term *school* so that community needs are the same as school needs. Realizing that this is a somewhat restricted view of the concept of community, we nevertheless feel that it is adequate because the school is composed of numerous subcultures that function in much the same way as in any other community. Returning to the main point, the community needs that would cause us to be concerned about setting up some type of career preparation program, the specific needs that we have focused on had to do with the fact that most mildly handicapped adolescents move directly from the school into the world of work. Therefore, these youth require the services of a program that will prepare them to enter this arena successfully.

In accounting for the specific program objectives that would aid mildly handicapped youth in preparing for a career, we return to the career preparation program objectives postulated at the beginning of chapter 7. These objectives are:

1. to increase the occupational awareness and aspirations of each student through career counseling;
2. to develop a preliminary assessment of each student's vocational skills and interests;
3. to provide each student with direct or "hands-on" job-related experiences and activities;
4. to aid each student in the development of entry level job skills; and
5. to provide a job placement service for students who complete the career preparation program.

According to Brolin's formula, the next matter requiring our attention (if we were actually evaluating a program already in existence) is that of the methods used to foster the objectives just mentioned. Without belaboring the point, we will simply say that in the last several chapters methods and strategies for achieving these objectives have been described. For example, assessing a student's vocational skills, counseling the student regarding vocational choices, and placing and following-up the student on the job have been discussed extensively.

Based on previous statements, we believe that the outcome evaluation that would be derived from this process would show that the career preparation program meets the needs of mildly handicapped adolescents. However, since we are not describing a program that is presently in force, we cannot determine whether these methods or strategies are effective and whether the outcome or product meets the conditions set forth in the program objectives. Even so, persons who have set up working programs would go through these same steps to determine the effectiveness of their programs.

Recommendations

In concluding this particular topic, we would like to make the following recommendations: (1) use the data that is gathered during follow-up sessions with former program participants as part of the total program evaluation; (2) use an outside evaluator for assessing program effectiveness—such an evaluator will probably have more skill in this area and will be less likely to be influenced adversely by management (Brashears, 1979); and (3) present the results of the evaluative efforts to the entire staff. This last point is crucial since evaluative data is often used to decide on program changes. By conveying this information to all staff members, program administrators pave the way for acceptance of change.

SUMMARY

In this chapter, the two related concerns of follow-up services and evaluation procedures were discussed. Follow-up services were perceived as related to evaluation because much of the information that one would use for evaluation purposes could be gathered while providing follow-up services to the employer and the employee. Initially, evaluation was defined as a process that seeks solutions to practical problems by comparing performance to a standard. Several types of evaluation were discussed, including external and internal evaluation. External evaluation is performed by either adjunct staff, by contract service, or by a consultant. Internal evaluation, on the other hand, is done for purposes of self-appraisal. All types of evaluation provide information for decision makers as well as others.

Follow-up services were then discussed. It was stated that by providing these services, both the employer and employee would be helped in their attempts to make the employee's work experience a success. The different roles of the placement specialist, the employer, and the employee were discussed at this point. Lastly, the process of evaluation was examined in relation to the total career program and it was shown how the different topics described in the past several chapters fit into the evaluation process.

REFERENCES

Brashears, J. Personal communication. 1979.

Brolin, D.E. *Vocational preparation of retarded citizens.* Columbus, Ohio: Charles E. Merrill Publishing Co., 1976.

Payne, J.S., Polloway, E.A., Smith, J.E., & Payne, R.A. *Strategies for teaching the mentally retarded.* Columbus, Ohio: Charles E. Merrill Publishing Co., 1977.

Provus, M. Evaluation of ongoing programs in the public school systems. *The sixty-eighth yearbook of the National Society for the Study of Education.* Chicago: University of Chicago Press, 1969.

U.S. Department of Health, Education, and Welfare. *Program Evaluation: A beginning statement.* Washington, D.C.: U.S. Government Printing Office, 1972.

Walker, R.A. The ninth panacea: Program evaluation. *Evaluation,* 1972, *1*(1), 45–53.

Weiss, C.H. The politicization of evaluation research. *Journal of Social Issues,* 1970, *26*(4), 57–68.

Weiss, C.H. Where politics and evaluation research meet. *Evaluation,* 1973, *1*(3), 37–45.

Worthen, B.R., & Sanders, J.R. *Educational evaluation: Theory and practice.* Belmont, California: Wadsworth Publishing Co., 1973.

Yavorsky, D.K. *Discrepancy evaluation: A practitioner's guide.* Charlottesville, Virginia: University of Virginia, 1976.

Epilogue

The last ten chapters of this book have examined the many intricate and diverse parts of the secondary school as they relate to the mildly handicapped learner. We have now come full circle in the sense that we are once again looking at the whole rather than the parts. Hopefully, you the reader now know more than when you began this volume. We the authors have learned a great deal.

In our search for material for this book, we saw a lot of people and programs, read a huge amount of literature about special and secondary education, and talked to a great number of high school students. In fact, during the writing of this book, one of our most pleasant moments with a student came near the end of our struggle to meet the production deadline for the final manuscript. On our way out of the building near the end of the day, we saw a teenager who looked vaguely familiar. As the teenager approached, we realized that he was Lonnie, the youth that we had referred to in chapter 2. After momentarily wondering why he was near our office, we all spoke since by this time we were very close to each other. Lonnie soon solved the riddle when he said, with a big smile, that he was receiving tutoring from the learning center at the university. He went on to tell us how he was doing much better in school and in all of his work. From his conversation and our questions, it certainly appeared that he was feeling good about himself and that he felt very successful. His behavior at this time was in marked contrast to what he had displayed to us previously. For example, in previous meetings he had been shy and withdrawn, rather defensive in fact; he now appeared to be the opposite. A check with the appropriate persons did reveal that Lonnie was doing well, in and out of school.

In reflecting on this particular situation, we concluded that this was a real life case of a student whose needs had been met. Here was a person who had a chance for success in life. That is also what this book and the programs and materials that we have described are about; a means to provide a chance for success in life for *all* mildly handicapped youth.

part four

Resource Materials

In the previous portions of this book, school characteristics, learner characteristics, strategies for teaching, career preparation, and other related topics have been discussed. This remaining part contains a listing of resource materials that have been used in the past to help the exceptional adolescent to learn. This list of materials was developed in two ways. First, we asked our colleagues to list all the materials that they had used in dealing with exceptional youth—generally many of these colleagues not only listed the materials, but they often allowed us to review on the spot the materials in their possession. Secondly, we perused the professional literature, as well as sales catalogues, for descriptions of lesser known materials that might be used with mildly handicapped adolescents.[1]

The materials that ultimately ended up in our listing were selected by using two criteria. Those two criteria were the potential usability of the product by either the teacher or student, and the appropriateness of the material for the secondary level student (whether the general

[1]Grateful appreciation is expressed to Richard G. Ward and Mary Lou Shunk for their help in evaluating many of the materials that are mentioned in the sections to follow.

format of the material appeared to be aimed at the secondary special needs learner). Additionally, we looked at all the materials to determine whether these materials possessed the following characteristics:

1. Enables the adolescent to achieve developmental tasks. *Our concern with this material characteristic was whether the material would actually foster maturation on the part of the adolescent in either a direct or indirect manner.*
2. Can be used in developmental or remedial teaching. *Since some mildly handicapped adolescents would need to develop certain skills while others would need to remediate faulty skill development, the abililty of the material to be used in different settings or ways was considered important.*
3. Must have high-interest / low-vocabulary level. *Without a doubt, many mildly handicapped adolescents will have some reading problems. Therefore, it was considered important that materials take these potential problems into consideration.*
4. Must be career oriented while teaching specific skills. *Because a large number of mildly handicapped adolescents will terminate their formal schooling after leaving secondary school, career-oriented materials for this group were perceived as a necessity. At the same time, the intricate learning problems of this group must be considered if these career materials are to be used successfully.* [2]

While the above characteristics indicate a number of variables tht must be considered in selection of materials for use with the special needs adolescent, the teacher must ultimately make the decision to use certain materials. Therefore, two cautionary notes are added to this selection information. We want to warn teachers that they must select materials for use with specific individuals, not because these materials were developed for the group with which these teachers presently work. Our second caution is that our review of a certain series, product, or material does not constitute endorsement of that particular entity. Our goal in describing these materials is to provide teachers with a means of quickly determining what material is currently available in a given area. Teachers are encouraged to contact personally the producers and distributors of those materials they feel would meet their needs and the needs of their particular students.

The following is a brief summary of what is contained in the resource sections. In sections one, two, three, and four, specific mate-

[2]Readers who are interested in determining further criteria for evaluating materials are referred to the following source: Wiederholt, J., & McNutt, G. Evaluating materials for handicapped adolescents. *Journal of Learning Disabilities*, 1977, *10*, 132–140.

rials relating to the four areas of reading and language, arithmetic, motor and physical development, and career preparation are described. Section five contains other materials we felt are important to the education of the special needs adolescent. However, these materials are usually overlooked in favor of materials that deal more directly with academic development and remediation. Section six is a professional bibliography composed of readings that, in general, have not been referred to in the body of the text. A brief statement provides the reader with a concise summary of each reading.

Reading and Language Materials

Scope Skills Books

Scholastic
$1.25/book
The 13 books in this series are designed to help the learner master and build skills in the areas of reading, word skills, language, and career/study skills. Each book has a different theme, for example, Driving, Fantastic Facts, et cetera. Skills covered in books include following directions and finding the main idea. Reading levels are grades 4–6. Suitable for persons in grades 8–12.

Most Used Words for Spelling

Fern Tripp
$1.75/book
This is a four-book series of exercises aimed at helping the student learn to spell. Each book contains 30 lessons that involve practicing

the words initially, using the words in sentences, and then being formally tested on spelling the words.

High Interest-Low Vocabulary Reading Center

McGraw-Hill
$120.00/entire set of 10 units
These reading centers are designed to promote better reading and to develop reading skills on an individual basis. Each center contains: five copies of title magazine (including story and accompanying activities), one tape cassette, four ditto masters, storage bag, and a teaching guide. Titles included are: Comprehension, Word Attack, S blends, R blends, and L blends; Vowel Combinations; Digraphs; Main Idea; and Details.

Programmed Reading for Adults

McGraw-Hill
$2.00/book $4.00/teacher's guide
The intent of this program is to bring older students up to a 6.0 reading level. The linguistic approach used is made up of a series of eight programmed workbooks. The author claims that by the end of the program the student will be able to read for meaning any material written at 5–6 level and have a vocabulary of 1500 words. Books begin with letters of the alphabet and range up to content analysis and functional reading.

Understanding English

Frank E. Richards
$1.95/book
This is a basic comprehensive text for students ready to cover such topics as punctuation marks and parts of speech. Designed to assist students with the mechanics of the English language. Provides practice in everyday usage.

Reading Skills Cards

McGraw-Hill
$25.00/set
This is a supplemental reading series with 224 cards in the set. Each

card contains a 180-word story on the front and comprehension questions on the back. Cards are numbered and coded for difficulty.

How to Write Yourself Up

Frank E. Richards
$1.95/book
This book is designed to give students practice in several areas, such as, writing letters, filling out job applications, applying for credit, social security, installment buying, and completing forms relating to banking, postal, and income tax. Much of the same material is covered in the "Using Money Series" and "Getting Ready for Pay Day," also published by Frank Richards.

Auto Phonics

Educational Activities, Inc.
$14.95/kit
Series of four games (Bingo style) designed for older students. Each card contains pictures and words related to cars (fender, engine, traffic signals, etc.). 1st game—Phonetic alphabet; initial sounds. 2nd game—Vowel review. 3rd game—All about consonants. 4th game—Vowel digraphs and diphthongs. Good supplement for older students. Could be used with vocational, prevocational training. The games are neither too complicated nor too juvenile. The kit also contains tapes with instructions and for calling out words.

The Venture Series

Follett Publishing Company
$3.33/book
A reading incentive program for 7th–12th grade students written on a 4–6.5 grade reading level. There are two levels to the Venture Library (I & II). Each level has six separate books with each book having a certain sport as its central theme. Within each book are approximately six stories related to that sport. Many stories are short biographies of famous athletes. Titles in *Venture I* include "On the Boards" (basketball); "Racing to Indy" (Indy Racing); "Inside Track" (track); "Flying High" (ballooning); "Gearing Down" (motorcycle racing); "Touchdown" (football). *Venture II:* "Match Point" (tennis); "Slap Shot" (hockey); "Split Decision" (boxing); "Line Drive" (baseball); "In the Chutes" (rodeo); "Fall Line" (skiing). The books have many full-color

pictures and each focuses mainly on the human aspect of sports. Also available are student "Inquiry" books to accompany the series.

Audio Reading Kit (ARK)

Education Progress Corporation (EPC)
Like many similar kits, this low-vocabulary, high-interest program is made up of written material accompanied by audio tapes. However, this program is unique in that each story and several related exercises are printed on laminated cards, which allows them to be reused. The readability level extends from 1.0 to 2.5 years. Stories are presented in a cartoon format.

Reading Incentive Series

McGraw-Hill
$4.50/book
Series contains five books ranging from 3.0 to 7.0 reading levels. Each book contains illustrated, reading for pleasure stories with an anthology type format. Strictly for independent reading levels. Might be good to have in a reading corner of Jr.-Sr. High classroom.

Good Literature for Slow Readers

Frank E. Richards
$79.50/10 volumes
A literature series designed for those who will never be able to read the "classics" in their original form. Stories have been stripped of long passages, difficult words, and lengthy chapters. No reading level available. Some titles included are: "Heidi," "Swiss Family Robinson," "Ivanhoe," "Prince and the Pauper," and "Treasure Island."

Read and Do With Professor Riddle

Frank E. Richards
$1.95/book
This book is designed and written for secondary special students. The programmed format gives practice in following printed directions. A controlled vocabulary is used throughout the book. The book is com-

posed of high-interest, limited reading materials. Looks like a helpful book—especially to begin a new school year.

Palo Alto Reading Program

Harcourt, Brace, Jovanovich
$1.00/book
The purpose of this ungraded phonetic and linguistic program is to develop skills in reading. The program contains a sequence of 20 pupil books with work pads, skill box, flannel board activities, pupil pocket charts, and criterion-referenced tests for each book. These tests are to be given after book and work pad are completed. The program covers single consonant sounds, short vowels, some sight words, and many pattern words.

Spiderman Reading Motivation Kit

McGraw-Hill
$120.00/kit
This is an intermediate-Jr. High reading kit using a multi-media approach to stimulate the slow reader. Each kit contains six color/sound filmstrips, three sets of eight story cards, seven comic book readers, one action poster, one teacher's guide. The teacher's guide was prepared by N. Link of Children's Television Workshop.

English in Action (1960)

Regents Publishing Company, Inc.
$1.75
For students who use English as a second language or use it poorly. This book is designed to teach the use of oral English. The book will make a good supplement to other reading and English materials.

Learning Functional Words and Phrases for Everyday Living

Frank E. Richards
$1.95/book
This book is to be used with students needing to learn basic survival words. Contains a pre-test, individual lessons, word signs, illustra-

tions displaying use with practice page for printing the sign, review lessons, and post-test.

Demon Spelling Words

Educational Activities, Inc.
$6.95/record—$7.95/tape
Contained on one record (cassette) are 105 hard-to-spell words—grade level 2–8. Record provides for repetitions so student can master words (memorize). Saves teacher from having to verbalize words over and over. Good for individual work (with headphones). For use with any grade student. Words that everyone has trouble with.

City Limits

McGraw-Hill
$1.65/book
Reading levels are 5.0–7.0. High-interest, low-vocabulary books dramatizing the inner-city life of young adults in realistic situations. There are three books in the series. Each is approximately 120 pages long, in paperback form.

Practical English/Grammar

Creative Visuals
Ten boxes of filmstrips with accompanying cassettes. Each box contains six filmstrips and cassettes. The kit is designed to be used individually, in small groups, or for whole-class presentation. Each filmstrip introduces a new concept (punctuation, parts of speech, usage, English sentences, and problem words). Some answers are included on the cassette tape and some are left unanswered to act as an evaluation of the pupils' knowledge. Best used for secondary students who have acquired English skills sufficient to merit further work.

Modern Short Biographies (1975; 2nd ed.)

Globe Book Company, Inc.
Book of biographies designed for mature students (secondary) reading below grade level. Written on a 5.5 grade reading level. The book has two purposes: (1) to provide interesting reading material at appropriate reading levels, and (2) to stimulate class discussion about

contemporary problems. The teacher's manual sets up each story and provides answers to comprehension and reading skills questions following each story. Discussion questions are included with each biography. Persons written about range from the familiar (John F. Kennedy and Martin Luther King, Jr.) to the unfamiliar (Daniel Hale Williams, the first open heart surgeon).

New Practice Readers

McGraw-Hill
$3.00/level
Short factual stories in each book are followed by comprehension questions. Answer key and teacher's guide for each level. Reading levels range from 2.5 to 6.8 across seven books (A through G). Good for supplemental materials.

Specific Skills Series

Barnell-Loft
$1.00/book
This series is a skill development program covering eight areas (Using Context, Locating Answers, Getting Facts, Following Directions, Working with Sounds, Getting the Main Idea, Drawing Conclusions, and Detecting Sequence). Each area has levels A through F, starting with 1.0 grade level up to 6.0 grade level (reading level). Students work through exercises using available answer sheets.

Monster Books

Bowmar Publishing Company
$70.00/series
Originated from language experience activity. These are high-interest, low-vocabulary books with a simple type of sentence structure. The books contain 12 stories intended for pleasure reading. Reading levels are approximately 1.2 to 2.1. These books can be used as motivation for creative writing and language experience activities.

Scope Play Series

Scholastic
$1.35/book $2.50/teacher's guide
Paperback anthologies containing current plays, teleplays, short

stories, screen plays, and open-ended dramas. Written on a 4–6 grade reading level for use in grades 8–12. Teacher's book offers extra activities to get students involved. This series offers a different way to approach reading with low vocabulary readers.

Scope Activity Kits

Scholastic
$30.00/kit
Fifteen kits available. Each is designed for the secondary student reading on a 4–6 grade level. Kits are mini-units containing theme related fiction, nonfiction, poetry, open-ended situations. Aimed at developing reading, reasoning, and language skills. Some include records to go along with ditto master activities.

Pro Fever

EMC Corporation
"Four Seasons at Lakeview" is a series of high-interest, low-vocabulary books that are primarily male-oriented. Other titles in the series are: "The Sixth Man," "The Unlikely Hero," and "Rip's Ups and Downs."

Reading Shelf

McGraw-Hill
$1.60/book
Reading levels are grade 4–6. High-interest, low-vocabulary series. Each book contains adaptions of popular short stories/novels. Some of the titles are: "Requiem for a Heavyweight," "Call of the Wild," and "The Year the Yankees Lost the Pennant." These books could be used to furnish a reading corner in a secondary classroom. There are 17 books in the series.

Guidebook to Better Reading (1976)

The Economy Company
This program is designed for those secondary students who need materials at low reading levels. The series provides for development of word attack and comprehension skill work. Reading levels range from 2.1 to 5.4. The series is built around the student's basic text with an extra skills book for 2.0 grade work. Supplemental readers (five novel-

ettes, five anthologies, one visual, and one functional reader, 2.0–6.0 reading level) are also available, as are duplicating masters, 16 cassettes with tear sheets, and an entire separate program entitled REACH. Content of readers is high-interest with mature and up-to-date illustrations.

Starting Line

Bowmar
High-interest, low-vocabulary series for beginning readers. Each of four reading kits contains six pupil books, one resource book, one tape, one filmstrip, two gameboards, and nine skill sheets. The series is aimed at improving vocabulary, word attack, comprehension, and writing skills. Pre-primer to 1.0 reading levels covered.

Reluctant Reader Libraries

Scholastic
$30.00/Library
Four libraries: Junior A & B and Senior A & B. High-interest, low-vocabulary books for grades 7–12. Each library contains two copies of each title and a teaching guide. Reading levels range from 4.7 to 5.10. Each library contains approximately 18 titles plus a selection of short stories.

The New Phonics We Use

Rand-McNally & Company
$2.00/book
Eight levels of workbooks A through G used to help students master basic phonetic and structural analysis skills to enhance independent reading. Pictures and exercises are not too juvenile for secondary students. Can be used effectively as supplementary work with poor/non-readers.

REACH (The Reading Extravaganza of American Cycling and Hydroplane Show) (1973)

The Economy Company
$3.27/book $159.60/Set of tapes
An individualized tape-reading program for students reading below grade level in grades 4–9. Skills covered in the program are: word

attack skills, vocabulary expansion, and comprehension development. Kit includes 21 tapes with one show (lesson) on each side of the tape, "A Show Magazine" (lesson book) for each student, and a teacher's program that utilizes the same supplementary readers as the "Guidebook to Better Reading" series. Available in two editions: to be used with any conventional cassette player, and to be used with a pacing cassette player.

Individualized English

Follett Publishing Company
$118.00/complete set
There are two sets to this series, "J" for Junior High and "H" for Senior High students. This is a programmed series designed to be used individually with only those students who need it. It begins with a diagnostic placement test to pinpoint the exact problems of the student. The series is designed to correct problems in grammar, usage, sentence structure, style, and punctuation. The lessons are contained on individual cards that the student uses with a sleeve to conceal answers until the task is performed. Reading levels extend from grade 5–8.

Red Line/Blue Line Series (1972)

EMC Corporation
Four titles are included in this series: *Making the Squad, Aiming to Please, The Tough Decision,* and *The Two That Count.* The books center around the theme of a boys' ice hockey team trying to win the city hockey championship. This series is a set of high-interest, low-vocabulary material. While the books are meant to be a series, each is complete in itself.

Everyone's Watching Tammy (1974)

EMC Corporation
This particular title is part of the series "Really Me." Other titles included in the series are: *Will the Real Jeannie Murphy Please Stand Up, A Candle, A Feather, A Wooden Spoon,* and *Checkmate Julie.* The stories in each of these high-interest, low-vocabulary books focus on the problems and lives of several girls and young women.

Report Writing Skills (1972)

Coronet
The publishers of this package indicate that it is to be used as a supplement to a language arts program. The general aim of the program is to improve students' writing skills. Eight lessons provide the information that the student must use in workbook exercises. The lessons are on cassettes. Two pages in a student workbook are used with each cassette lesson.

Scope Visuals

Scholastic
$7.00/unit
Each unit contains four to eight lessons printed on ditto masters with matching overhead transparencies. Written on 4.0–6.0 grade level. There are 26 units covering the areas of reading skills, reference skills, and career skills. Each includes its own teaching guide. Good for supplemental work with slow learners.

The Everyreader Series

Webster/McGraw-Hill
$40.00/entire series
There are 20 books in this series that contain popular stories adapted to a 4.0 reading level or below. This material could be used in a literature course for secondary students needing a specific required number of credits. High-interest, low-difficulty. Should be of interest to ages 10–18. Examples of titles are: "Call of the Wild" "King Arthur and His Knights," and "Treasure Island."

A Better Bit and Bridle (1975)

EMC Corporation
This book is from another series of books about young women. The series includes three other titles: *Open the Gate, Trailering Troubles,* and *A Chance to Win.*

Webster Word Wheels

McGraw-Hill, Inc.
Kit of 63 word wheels covering two-letter consonant digraphs, initial

blends, prefixes, and suffixes. The wheels are intended to teach word analysis skills and to develop word recognition. Vocabulary used comes from Thorndike-Lorge word count. Blank wheels are also available for making new exercises. Definitions of words used are on the back of each wheel.

Guidebook to Better English (1978)

The Economy Company
$1.98/book $17.34/Set Duplicating Masters
A success-oriented remedial language program in four levels (I–IV). Written on a 4–7 grade reading level. This series is designed to teach basic English skills to high school or adult students, with attention given to reinforcement and application of skills acquired. A good series that helps provide students who do not use correct English with the fundamentals of good English usage. The series is not designed to be a starting point for an English program; rather, it is designed to build on minimal skills acquired via a less complex series.

The Turner-Livingston Communication Series (1974)

Follett Publishing Company
$1.44/book
A series of six workbooks designed to help students understand facts concerning communication in our world. Written on a 3–4 grade reading level, each workbook covers a different facet of communication in short selections to be read by students. Each workbook also contains several structured lessons emphasizing skills in English work and in social studies areas. Titles include: "The Television You Watch," "The Phone Calls You Make," "The Newspapers You Read," "The Movies You See," "The Letters You Write," and "The Language You Speak." Each book explores related job opportunities, how to evaluate the various media, and provides much general information relating to communications.

Corrective Reading (1978)

Science Research Associates (SRA)
A highly structured reading program for any age student who has learned incorrect reading skills, especially how to decode words. The teacher determines program participants by giving a placement test.

Then the teacher begins with one of the 155 written lessons, which must be followed verbatim to insure success. The students are required to respond in a prescribed manner according to rules agreed on by the students and the teacher. According to the publisher, it's appropriate for grades 4–12.

Getting It Together—A Reading Series About People (1973)

Science Research Associates (SRA)
$4.65/book
This reading series is composed of one book written on three levels (Level I on a 2–3 grade level, Level II on a 3–4 grade level, and Level III on a 5–6 grade level). This technique was used so that a class of varying reading levels could use the same materials without obvious grouping. Each book contains 50 short stories featuring life problem themes, and information on dealing with personal problems. The accompanying workbook is the same for all three levels. Exercises cover comprehension skills and are designed to stimulate some problem-solving processes in the student.

Spelling Word Power Laboratory (1966)

Science Research Associates (SRA)
$135.00/complete kit
This is a personalized spelling program for use with students up to grade 7. It is not specifically intended for use in special education programs, but due to the nature of the individualized format it could easily be used with the student who is unable to keep up with peers in a regular spelling program. The kit consists of a word wheel that teaches a specific spelling principle (changing "y" to "i," adding suffixes, etc.). The student uses a record book in conjunction with the word wheel and a check test card to determine if he or she has mastered the principle well enough to go on to the next card. The record book allows for practice of missed words and/or principles.

English Grammar

BRL
$9.00/book $4.00/teacher book/test book
This is a two-volume programmed English series that focuses on function. Beginning with the noun, all words must have a purpose be-

fore they are classified. Each passage contains small amounts of information, which the student must respond to before proceeding. The books show the student why language is important, and attempt to assign a logical reason for the way English grammar is assembled and used today.

Action Library

Scholastic Book Services
A complete set of reading materials developed for secondary students (grades 7–12) who are reading as low as a 2.0 grade reading level. "New Unit Action" (1977) provides a full semester's program of word attack skills and comprehension for students reading at the 2.0–4.0 level. "Original Action Library" (1969) high-interest, low-vocabulary paperbacks provide four different levels of reading ability. There are four books per level and five copies of each book. The program gives lots of extra material for those students unable to progress to the next level. "Double Action" follows the other two action series.

Point 31 (1975)

Reader's Digest
This is a comprehensive remedial reading program. The program is presented to the student in a magazine format. High-interest, low-vocabulary stories provide the basic content and also provide the means for instruction in basic and additional reading skills. The program encompasses four different levels, from a 1.0–5.0-year readability range.

Cracking the Code (1968)

SRA
$3.20/book and $2.10/workbook
This is a supplementary program for beginning readers. The material is suitable for students up to grade 9 who are not reading on the independent reading level. The program focuses on developing skills. It is not designed for nonreaders. The books contain a variety of reading selections including short stories, poems, and limericks.

A Linguistic Grammar of English

BRL
$5.00/book
With this book, students become involved in the study of underlying

patterns of English grammar as opposed to memorizing usage rules in this programmed approach. Each page has approximately ten frames to which the student responds. Concepts are presented in a limited manner and consistently reinforced throughout the rest of the book. The book focuses on identifying word types and their specific functions.

Reading Laboratory 3A–3B and 4A (1964)

Science Research Associates (SRA)
$135.00/kit
An individualized approach to building comprehension, vocabulary, and word attack skills. Kits 3A and 3B are written for grades 7–10. Kit 4A is written for grades 9–14. Reading levels are 3.5–12.0 for kit 3 and 8.0–14.0 for kit 4. Students can begin at their own level and progress at their own rate with these reading kits. Each kit contains 10 levels with 15 selections per level. A student who would start at a 3.5 reading level would have 15 stories to read before moving to the next (4.0) reading level, and so forth. Also included in the kits are student record cards, rate builders to develop faster reading habits, key cards for the exercises, and colored pencils.

Spelling (1972)

BRL (Behavioral Research Laboratories, Inc.)
$2.25/book
A programmed spelling series designed to teach first-year spelling skills in conjunction with reading skills. Students learn to read the word then spell it. This linguistic approach enables students to use the spelling program that they learn to read. After the sound-symbol relationships are learned, students use the known words as clues to sound out new words. Spelling words used in the series are also vocabulary words from the "Sullivan Programmed Reading" series. The series goes from level 1 to level 8.

GO—Reading in the Content Areas

Scholastic Book Services
In this reading program, the four areas of literature, social studies, mathematics, and science are used to develop skills related to these areas as well as to develop reading skills. Reading levels start at 2.0 grade level (Book 4) and end at 7.5 grade level (Book 8). Included in the program are four skills texts, a teacher's guide for each skills text, and duplicating masters to be used for supplemental work.

Comics Reading Libraries 1 & 2

King Features Syndicate
$59.50/set plus postage
This is a supplemental reading series for use with any age student. The program contains high-interest, low-vocabulary comic books that portray numerous popular comic book characters in different roles, for example, Popeye and Beetle Bailey. Reading levels are not disclosed due to strong context clues of the pictures. Twelve books of eight different titles, four word skill posters, teacher's guide, eight spirit master sheets, and a display/storage rack are included. Exercises readers. Reading difficulty varies from book to book. © King Features Syndicate, Inc., 1977. Described by permission of the publisher.

Superstars of Soul (1978)

Steck-Vaughn Company
Stories about various soul rock groups are to be read by the student. The student then has to do different activities concerning comprehension of the story. Some activities are titled "Remembering Facts," "Finishing Sentences," and "Using Words." There is a glossary at the end of the workbook. Student may check answers with the key provided.

Hip Reader's Reader (1978)

Book-Lab, Inc.
Stories followed by different group activities help to develop necessary reading skills and writing skills. Some activities act as comprehension tests. Other activities tap other reading skills, such as, word analysis (vowels, vocabulary, etc.) and sequencing. Writing skills are developed by having student write correct answers to questions.

Turner-Livingston Reading Series (1974)

Follett Publishing Company
This reading series includes the following workbooks: (1) The Family You Belong To; (2) The Friends You Make; (3) The Person You Are; (4) The Jobs You Get; (5) The Town You Live In; and Teacher's Guide. The workbooks have short stories accompanied by comprehension

questions of various form (multiple choice, true and false, etc.), and other related instructional activities. There is a final examination at each workbook's end.

Hip Reader (1977)

Book-Lab, Inc.
This two-volume series is for the older student who wishes to learn to read or read better. Volume One introduces letters accompanied by word families and sentences. With practice, more words and sentences are included on each page. Also, sentences become longer and build into more difficult paragraphs. There are no activities included in this workbook. Through stories, Volume Two introduces sounds and their different spellings, for example, $\bar{a}$ = ay, ai, a̲t̲e̲. A list of the words with the new spelling is on the side of each story. Volume Two also introduces concepts such as syllabication and superlatives.

2

Arithmetic Materials

Reading for Mathematics

Frank E. Richards
$1.95/book
This is a reading book series designed to teach and give practice in use of mathematical terms and in solving word problems. Each unit introduces new words and stresses development of word recognition skills in a math context.

Consumer Math Series (1972)

BRL
$9.00/text; $2.00/teacher book; $2.00/test book
A programmed math series aimed at secondary students who need easy-to-read facts concerning practical, life-situation mathematics. Seven books are included in the series: Book 1, Vocational Opportunities and Lifetime Earnings; Book 2, The Pay Check; Book 3, The Household Budget; Book 4, The Wise Buyer; Book 5, Income Tax;

Book 6, Insurance; and Book 7, Investments. The books contain very structured step-by-step exercises the student must answer.

Adventures With Arithmetic

Creative Publications
$4.00 each or 4 for $14.00
The four books in this package cover the topics of decimals, fractions, and percents. Activities begin with stories with a number-coded ending that has to be solved by the student.

Arithmetic Skill Text for Daily Living (1970)

Special Service Supply
This is a series of practical math found in newspaper magazine format. Included in each of the three books of this series are word problems related to newspaper type ads found on various pages throughout the book. The student must check ad prices to answer each problem. Topics of different ads relate to the food store, the clothing store, recreation, the department store, and the hardware store.

Mathematical Balance

Sigma Scientific
$11.00
A plastic teaching device that can be used to teach many operations, from simple addition to more complex fractions. Weights can be placed on either side to formulate an answer to the problem. Also available are extra weights, a teacher's guide, and additional activity cards.

Mastering Arithmetic Facts (1972)

Charles E. Merrill
Five topics relating to arithmetic facts are covered by this program: (1) readiness, (2) addition facts, (3) subtraction facts, (4) multiplication facts, and (5) division facts. The program is meant to be used as a supplement to the regular arithmetic program. It can easily be used in remedial programs to develop missing skills. Included in the program

are workbooks and skill tapes that actually take the student through each level or topic.

The Bank Book

Frank E. Richards
$1.95/book
This book attempts to explain in detail several topics relating to banking, such as, "Choosing a Bank," "Safe Deposit Bank," "Traveler's Checks," "Loans," "Christmas Club," "Savings Bonds," and "Money Denominations". The book provides a good basis for introduction of a hands-on approach to banking.

Learning About Time

Frank E. Richards
$1.95
This book can be used with secondary students who have little or no working concept of how to tell time. The book is simple to read and it includes a clock face with movable hands to be used with exercises within the book. The book covers such topics as telling and writing time, writing a date, and other related matters. Good for a basic unit on time telling.

Banking, Budgeting and Employment

Frank E. Richards
$1.95/book
This book employs a basic approach to simplifying terminology relative to banking operations, budgeting money, and employment. Included in the book are examples of forms on which to practice. It also contains vocabulary lists, maze puzzles, worksheet questionnaires, and story problems.

Cross Number Puzzles

Ideal
This math material consists of 24 plastic laminated cards containing puzzles in a crossword puzzle format. These puzzles could be used by the student needing remedial drill work in the areas of addition, multiplication, et cetera. This would be a good learning center activity for any age student.

Metric System Skills

Educational Activities, Inc.
$127.00/records—$31.00/4 cassettes
This set of records on the metric system contains material to develop sequential skills in the area of length, weight, and capacity. The records are self-directing and self-correcting. A concept is first introduced to the student, then questions are asked, followed by the correct answers.

Basic Mathematic Series

Educational Activities, Inc.
This is a comprehensive developmental math series consisting of three levels with ten records (cassettes) per level. Records provide very specific drills with recorded answers for immediate reinforcement. The records are nongraded so they can be used with different age levels. Drills include the following topics: basic facts (addition, subtraction, etc.), problem solving, decimals, and Roman numerals.

Using Money Series

Frank E. Richards
$1.95/book
Four workbooks dealing with different money concepts are included in this series. Book I, "Counting My Money," calls for recognition of coins, relative value, comparing and writing amounts of money, and totaling groups of coins. Book II, "Making My Money Count," involves different coin problems, such as, making change, adding the amount of several purchases, counting change from bills, buying supplies, and choosing the correct change. Book III, "Buying Power," centers around the topics of buying food, household goods, clothes, comparing prices, figuring costs of tools, and an allowance. Book IV, "Earning, Spending, Saving," deals with the topics of working part-time, spending money, wage deductions, saving money, planning how to spend, and banking services. The books would be especially helpful in setting up an ongoing unit on budgeting and spending money. (Also available in Spanish editions.)

Learning About Measurement

Frank E. Richards
$1.95/book
For use in secondary classroom for those who were unable to grasp

certain measurement concepts the first time around. The book covers the different kinds of measurements, tools of measurement, the ruler, liquid measurement, solid measurement, measuring temperatures, time as a measure, and tables of measurement.

Basic Mathematics (1974)

Charles E. Merrill
$79.00 each
Three separate kits (A, B, and C) are included in this mathematics package. Each kit contains 18 units with pre-tests and post-tests. According to the teacher's guide, "*Basic Mathematics* was developed as a complete mathematics program for students in the lowest quartile in achievement in grades 7, 8, and 9" (p. 1). Spirit duplicating masters in a cartoon format provide the means for the student to demonstrate knowledge of different arithmetic operations. Kit A reintroduces the student to the number system and arithmetic processes. Kit B continues this procedure, while Kit C gives the student a chance to engage in systematic review.

Understanding Decimals (1975)

Enrich, Inc.
This is a self-instructional system intended to aid the student in developing a knowledge of decimals. The system consists of 10 visual cartridges with 40 frames. The student chooses one of several answers to a particular exercise and advances to the next frame. A wrong answer on the "Telor," the cartridge holder, results in the cartridge failing to advance; a right answer does the reverse. Materials for performance testing and charting the pupil's response are provided. A teacher's manual is also included. Similar kits are available for other academic subjects.

The Learning Skills Series: Arithmetic

Webster/McGraw-Hill
$3.54/book
This arithmetic series is designed to interest high school age students with IQs in the 50–75 age. Uses real life situations to build skills. The series is based on four levels that can be used simultaneously in the same class. The different levels cover time (clocks, calendar), money, budgeting, shopping, recipes for cooking, and measurement. The teacher's guide provides an overview of concepts to be developed, as

well as spelling lists to correlate all materials. Each level builds on previously learned skills and teaches new ones.

Merrill Mathematics Skill Tapes (2nd ed., 1977)

Charles E. Merrill
This package aims at providing comprehensive treatment of mathematics. Included in the program are several workbooks and tapes, which the student uses to complete individual work in such areas as addition, subtraction, and fractions. The program also provides a means for determining the specific weaknesses of each student. The program can be used instead of a regular math program, or used to provide individual students with remedial instruction. Unlike some similar programs, the many components of this program can be used independently.

Mastering Mathematics Series (1973)

Sadlier-Oxford
$2.37/book
This is a math series that covers math from readiness through 8th-grade levels. Although the series was designed for elementary students, the format is more like a nongraded approach to teaching math. The pages are relatively clear of confusing stimuli. The problems are clearly printed in large type. Some topics covered are: computational processes, geometry (shapes), measurments, and fractions. Each book deals fairly heavily with sets, which some might elect to eliminate from a remedial program.

Think Metric

Educational Activities, Inc.
$55.00/record kit—$59.00/cassette kit
This kit contains four records, four filmstrips, and practice Ditto sheets to introduce metric concepts and relate metric skills to known areas. The kit includes an introduction of terms, as well as material on units of weights, length, and capacity. The different filmstrips involve students in problem-solving activities that can be used for individual, small, or large group instruction.

Math From Rock Bottom (1972)

Charles E. Merrill
According to this interesting math supplemental program, math de-

veloped in a land called "Rock Bottom." By reading the story of the folks in "Rock Bottom," the student learns how counting and the number system might have developed. Even though audio tapes are provided with the program, the students need to be competent readers in order to read and understand certain passages.

Project Math (1977)

Educational Progress Corporation (EPC)
In this multilevel math program, which was developed for use with students with learning problems, the teacher and student are provided with several input/output options when dealing with different math concepts. Materials relating to each level (four levels) show clearly how the individual is progressing. Records for indicating group progress are also included. Six major strands of mathematics are covered in the program: patterns, geometry, measurement, fractions, numbers, and sets.

Clues to Math (1978)

Education Progress Corporation
This is an audio-tutorial program for use with students who are studying decimals, percents, and metrics. Three student magazines present stories with number-related concepts. All stories are read or heard on audio tapes. Each magazine is accompanied by eight audiotapes, which provide instruction, as well as four additional tapes that provide an opportunity for further practice. Diagnostic and evaluative tests are also included in the program.

Getting Ready for Payday

Frank E. Richards
$1.75
The three books in this series are *Checking Accounts, Savings Accounts,* and *Planning Ahead.* The books cover such topics as, "How I Make My Money," "Opening a Checking Account," "Spending My Money," "Opening a Savings Account," "Payday," "My Budget," and "Taking Care of My Needs."

3

Motor and Physical Development Materials

The American Health and Safety Series (1972)

BRL
$10.00/kit
This series contains six different units—all programmed materials. They can be used as one course or as separate units. Units included are: *SAFETY*—the student learns fundamentals of good safety practices relating to driving, swimming, hunting, poisons, and other activities; *FIRST AID*—the student learns skills needed to give first aid in extreme emergency situations, such as, bleeding, shock, bites, or drowning; *NUTRITION*—the student learns elements of a balanced diet and elements relating to good nutrition, for example, vitamins, digestion, and calories/body weight; *PREVENTION OF COMMUNICABLE DISEASES*—the student learns how micro-organisms enter the body and how the body defends itself against diseases; *BODY STRUCTURE AND FUNCTION*—the student learns how the body is or-

ganized from cells, tissues, organ systems, and skin to skeletal system; *PERSONAL HEALTH*—good health habits including skin care, hair care, care of teeth, exercise, and information on tobacco, alcohol, and narcotics are discussed. Well-rounded series for students not able to participate in regular health program at the secondary level.

Royal Canadian Air Force Exercise Plan for Physical Fitness (1962)

Simon & Schuster, Inc.
$2.50
Included in this program, which was originally developed for members of the Royal Canadian Air Force, are two basic plans for developing and promoting physical fitness. Plan XBX is the daily physical fitness program for females (12 minutes a day). Plan 5BX is the daily fitness program for males (11 minutes a day). With daily use, these two fitness plans can increase and/or maintain good physical fitness throughout one's life span.

Your Body and How It Works (1977)

AMA (American Medical Association)
A booklet put out by the AMA written for parents and children. The book begins with a human cell and briefly depicts various parts of the body, such as, the muscles, brain, and teeth, and ends with good health hints. Although it is intended for use with 6–9 year olds, it can be used with intermediate and/or secondary students as well. The illustrations are in cartoon form and the language used is informative and straightforward. Good for use with students who have not been made aware of their body and how it functions.

Safe and Sound (1965)

Gary D. Lawson
$1.75
Health and safety topics, such as, planning parenthood, caring for unborn and newborn babies, accident prevention, and first aid are explored throughout this workbook. Case histories are cited to explain certain points. Several exercises are provided at the end of each section to test the student's knowledge of concepts discussed.

Better Living (1964)

Gary D. Lawson (Lawson Book Company)
$1.60
Morals and virtues, marriage, and parenthood are topics discussed in this workbook. Following specific topics or topical questions are "things to do" or activities that help reinforce the knowledge that the student has acquired.

The Me I Want to Be

Kimberly-Clark Corporation
$19.95
This program tells the story of a ninth-grade girl who is moving toward adulthood. Transparencies and a guide book make up the program. The guide book contains a wealth of resources relative to the maturing adolescent.

The Fullest Life

NARC (National Association for Retarded Citizens)
Recreation for the exceptional person is the topic discussed in this pamphlet. Numerous recreation programs located throughout the United States are described. Addresses and names are also given so that the reader can contact these programs for more specific information.

Your Body: Fitness, Growth, Appearance (1975)

Guidance Associates
The three filmstrips and accompanying audiotapes, as well as the study guide in this package discuss various topics relating to the matters of fitness, growth, and appearance.

Listed next are several books and articles that will provide the reader with information on the development and organization of physical education and recreation programs for special needs adolescents.

Amary, I.B. *Creative recreation for the mentally retarded.* Springfield, Illinois: Charles Thomas, 1975.

Organizing recreational programs for the retarded is the primary focus of this book. However, many of the activities mentioned in the book can be used with other mildly handicapped youth.

Carlson, B.W., & Ginglend, D.R. *Recreation for retarded teenagers and young adults.* Nashville: Abingdon Press, 1968.

The many complexities of developing recreational programs for retarded adolescents and adults are explored in this volume. Such topics as understanding the maturing retarded person, organizing the recreation program, and different kinds of activities are discussed in detail.

Guide to information systems in physical education and recreation for impaired, disabled, and handicapped persons. Washington, D.C.: AAHPER, (N.D.).

Physical activities for the mentally retarded: Ideas for instruction. Washington, D.C.: AAHPER, 1968.

Activities for developing fundamental motor skills are described in this volume. Simple activities (Level I) are described initially; then other activities that get progressively more complex are described (Level II and Level III). A selected bibliography is included.

Physical Education and Recreation for the Handicapped: Information and Research Utilization Center. Individualized education programs. *Practical Pointers,* 1977, *1*(6), 1–14.

Testing for impaired, disabled and handicapped individuals. Washington, D.C.: AAHPER, 1975.

This book explains considerations that must be brought to bear in physical fitness programs for the handicapped. Numerous physical fitness tests, components of a physical fitness program, and other topics are explained throughout this book.

Vannier, M. *Physical activities for the handicapped.* Englewood Cliffs, New Jersey: Prentice-Hall, 1977.

This comprehensive book covers physical education and recreation programs for all types of handicapping conditions. Part One of the book is a broad overview of programs for the handicapped in this area. Part Two examines specific programming for different categorical groups of the handicapped. Part Three contains materials on general aspects of physical education and recreation programs. This section is especially pertinent to the older pupil. The several different appendices at the end of the book contain a large amount of information that has been reduced to a list format.

4

Career Preparation Materials

AAMD-Becker Reading-Free Vocational Interest Inventory

American Association on Mental Deficiency

This is a nonreading vocational preference test designed for use with EMRs at the high school level. The instrument is used to identify areas in which these individuals have vocational interests. Scores from the instrument are provided in eleven male and eight female interest areas and are derived from pictorial triads. In each triad the individual is asked to select the one activity that he or she would most like to do. The inventory can be administered in 45 minutes or less to an individual or a group.

Everyday Business (Rev. 1976)

Gary D. Lawson
$2.00
In a simple format, this student workbook covers such everyday business matters as banking, budgeting, buying, federal income tax, and

different kinds of insurance. A teacher's guide that is used with the workbook lists behavioral objectives to be used with each subject area (units) mentioned above. This guide also lists supplemental activities that can be used with different workbook exercises.

Why Work Series (1966)

BRL
$95.00/complete kit
This series consists of 21 stories (short story form) written by well-known fiction authors. In the kit there are 30 copies of each story. The stories are aimed solely at motivating the reader to want to work. The stories can be classified into three groups: A stories that center on a definition of manhood in terms of work; B stories that focus on one's personal identity in terms of work; and C stories that center on one's group identity in terms of work. The authors talk of the work world in frank and forceful terms. Each selection includes a comprehension test. Also included is a tape cassette with 8 of 21 stories recorded on it by the authors. Reading levels range from 4.0 to 7.0.

Turner Guidance Series (1974)

Follett Publishing Company
$1.44/book
The six books in this series, written on a 4–5 grade reading level, are aimed at high school age students. Each book covers a basic career topic, such as, "Wanting a Job," "Training for a Job," "Starting a Job," "Looking for a Job," "Holding a Job," and "Changing a Job." Each lesson consists of a short reading selection followed by several exercises for the student to complete. Some exercises check reading comprehension, while others are aimed at values clarification.

Prevocational Series (1970)

Delmar Publishers
This series of short workbooks provides the student with a broad exposure to several different occupations and occupational concepts. Titles listed in the series are: "Start in the Right Direction," "Finding and Holding a Job," "Finding a Job Through the Newspaper," "Choosing Your Job," "Air Conditioning/Refrigeration," "Repairman," "Automobile Mechanic," "Building Maintenance Worker,"

"Electronics Technician," "Food Service Worker," "Heating Technician," "Household Appliance Repairman," "Office Machine Repairman," and "Office Occupations."

Help Yourself to a Job

Finney Company
Student workbooks I & II explain in a simplified format how to go about getting a job. Workbook I details the process of getting a job, holding the job, and changing jobs. This workbook also attempts to help the student build newspaper (ads) reading skills. Workbook II lists and describes many different jobs that may help the student in the job selection process. Several sections are provided in this second workbook to explain different aspects of job payments.

Job Application Skill Test (1968)

Special Service Supply
This skill test contains 36 job applications that could be found in almost any type of personnel office in the "real world." It begins with samples that are very basic, requiring basic personal information. The rest of the pages are actual sample job application forms. Good to show students how they all look different, but most require the same types of information. Some applications contain problems to be solved in order to complete the application.

Jobs (1972)

BRL
$14.50/kit
This is a programmed series that includes a student textbook, a job book, and a teacher's manual. The textbook is a series of stories about Joe who enters the world of work with many potential vocational problems (no diploma, an arrest record, etc.). However, by the end of the book, he overcomes his handicaps and learns how to find a job. He also learns how to take interviews, and how to examine his own qualifications. The "Jobs" book coincides with the text and provides pages for students' responses according to the text. This series helps students at a secondary level realize what is expected of them as they enter the work world. Written on a 4.9 reading level.

Vocational Job Skills

Interpretive Education
These three workbooks (application forms, budgeting, and banking) provide good forms for the student to practice on before actually looking for a job. The workbooks can easily be used in conjunction with arithmetic lessons. Other workbooks and materials relating to this area are also available.

Application Forms

Frank E. Richards
$1.95/book
This book is a step-by-step approach to learning how to fill out job applications. The book aids the student in understanding important application words, and also how to learn to respond accurately to direct demands. The material in the book covers: name, address, telephone number, social security number, training references, data of birth, sex, marital status, dependents, height/weight, and other topics.

Unemployment is Non-Cents (1970)

Gary D. Lawson
$1.60
This workbook provides several units that acquaint the student with the many facets of getting a job, keeping the job, and quitting a job. Sample forms and case histories are interspersed throughout the volume to aid the student in understanding this particular topic.

Out of Work (1975)

News Readers Press
The four primary aims of this book are: (1) to describe unemployment; (2) to describe ways and means to survive the crisis of unemployment; (3) to describe the process of improving job skills; and (4) to encourage the reader to make his or her own decisions concerning unemployment. These aims are fostered as the reader learns what can happen after a person loses a job.

The Be-Informed Series (1976)

New Readers Press
$25.00—Units I & II (Bound)

A consumer information series written on grade 3–7 reading levels. There are 20 units in the series. Each unit contains informational passages for oral or silent reading as well as review exercises. Topics covered in the series are personal credit, buying a house, taxes, drugs, and population problems. Activities involving this series must be carefully structured and carried out, since much of the material either needs further explanation or the review exercises must be checked for accuracy.

How to Get a Job

(Distributed by) NARC
This guide describes in very brief form how to get a job and other matters pertinent to the career process. A teacher's manual listing teaching suggestions and exercises for the student is also provided.

Career Education Program

Educational Progress Corporation (EPC)
In this program, the student is helped to make difficult career choices through a branching technique; that is, each choice is based on a previous career decision. The reading level is somewhat high, but the format does appear very engaging. Audio material also accompanies the program.

Comics Career Awareness Program (1973)

King Features
$59.50/set plus postage
Fifteen career clusters established by the U.S. Office of Education are covered in "Popeye" comic book format. The kit includes five books in each career area, two student involvement posters, a career awareness Bingo game, a teacher's guide, and a display/storage rack. Can be used supplementally with various subject areas in an indirect approach or directly with daily lessons, exercises, reports, et cetera. © King Features Syndicate, Inc., 1973. Described by permission of the publisher.

5

Other Materials

DRIVER'S EDUCATION

Becoming a Car Owner (1976)

New Readers Press
This booklet explains the ins and outs of buying a car. Such topics as shopping for a used car and testing the car (new or used) are more than adequately covered. An end section explains how to convert present U.S. measurements to metric measurements.

Studying for a Driver's License (1973)

New Readers Press
A simplified driver's manual based on the New York state manual provides the format for this book (the same basic information is provided but is separated into smaller units). Review questions are designed to structure the way a student approaches his or her review of the

manual. Over 100 multiple choice questions are also provided to show the student what the exam questions will be like. These questions are grouped into several different tests (20).

FILM MATERIALS

If a Boy Can't Learn (1975)

Lawren Productions, Inc.
A young man who has experienced great difficulty in school is portrayed in this 16mm film. The film describes his past problems and also shows how the educational problems were treated so that the young man was able to graduate from high school. As with many other films produced by this company, a film/study guide accompanies the film.

Adolescence and Learning Disabilities (1975)

Lawren Productions, Inc.
Youths with several different types of specific learning disabilities are discussed. Sol Gordon, who is widely known for his writings on sexuality, discusses this and other topics in the film. A study guide accompanies the film.

The Reluctant Delinquent (1977)

Lawren Productions, Inc.
In this film, an attempt is made to show the relationship between learning difficulties encountered in school and juvenile delinquency. The lives and problems of several persons who have experienced learning problems in the school are examined. Certain treatment methods are also discussed. A study guide accompanies the film.

The How and What of Sex Education for Educable Persons

Hallmark Films & Recordings, Inc.
How to handle the sexual feelings, desires, and needs of educable mentally retarded persons is the subject of this film. Frank discus-

sions between teachers and students are illustrated throughout. Although the title indicates that the film is aimed at persons who will work with the mentally retarded, much of the material is appropriate for other audiences.

Fertility Regulation for the Mentally Handicapped

Hallmark Films & Recordings, Inc.
The various methods of fertility regulation, pros and cons of the different methods, and how various methods of contraception work are discussed in this film. Certain community agencies that offer assistance to the mentally handicapped individual and his or her family are also mentioned.

Sexuality and the Mentally Handicapped (2nd ed.)

Stanfield Film Associates
This sex education program is composed of nine subparts that may be used individually or in any combination the teacher views as appropriate. Major components of the program are the teacher's guide and the accompanying slides. The program has been field tested extensively and is now marketed in a second edition.

The Blackboard Jumble (1978)

Lawren Productions, Inc.
This film focuses on the dual problem of having a learning disorder and being in trouble with the law. Gabriel Kaplan of "Welcome Back Kotter" lists a number of characteristics that are usually ascribed to LD/JD persons. He also takes the viewer through the inner workings of a model juvenile rehabilitation program.

Cry Help

Films Incorporated
Two teenage females with emotional problems are the subjects of this film. The film (actually three films) describes the attempts of personnel at a large state mental hospital to help these two maturing females to solve their emotional problems. Other persons with different types of emotional difficulties are also interviewed and/or described.

A Place Among Us

Films Incorporated
Deinstitutionalization, vocational placement, and community adjustment are several of the topics that are briefly but succinctly discussed
in this film. The film focuses on the lives of many former residents of
Mansfield Training School. Mentally retarded persons in the film
range from young to old, and from mildly to severely retarded.

Graduation

Stanfield Film Associates
The many problems that face the mentally retarded person who is beyond school age are discussed in this film. Problems of what to do
with leisure time, finding work sites, and alternatives to work are
closely examined.

People First

Stanfield Film Associates
This film shows the very personal strivings of mentally handicapped
persons as they attempt to be accepted by society. Each person in the
film wants to be viewed as a person, and seeks to communicate these
feelings to the viewer. A very important point of this film is that the
mentally handicapped are telling their story about their feelings and
perceptions rather than someone telling it for them.

The Sexually Abused Child (1978)

Lawren Productions, Inc.
The many intricate aspects of handling the problems of sexually
abused children are discussed in this timely film. While the film tends
to concentrate on the criminal justice system, educators can certainly
profit from viewing this film.

A Time for Caring: The School's Response to the
Sexually Abused Child (1979)

$390
Lawren Productions, Inc.
This excellent film attempts to provide a framework for the school to
establish policies for dealing with child abuse that is of a sexual ori-

gin. A list of behavioral, physical, and family indicators of sexual abuse is discussed throughout the film.

SEX EDUCATION

Growing Up Young (Rev. 1975)

Kimberly-Clark Corporation
Explanations of menstruation are provided in this concise booklet. These explanations are meant to help parents and teachers explain menstruation to retarded females.

Your New Self-Discovery (1976)

Kimberly-Clark Corporation
Free
This particular booklet covers sex education including male and female reproductive systems. Other topics relating to questions a person may have regarding sexual matters are also discussed (venereal diseases, masturbation, etc.).

VD Claptrap (1971; 1975)

Ed-U Press
In this educational comic book, problems associated with venereal diseases are discussed. The various forms of VD, as well as other non-VD infections are examined as to their possible effects, and the treatments or procedures used to eradicate these conditions are discussed.

Tell It Like It Is: Straight Talk About Tampons (Rev. 1974)

Kimberly-Clark Corporation
Free
Questions concerning tampons and their use are discussed in this short booklet.

Puberty in the Girl Who Is Retarded

NARC
This booklet is designed primarily for mothers of retarded girls. It seeks

to provide information and suggestions as to how these mothers can deal with the onset of puberty and other sexual problems of the retarded girl.

A Resource Guide in Sex Education for the Mentally Retarded (1971)

SIECUS
While this guide for sex education is intended primarily for the mentally retarded, it can also be used with other mildly handicapped persons. Included in the guide are sample lessons, curriculum materials, and a large section relating to resource materials.

Having a Baby Series (1973)

New Readers Press
There are six pamphlets in this series that discuss several topics associated with having a baby. The six titles of the series are: "Conception and Pregnancy," "Giving Birth," "Prenatal Care," "The First Six Weeks," "The Baby and the Family," and "Unwed Mother." An attempt has been made to reduce the vocabulary used in the books so that low-level readers can use them.

Facts Aren't Enough (1973; Rev. ed.)

NEA/AMA
This pamphlet was written for parents. Basically, it attempts to explain the human reproduction system in frank terms so that parents of any age children will be able to discuss the subject of sex openly and intelligently without embarrassment. A good, easy-to-read, informative guide for sex education in the home.

Venereal Disease: Facts About Syphillis and Gonorrhea (1972)

BRL
$6.00/book
A channelled textbook covering the topics of syphilis and gonorrhea. The book provides basic information, then asks the students several questions. The student picks the best answer and then turns to another page to discover if the answer was right or wrong. If wrong, he or she is given additional information to clear up any misunderstandings

concerning the particular question. If right, he or she is directed to the next selection or given additional information to reinforce this correct response. Material is presented in a very straightforward manner in an effort to enable the student to understand clearly the facts about venereal disease.

The Miracle of You (Rev. 1977)

Kimberly-Clark Corporation
Free
In this booklet menstruation is placed in a total life perspective. Different facets of the life cycle are thoroughly explained. Available in Spanish.

Very Personally Yours (1976)

Kimberly-Clark Corporation
Free
Like "Growing Up Young" this booklet explains menstruation. However, this booklet is intended to be read by females with a fairly extensive reading vocabulary. Available in Spanish.

Learning About Sex (1969)

Guidance Associates
This filmstrip and accompanying cassette give the student some ideas about the different sex roles and relationships that occur in our society. A discussion guide accompanies the other material.

Becoming a Woman/Becoming a Man (1971)

Guidance Associates
The "growth spurt" and the maturing male and female are the two primary topics explored by this two-part set of filmstrips and cassettes. A discussion guide accompanies the other materials.

Sexual Values in Society (1969)

Guidance Associates
The aim of this particular package is to help the developing adolescent

understand the changing sexual values in this society. Two filmstrips and audiotapes, and a discussion guide are included in the package.

Understanding Human Reproduction (Revised)

Guidance Associates
The two filmstrips and other materials in this package are designed to acquaint the student with the numerous facts associated with the human reproductive system.

Growing Into Womanhood / Growing Into Manhood (1971)

Guidance Associates
This two-part program attempts to explain the human growth process. Part One deals with general growth concerns that relate to both males and females. Part Two is divided into two sections, one relating specifically to males and the other to females. Two filmstrips and audiotapes, and a study guide are included in the program.

Sex Education in America (1971)

Guidance Associates
Three pairs of filmstrips and cassettes and the accompanying discussion explore the topic of sex education in our culture.

To Grow Up, Now—An Instructional Guide for Teachers

Kimberly-Clark Corporation (Revised 1975; 1977)
This instructional guide for teachers includes a dramatization, three spirit masters (with instructions), suggested follow-up projects and activities, and suggested sources of additional information concerning the topics of menstruation and personal hygiene. The guide and the samples provided (Kotex products) will help teachers introducing these topics. The samples are actual products on today's market.

Personal Development Series (1970)

Delmar Publishers
This series of *programmed* instruction includes booklets on: (1) Venereal Disease; (2) Keeping Your Body Healthy; (3) Finding Your Way; (4) Telephone Talk; (5) Alcohol and Health (Books One and Two), To-

bacco and Health (Books One and Two), Drug Abuse (Books One and Two), and The Facts About Sex (Books One and Two). Booklets include instructions to students about answering questions. Answers to questions are on the side of each page. There is a post-test without answers at each booklet's end. An answer key is provided for the teacher.

Young, Single, and Pregnant (1972)

Guidance Associates
The two filmstrips and cassettes that make up this program deal with the issue of young pregnant females. This material and the accompanying discussion guide intricately explore this problem.

Venereal Disease: Who, Me? (1973)

Guidance Associates
The various problems associated with VD are discussed in the two filmstrips and record that compose this set of materials. The filmstrips have several test segments that are followed by review answers.

VD: What You Should Know (1973)

Guidance Associates
Three filmstrips and three cassette tapes make up this mini-series on venereal disease. The first filmstrip and cassette discuss the facts associated with VD, the second set explains how to get help, and the third set explores attitudes about this subject. A discussion guide is also included.

The Story of Menstruation (1977)

Kimberly-Clark Corporation (Life-Cycle Center)
The filmstrip (color) and accompanying cassette discuss the menstruation cycle. Personal hygiene and sanitary protection are also discussed. The filmstrip is about fifteen minutes in length.

Sex Education Series (1970)

Joint Committee on Health Problems in Education of the National Education Association and the American Medical Association. This series includes the following booklets: A Story About You (grades 4–6); Finding Yourself (Junior High); Approaching Adulthood (high school and college); and Parents' Responsibilities (parents and other adults). Each booklet discusses human reproduction at the appropriate level for its readers. At each level, discussions of other problems and responsibilities facing that age group are also included.

SOCIAL STUDIES

Where It's At (1973)

Gary D. Lawson
$1.75
Geographic, cultural, and economic facts concerning different parts of the world are examined in the several sections of this workbook. Questions and activities concerning each of these topics are explored.

Color Me American (1967)

Gary D. Lawson
$1.75
Topics relating to citizenship and participation in the affairs of the local government and community are covered in this workbook. The U.S. Constitution, branches of government, and the Bill of Rights are also discussed. Following each topic are activities aimed at further developing the student's knowledge.

Basic Illustrated History of America

Pendulum Press
This social studies program uses many interesting illustrations to motivate students. Illustrations provide clues to meanings of words. Footnotes help define unfamiliar vocabulary. There are 12 readers along with activity books for each reader. The program covers the period from 1500–1976.

America's Story (1978)

Steck-Vaughn Company
Book One
The story of America's growth is divided into twenty chapters. At the

end of each chapter there are test activities for the student, including true-false items, sequencing, and fill-in-the-blanks. There are four unit-type reviews and a final review located at the end of the workbook.

PUBLISHERS LISTING

Listed in alphabetical order are the names and addresses of the publishers of materials that were reviewed in this section.

Academic Therapy Publishers. P.O. Box 899–1539 Fourth Street. San Rafael, California 94901

Allyn & Bacon, Inc. 470 Atlantic Avenue. Boston, Massachusetts 02210

American Association of Health, Physical Education, and Recreation (AAHPER). 1201 16th Street, N.W. Washington, D.C. 20036

American Medical Association. Order Department OP–176. 535 N. Dearborn Street. Chicago, Illinois 60610

Barnell-Loft. 958 Church Street. Baldwin, New York 11510

Behavioral Research Laboratories, Inc. (BRL). Ladera Professional Center. Box 577. Palo Alto, California 94302

ALSO: 115 Charter Street. Redwood City, California 94063

Benefic Press. 10300 W. Roosevelt Road. Westchester, Illinois 60153

Book-Lab, Inc. 1449 Thirty-Seventh Street. Brooklyn, New York 11218

Bowmar Publishing Corporation. 4563 Colorado Boulevard. Los Angeles, California 90039

Burgess Publishing Company. 426 S. 6th Street. Minneapolis, Minnesota 55415

Coronet Instructional Films. 65 South Water Street E. Chicago, Illinois 60601

Creative Publications. 3977 E. Bayshore Road. P.O. Box 10328. Palo Alto, California 94303

Creative Visuals. Division of Gamco Industries. Box 1911. Big Springs, Texas 79720

John Day Company. 257 Park Avenue, S. New York, New York 10010

Delmar Publishers. (Litton Educational Publishing, Inc.) 7625 Empire Drive. Florence, Kentucky 41042

Economy Company (The). P.O. Box 68502. 5455 W. 84th Street. Indianapolis, Indiana 46268

Education Progress Corporation (EPC). P.O. Box 45663. Tulsa, Oklahoma 74145

Educational Activities, Inc. 1937 Grand Avenue. Baldwin, New York 11510

EMC Corporation. 180 E. Sixth Street. Saint Paul, Minnesota 55101

Encyclopedia Britannica Educational Corporation. 425 N. Michigan Avenue. Chicago, Illinois 60611

Enrich, Inc. 760 Kifer Road. Sunnyvale, California 94806

Fearon Publishers. Pitman Publishing Corporation. 6 Davis Drive. Belmont, California 94002

Film Incorporated. 733 Greenbay Road. Willamette, Illinois 60091

Finney Company. 3350 Gorham Avenue. Minneapolis, Minnesota 55426

Follett Educational Corporation. 1010 W. Washington Boulevard. Chicago, Illinois 60607

Ginn & Company, P.O. Box 2649. 1250 Fairwood Avenue. Columbus, Ohio 43216

Globe Book Company, Inc. 175 Fifth Avenue. New York, New York 10010

Guidance Associates. 757 Third Avenue. New York, New York 10017

Hallmark Films & Recordings, Inc. 51–53 New Plant Court. Owings Mills, Maryland 21117

Harcourt, Brace, Jovanovich, Inc. 757 Third Avenue. New York, New York 10017

Ideal School Supply Company. 11000 South Lavergne Avenue. Oak Lawn, Illinois 60453

Interpretive Education. 400 Bryant Street. Kalamazoo, Michigan 49001

Kimberly-Clark. P.O. Box 551. Neenah, Wisconsin 54956

King Features Syndicates. 235 E. 45th Street. New York, New York 10017

Lawson Book Company, 8488 Sara Street. Elk Grove, California 95624

Learning Pathways, Inc. P.O. Box 1407. Evergreen, California 80439

Litton Educational Publishing, Inc. (Delmar Publishers.) 7625 Empire Drive. Florence, Kentucky 41042

Mafex Associates, Inc. 90 Cherry Street. P.O. Box 519. Johnstown, Pennsylvania 15902

McGraw-Hill Book Company. 1221 Avenue of the Americas. New York, New York 10020

Charles E. Merrill Publishing Co. 1300 Alum Creek Drive. Columbus, Ohio 43216

National Association for Retarded Citizens (NARC). 2709 Avenue East. P.O. Box 6109. Arlington, Texas 76011

National Education Association (NEA). 1210 16th Street, N.W. Washington, D.C. 20036

New Reader's Press. 1320 Jamesville Avenue. Box 131. Syracuse, New York 13210

Rand-McNally & Company. Box 7600. Chicago, Illinois 60680

Reader's Digest Services, Inc. Educational Division. Pleasantville, New York 10570

Regents Publishing Company, Inc. Southeastern Division. 265 University Drive. Suite 103. Coral Gables, Florida 33134

Frank E. Richards Publishing Company. P.O. Box 66. Phoenix, New York 13135

Sadlier/Oxford. 11 Park Place. New York, New York 10007

Scholastic. 904 Sylvan Avenue. Englewood Cliffs, New Jersey 07632

Scholastic Book Services. 2931 E. McCarthy Street. Jefferson City, Missouri 65101

Science Research Associates (SRA). P.O. Box 4924. Chicago, Illinois 60680

Scott, Foresman and Company. 99 Bauer Drive. Oakland, New Jersey 07436

Simon and Schuster, Inc. 1 West 39th Street. New York, New York 10018

Special Service Supply. Box 705. Huntington, New Jersey 11743

Stanfield Film Associates. P.O. Box 851. Pasadena, California 91102

Steck-Vaughn Company. P.O. Box 2028. Vaughn Building. Austin, Texas 78767

Fern Tripp. 2035 East Sierra Way. Dinuba, California 93618

Webster/McGraw-Hill. Webster Division, McGraw-Hill. Manchester Road. Manchester, Missouri 63011

6

Professional Bibliography

GENERAL ARTICLES AND BOOKS

Becker, R.L. The reading-free vocational interest inventory: Measurement of job preference in the EMR. *Mental Retardation,* 1973, *11*(4), 11–15.
Development of the RF VII is discussed in some detail in this article.

Blue, R. *Sex education and the mentally retarded: A community approach.* Nashville: Tennessee Assocation for Retarded Citizens, 1974.
Roger Blue discusses methods and procedures for teaching sex education to the mentally retarded. A good deal of resource material relating to this topic is located throughout this book.

Brolin, D.E. (Ed.). *Life-centered career education: A competency based approach.* Reston, Virginia: Council for Expectional Children, 1973.
Brolin discusses the definition of career education and a curriculum to encompass it. Included in the book are chapters concerned

with instructional materials, resource lists, and student competency (assessment and planning for individualized education programs). Appendices contain competency scale manual and master forms for duplication.

Cawley, J.F., Fitzmaurice, A.M., Shaw, R., Kahn, H., & Bates, H. LD youth and mathematics: A review of characteristics. *Learning Disability Quarterly,* 1979, *2*(1), 29–44.

Cawley and his associates discuss math learning characteristics of several groups of LD children and youth. (See also: Cawley, J.F., Fitzmaurice, A.M., Shaw, R.A., Kahn, H., & Bates, H. Mathematics and learning disabled youth: The upper grade levels. *Learning Disability Quarterly,* 1978, *1*(4), 37–52.)

Davis, S., & Ward, M. *Vocational education of handicapped students: A guide for policy development.* Reston, Virginia: Council for Exceptional Children, 1978.

Davis and Ward discuss policies concerning the development and implementation of vocational education for handicapped students. There are nine policy areas discussed: five are concerned with identifying and serving handicapped students; four address administrative concerns of managing the program and providing appropriate resources.

Fantini, M.D. (Ed.). *Alternative education: A source book for parents, teachers, students, and administrators.* Garden City, New York: Doubleday and Company (Anchor Books), 1976.

Reprints of articles on the alternative school movement are collected in this sourcebook.

Fantini, M.D. *Public schools of choice.* New York: Simon and Schuster, Inc., 1973.

In this volume, Fantini discusses the many intricate variables associated with altlernative schools, for example, how to legitimize and finance this type of school.

Hauser, C. Education for mildly handicapped adolescents: Structure and quality of published information from the past decade. *The Journal of Special Education,* 1978, *12,* 285–301.

This article takes a very critical look at published material relating to mildly handicapped adolescents. The author concludes that this published material has been very meager and that programs as they now exist for this group are woefully inadequate. The article ends with a set of recommendations to correct this situation.

Levy, Marvin R. *Resource book for drug abuse education.* Washington, D.C.: American Association for Health, Physical Education, and Recreation (no date).

Levy has gathered together a series of papers written by medical authorities and social scientists reflecting a wide range of views regarding drugs. It is hoped that a teacher familiar with a variety of viewpoints can more effectively discuss drug-related problems with young people.

Touzel, S.W. Secondary LD curricula—A proposed framework. *Learning Disability Quarterly,* 1978, *1*(4), 53–61.

In this article, which is based on the author's doctoral dissertation, several key elements of a curriculum for the secondary LD student are discussed, for example, basing the curricula content on the development of survival and coping skills, as well as developing career and vocational skills.

Vockell, E.L. Sex education for the mentally retarded—A bibliography. *The Journal for Special Educators of the Mentally Retarded,* 1975, *12*, 36–38.

As indicated, this is a bibliography concerning sex education for the mentally retarded. However, a large amount of the material would be relevant to other youth who may have learning deficits.

Weisgerber, R. (Ed.). *Vocational education: Teaching the handicapped in regular classes.* Reston, Virginia: Council for Exceptional Children, 1978.

Weisgerber has gathered information to help the vocational instructor provide practical knowledge and work skills to the handicapped student. Special consideration has been given to four major disabilities (orthopedic/health impairments, visual impairments, mental retardation, and communication impairments). Steps involved in developing individualized instruction are also included. Lists of selected publications are provided to help in further investigations of these topics.

POPULAR BOOKS AND NOVELS

Green, H. *I never promised you a rose garden.* New York: New American Library (Signet), 1964.

Deborah, a teenage girl, is placed in a hospital for the severely disturbed. Events that follow this placement are graphically related to the reader in the subsequent portions of the book.

Grossman, H. *Nine rotten lousy kids.* New York: Holt, Rinehart & Winston, 1972.

    An experimental school for emotionally disturbed boys in New York City is described. Initially, the book focuses on the behaviors of nine of the boys; later, other boys are added to the group.

Herndon, J. *How to survive in your native land.* New York: Simon and Schuster, Inc. (Bantam), 1971.

    The author describes his and his students' experiences as he learned to teach (secondary students) in a middle-class school.

Herndon, J. *The way it spozed to be.* New York: Simon and Schuster, Inc. (Bantam), 1968.

    This is the first of Herndon's books. In it, he describes what it is like to work in a ghetto school, his experiences at this school, and how students behaved and were treated at the school.

Rothman, E.P. *The angel inside went sour.* New York: David McKay, 1970.

    A public school for "girls in trouble" is described in this interesting book. The story is told from the perspective of Esther Rothman, who is the principal.

SECONDARY SPECIAL EDUCATION BOOKS

Alley, G., & Deshler, D. *Teaching the learning disabled adolescent: Strategies and methods.* Denver: Love Publishing Co., 1979.

    The authors of this text describe an alternative approach for teaching LD youth. This approach, called the *learning strategies model*, is based on the belief that LD adolescents can learn to acquire, store and retrieve information on their own. Throughout the book, strategies and methods for helping LD youth demonstrate the above skills are described.

Bailey, E.J. *Academic activities for adolescents with learning disabilities.* Evergreen, CO.: Learning Pathways, Inc., 1975.

    Specific activities for reducing or eradicating the learning deficits of LD youth are extensively discussed. Quite a number of these teaching/learning activities are also appropriate for use with other adolescents who have learning problems.

Cullinan, D., & Epstein, M.H. (Eds.). *Special education for adolescents: Issues and perspectives.* Columbus: Charles E. Merrill Publishing Co., 1979.

    The editors and contributors to this volume have done an excellent job of covering the topic of secondary education for mildly handicapped youth. Topics covered from a personal perspective of the several contributors include vocational education, career education, drug abuse prevention, and legal issues.

Goodman, L., & Mann, L. *Learning disabilities in the secondary school: Issues and practices.* New York: Grune & Stratton, 1976.

The authors of this book take a strong look at the field of learning disabilities and the way this field has traditionally responded to the secondary LD youth. As they state in the preface, there are some controversial matters within the book with which the reader may take issue.

Mann, L., Goodman, L., & Wiederholt, J.L. *Teaching the learning-disabled adolescent.* Boston: Houghton Mifflin, 1978.

The primary focus of this book is on instructional strategies for alleviating the learning difficulties of LD adolescents. While the subjects of reading and mathematics are discussed extensively, a good amount of attention is also directed at career topics, and teacher competencies in this area.

Marsh, G., Gearheart, C.K., & Gearheart, B.R. *The learning disabled adolescent: Program altelrnatives in the secondary school.* St. Louis: C.V. Mosby Co., 1978.

As the title of the book states, secondary programs for learning disabled adolescents are examined in this volume. The book is divided into three primary sections: (1) an overview of the field of learning disabilities, adolescence, and the secondary school; (2) a description of various components of a secondary LD program; and (3) a description of various existing programs for LD adolescents.

Sabatino, D.A., & Mauser, A.J. (Eds.). *Specialized education in today's secondary schools.* Boston: Allyn & Bacon, 1978.

Characteristics, programs and services, and methods for working with behaviorally disordered and learning disabled youth are discussed.

Index

AUTHOR INDEX

SUBJECT INDEX